Price and Value in the
Aristotelian Tradition

ODD LANGHOLM

Price and Value in the Aristotelian Tradition

A study in scholastic economic sources

UNIVERSITETSFORLAGET

BERGEN · OSLO · TROMSØ

ISBN: 82-00-01840-7

Distribution offices:

NORWAY
Universitetsforlaget
Box 6589, Rodeløkka
Oslo 5

UNITED KINGDOM
Global Book Resources Ltd.
37 Queen Street
Henley on Thames
Oxon RG9 1AJ

UNITED STATES and CANADA
Columbia University Press
136 South Broadway
Irvington-on-Hudson
New York 10533

Printed in Norway by A.s John Grieg

Preface

Based on some hundred scholastic and early post-scholastic texts, this book seeks to trace the several branches of the tradition in economic value theory which developed in commentary to the *Ethics* of Aristotle, from the first Latin translations in the thirteenth century, down to the waning of scholastic philosophy and the assimilation of some of its ideas into the bases of modern theory. Economics, as an academic discipline, grew out of the mediaeval course in Moral Philosophy. For many centuries, the *Nicomachean Ethics* and its commentary literature provided the standard texts for this course. In Book V of the *Ethics*, on Justice, Aristotle treats of economic exchange, price and money in a brief chapter of exceptional suggestiveness and analytical potential. We can therefore look to the Aristotelian tradition for much of what is best and most relevant in scholastic economics. It did not, of course, develop in isolation; we shall frequently note points of entry from and exit to other schools and traditions. But the peculiar circumstances of the scholastic commentary, preserving and augmenting a common stock of ideas about the meaning and significance of an ever present classical text, tended to sustain a certain analytical core, the development of which defines the Aristotelian tradition in its narrow sense and forms the subject matter of the present study. It is thus a partial study, but I believe the partition to be valid and instructive.

Recent critical editions of some decisive early translations and commentaries invite a reexamination of the very bases of Latin Aristotelian economics, while a number of excellent new bibliographical surveys greatly facilitate research into later sources. With these aids at hand there is no longer any excuse for a practice which has confounded the study of mediaeval economics since its inception more than a century ago, namely that of basing the most sweeping historical generalizations on a few familiar names, with no regard for context and continuity; even the best textbooks in the field still skip and jump from one century to the next, in and out of different traditions. But a scholastic commentator superposed his own ideas on those accumulated in the particular tradition in which he wrote, accepted its premises and adopted its language. He cannot be fully understood until this foundation is also dug out. The most important points to establish are often semantic. Modern value theory has inherited a string of exact terms; the words *want, utility, demand,* for instance, all have precise meanings and precise analytical relations to each other. But those who initiated systematic study of economic phenomena had to shape their own terms from the blunter tools of non-professional language. The Latin Aristotelian concept of *indigentia* thus emerged from the first translator's notes as a vague term meaning perhaps want or need in an individual, physiological sense. Over an extended sequence of commentaries, it developed into a precise technical term closely approaching what we now mean by effective demand. To pick a single commentator, like Aquinas or Buridanus, and say that he made value depend on *indigentia* which means demand (as has often been done in both cases), makes very little sense unless it can also be stated precisely how far the term had come as used by that particular commentator. We are now in a position to do this.

But tracing the evolution of terms is not to be undertaken solely as a philological exercise (fascinating though it may be), for in step with the semantic process there is the analytical one. As the meanings of words are clarified, it will also become clearer to those who use them, how the functional relationships must be in that segment of reality which the words describe. As the Aristotelians developed the concept of *indigentia* (and other concepts), they developed a theory of value. It was a slow process to which many commentators, perhaps unprinted and now forgotten, contributed along with those whose works have since become famous, sometimes for reasons unrelated to economics, which takes up only a small part

6

of the *Ethics*. To get to the meanings of the terms as used by each and so to his analytical insight, we have to quote him directly, often in broad context and, needless to say, in the language in which he wrote, which was usually Latin. This need not scare off all those economists whose classical educations may be a little uncertain or a little rusty, leaving this book and its subject entirely to the historian and the linguist. For this is mostly the plain Latin of the mediaeval schools and it is highly repetitive; it is the same page in Aristotle which is commented upon, again and again. That page is reproduced in the Appendix (over three pages) in the several versions of the mediaeval Latin translation; it is available, for comparison, in a number of modern English editions of the *Nicomachean Ethics*.

*

Mentioning only one name, I have not forgotten the many others who also aided and encouraged me in this project. Anyone now engaging in literary work on the Latin *Ethics* can climb onto the shoulders of a giant. I saw the practical possibility of a study like this almost ten years ago when reading R. A. Gauthier's bibliographical history of the *Ethics* prefixed to his French edition (with Jolif); since then, I have become acquainted with his critical work and have come to share the admiration for his scholarship. I am deeply grateful to Father Gauthier for his detailed criticism of this book in its first complete draft and can only regret the shortcomings which remain in its final version and for which I can blame no one but myself.

This is a book about books and manuscripts. It has made me a connoisseur of libraries and an admirer of librarians. I wish to thank all those gentle caretakers of old volumes, in more than forty libraries from Uppsala to Naples and from Oxford to Vienna, who helped me locate and sort out this enormous material. I can only hope that some of the note material appended here can repay a little of their kindness with a modest contribution to Aristotelian bibliography.

O.L.

Contents

Introduction

The role of the Ethics in economic analysis

The aim of this book is to uncover a section of the mediaeval sub-structure of that part of economic science which we now call the theory of value. The mediaeval students of the subject did not use that name for it. Well into the seventeenth century, most contributions to the gradually increasing insight into the difficult problem of economic value were couched in the now unfamiliar terms of scholastic philosophy. And ever since the Enlightenment, economists have been taught to fight shy of the problem of the *iustum pretium* — for reasons which are certainly not all bad. But a change of terms to herald a new approach is sometimes a symbol of an ideological protest which does not correspond to a liberation from intellectual influences. It is easy now to forget that those who laid the foundation of modern economics in the eighteenth century were as familiar with the accumulated knowledge of scholastic analysis as the average twentieth century economist is ignorant of it. Vital elements of the new theories, on which these authors did not elaborate because they took them for granted, were inheritances from the mediaeval schools. Since it is so obvious that economics was in part renewed in the eighteenth century, it is particularly important to know what was in fact *not* new. Moreover, the nature of the ideological protests of the Enlightenment and the fact that these particular lights are now themselves definitely receding back into history, call upon us to inquire if there were valuable parts of the inheritance which were lost. We are again increasingly conscious, even in our theoretical preoccupations, of the question of justice in pricing, and this trend is surely partly brought upon us by social concerns which survived the sterile individualism of professional economics. So even when we keep strictly to positive theory, the moral intent of the mediaeval economists constitutes no valid objection to a systematic search for their analytical contributions. This point must assume added relevance in introducing the present study, which addresses itself to source-material explicitly ethical in content. From the middle of the thirteenth century, when Aristotle was rediscovered in the West, a considerable part of the analytical contribution to any science is to be found in commentary on the works of the *Philosopher*. But economic value theory is an extreme case, in that its dominant mediaeval tradition springs from a single brief locus in Aristotle's *Ethics*. In the course of what may be called the four scholastic centuries, from Thomas Aquinas to Thomas Hobbes, several hundred commentaries were composed on this work, and there are still extant a considerable number which offer something of interest to economics. Only a handful of these contributions have been examined before. Many more are to be examined here, and the several branches of the Aristotelian economic tradition sorted out and traced until they peter out in the late seventeenth century. In some of these branches the basic textual problem of ethics in exchange had inspired analytical attempts on which later authors could draw when they built what we think of as the new economics.

A work called *Economics* was ascribed to Aristotle in the Middle Ages but it is not authentic and it does not deal with economics in the modern sense. The *Politics* deals with some economic topics; many of our authors commented on it along with the *Ethics* and discussed usury.[1] The Latin Aristotelian corpus included four ethical works. A brief tract, *On Virtues and Vices*, is spurious and quite trivial. The *Magna Moralia* seems to be spurious too, though the point was long disputed; this brief epitome (in spite of its given title) has a curious point in our section to which we must return briefly below.[2] There remain the *Eudemian* and the *Nicomachean Ethics*, both authentic beyond question but presumably, like many

1 Aristotle's account of how to create a monopoly and profit from it (*Politics*, I, iv, 5–8) is played down by the scholastic commentators, who obviously disapprove on ethical grounds.
2 See p. 37.

other extant works of Aristotle, edited by others on the basis of his lectures, Eudemus being a pupil of Aristotle and Nicomachus his son. The works overlap in three books, as noted in the manuscripts of the *Eudemian Ethics*, which consequently omit them, as do the translations and the commentaries. Since it is only one of these common books which concerns us, its whole tradition harks back to the *Nicomachean Ethics*. When the scholastic authors spoke of *Aristotelis Ethica*, that is the work to which they referred. It drew a volume of commentary larger than most other works of Aristotle. In Book V (of ten, corresponding to the omitted Book IV of the *Eudemian*) on Justice, there occurs the brief section about justice in exchange, the comments on which constitute the source-material for the present study.

*

Ethics is the strangest of intellectual disciplines. Recently, analytical contributions to ethics have come to look like nothing so much as determined efforts to disprove its very existence. But prior to the logical revolution in philosophy, ethics was something else. Taking for granted the possibility of establishing meaningful bases for universal principles of ethics, philosophers taking to this field attempted to make this wisdom useful by working out rules of moral conduct, frequently aided by an analytical scheme derived from Greek antiquity, the list of virtues. The list itself would vary with the social and personal tempers of which it was born, as would the interpretation of individual items (though some philosophers would not willingly have admitted that). In addition, the invention of systems and techniques for analysing conduct in relation to these ideal types was a part of ethics. Aristotle, father of European ethics, formalised moral analysis in terms of the "ethos of the mean": ideal conduct in the dimension of each virtue is a mean between extremes. For instance, in terms of confidence in oneself, the virtue of courage is a mean between cowardice and rashness, etc. The ethos compounded of such behavioural norms is that of moderation, the eternal gentleman's "nothing too much". But as applied to the virtue of justice, the norm tends to shed this image.

Justice enters the Aristotelian ethical system in two ways. In one

13

sense, that of *universal justice*, it does not exactly correspond to virtue itself in a general sense, since "justice" particularly emphasizes the social aspect of moral conduct; however, it is a general term covering all virtues and referring to this aspect as implied in each of them. In the other sense, that of *particular justice*, it is simply one of these individual virtues on Aristotle's list. This virtue is also a mean between extremes, but in a sense different from other virtues; it is a mean between acting unjustly and being unjustly treated. Identification of the just mean then becomes a matter of comparing (or weighing) what is unjust to one against what is unjust to the other of two interacting persons. As with all classical authors, the "just" is what is "fair": "to give each one his due"; but with Aristotle "fair" comes to mean "equal", justice is an equation involving opposing "dues". The form of this equation differs with different kinds of particular justice. There are two kinds. *Distributive justice* applies to the distribution of goods among cooperating persons, for instance a state's collective gains from war or some other enterprise among its citizens; the equation of justice then involves a geometric proportion, taking account of relative merit (social worth, position, dignity) of the sharing persons. *Commutative justice* applies to the correction of injury inflicted on one person by another, and this is taken in a broad sense to include injurious transactions in physical goods so that the principle applies even to contractual justice; the equation in this case involves an arithmetic proportion, the persons being treated as equal.

Justice in economic exchange comes under this heading. At least, that is how the mediaeval commentators presented Aristotle, so that is how we shall read him here. Actually, the classification of economic justice in relation to the two main kinds of particular justice is one of the many unsettled questions of Aristotle's exchange analysis. It has even been maintained[3] that the failure to distinguish it clearly as a third kind, a failure for which the mediaeval commentators must in fact take the original responsibility, is the cause of some of the confusion which clouds this point. But it is just as well to state at once that what Aristotle himself intended at this or other disputed points really does not concern us here, since the subject matter of

3 Hardie 188ff.

this study is not the Greek but the Latin Aristotle, i.e. the Philosopher according to his Latin interpreters, as they read the available translations, truly or falsely. For that is all that matters to the analytical developments which they based on the book. This does not mean that I shall not occasionally have to quote classical scholars on the interpretation of the original Greek phrases and even suggest personal opinions, but this is always done in order to clarify the mediaeval Latin interpretations. On points where that interpretation is clear from the start, as with the subdivisions of commutative justice, there is nothing to add.

Aristotle turns to justice in exchange in a brief chapter which is in most editions, Chapter 5 of Book V of the *Nicomachean Ethics* (*EN*, V, 5). In Bekker's standard edition, the section of text which concerns us takes up slightly less than a page of book space.[4] Of this, several sub-sections can be passed over here since they deal with the nature and role of money rather than value as such. Justice in economic exchange, according to *EN*, V, 5, requires ἀντιπεπονθὸς — reciprocity, which the mediaeval Latin translation rendered as *contrapassum* — but according to a proportion which takes account of the different values of the goods exchanged. Aristotle presents a cast of economic characters: a doctor, a builder, a shoemaker, a farmer, and some of their products: a house, shoes, food, stressing their social interdependence and the need for exchange, all in the scope of an obviously Platonic reference.[5] It is not two doctors that exchange, but a doctor and a farmer. The existence of the state depends on such exchange, and it must be just. Justice of proportionate reciprocity is effected by diagonal conjunction. With this obscure saying Aristotle introduces a quasi-mathematical argument in four terms, corresponding — according to the Latin tradition — to the angles of a square, and concludes the argument with slight variation for different pairs of producers and products: as builder to shoemaker, so shoes to a house.

In Aristotle there is no clear pointer to what this means in terms of economic variables; a catalogue of suggestions, mediaeval and modern, would include references to proportionate social status,

---

4 1132b31–1133b28. According to an alternative subdivision, this is in V, 8.
5 *Republic*, II, xi.

productive worth, labour time, even market valuation. The latter suggestion is based on the text, but strictly speaking out of the proper context. Returning twice again to the square of exchange, Aristotle intermittently speaks of the market, since the actual evaluation of goods in exchange is normally made in the market by means of money, to a discussion of which he devotes somewhat less than half the page. On the whole this does not, as I said, concern us, but Aristotle in this connection makes a remark to the effect (or so most mediaeval and modern interpreters read him) that money as an institutional value measure derives from a natural one, which is χρεία. Whatever Aristotle meant by that, it came after a while to be rendered as *indigentia* and gradually took on the meaning of "demand". Consequently, to the catalogue of suggestions as to what constitutes the basis of proportionate reciprocity — in other words, the basis of the just price — there is added a market evaluation to supplement those suggested directly by the square of exchange itself, and among which production costs came to figure prominently. In the broadest outline, therefore, what emerges from this obscure passage is a picture composed of the main elements of a theory of value: the production and marketing determinants of the exchange rates of commodities.

*

In 1240 at Toledo a scholar known as Herman the German translated into Latin the commentary on the *Nicomachean Ethics* by the twelfth century Arabian philosopher, Averroes. A few years later, Robert Grosseteste, bishop of Lincoln, started the work of translating directly from Greek the entire text of the *Ethics* itself, supplying each book with a translation of a Greek commentary — two, in the case of Book V — as well as his own notes. The *Translatio Lincolniensis*, in a revised version, held sway until gradually superseded by the Renaissance translations of Aretinus and Argyropulus; after 1530 there is a whole host of new ones. A translation is always in a sense a commentary, and a first text in a language may deeply influence the subsequent trend of interpretation. All later scholastic translators reflect Grosseteste, and the notes and translated commentaries which he provided set in motion the various lines of interpretation and analysis which developed down through the centuries.

To get to the roots of the Aristotelian economic tradition, we must therefore devote a chapter to the *tradition of Robert Grosseteste.* Immediately included in university curricula, the thirteenth century *Ethics* translation became the object of summaries and brief paraphrases as well as other aids to learning and memorizing.[6] This type of summary literature continued to pour out as long as the *Ethics* was used as a textbook, but it is of limited interest here. A difficult and somewhat peripheral part of the work, the exchange model was often left out of summary expositions or reduced to some insignificant phrases. It seems that it took somewhat more space and some commitment to tangle with the problem of justice in exchange. But the *Translatio Lincolniensis* was not long out before it was subjected to the first regular commentary.

The typical scholastic commentary is either a close textual exposition or a set of disputed questions or a combination of the two. Not all commentators on the *Nicomachean Ethics* go into the problem of value in exchange and many of those who do just copy the ideas and frequently the very words of a previous authority. On closer inspection, however, such borrowings usually turn out to be not entirely verbatim; there will be omissions, interpolations, slight changes in wording and emphasis. To study the history of scholastic thought is partly to record these changes as they slowly turn the train of ideas into new channels, the better thus to evaluate those few authors who suddenly stand out in the sources as apparently saying something new in their own words. The commentary history of the *Ethics* will naturally come to centre on a few such important names, each creating a distinct branch tradition. The best way to organize our extensive material is to renounce chronology and record the development of these branch traditions in turn, devoting a chapter to each. I propose to call them the *traditions of Albertus Magnus, Thomas Aquinas, Henricus de Frimaria, Johannes Buridanus,* and *Geraldus Odonis.*

Albertus Magnus, the first Latin regular commentator, made some important suggestions but otherwise leaned heavily on the Grossetestan material, and each of the other four drew some support

6 See the classical study by Grabmann (4). To the origins and nature of Latin Aristotelianism there is a useful introduction by Van Steenberghen.

17

from one or more of the previous ones. These five traditions thus are not independent but are rather in the nature of branchings ever higher up on the tree. This means that a commentator may well be influenced, say, by Thomas Aquinas and still be classified in the tradition of Buridanus; as a matter of fact, most of the interesting users of Thomas will not be found in the Thomist branch as defined here but rather in branches situated higher — those to be treated of in the chapter about Thomas being a kind of residue of less interesting authors not taking part in important later developments. Still, there is development in each branch and considerable development in some. All the five commentators after whom branches are named wrote before the middle of the fourteenth century, and the survey made here can only confirm the general impression of a gradual decline in the quality of scholastic analysis. But I wish strongly to preclude the possible inference that we could have covered Aristotelian economics simply by reading these five early commentaries. Their significance is rather that they introduce one after another of a set of distinct elements which must go into a comprehensive explanation of value, thus lifting the potential level of analysis another notch. In some instances, all that their successors could hope to do was maintain this level, holding some brilliant early scholastic ideas over for the first post-scholastic economists. But among a mass of copyists there are eminent analysts to be found among the *Ethics* commentators throughout the scholastic period, and the Aristotelian economic tradition itself bore some late fruits of considerable theoretical interest.

When at some point during the period under study, certain commentators started to bypass the mediaeval authorities, thus creating new traditions, their aims were no longer those of the scholastic philosopher, but those of the humanist; their notes and comments were increasingly in the nature of textual criticism and of literary and historical support to the locus. The humanists started to take over the *Ethics* quite early, but this did not happen overnight in what we have become used to call the Renaissance. Another view of this age has arisen from renewed inspection of the sources[7] and it is fully

---

7 "The Renaissance is still in many respects an Aristotelian age which in part continued the trends of medieval Aristotelianism, and in part gave it a new

born out by our material: scholastic arguments over the text of the *Ethics* continued all through the Renaissance and only slowly gave up ground. But from the late fifteenth century onward, an increasing number of regular commentaries approach Aristotle with purposes irrelevant to the present study. At the same time, for the purpose of philosophical study, the regular commentary itself is gradually eased off the field by different types of textbook. Not all mediaeval commentaries were actually meant to be read in class, but their basic forms were designed to accommodate oral instruction: either an oral dispute over a point in the text or a reading of the text with consecutive comments. The art of printing was decisive for the breaking up of these forms. Through cheaper, printed books the student could be approached in a larger variety of forms suited to different purposes and levels of study — and to professors' tastes. In Moral Philosophy an increasing number were able to publish textbooks of their own design rather than follow Aristotle line by line or problem by problem. The appearance of such books does not mean that Aristotle was discarded as an authority. Though it became easier to combine several authorities, the prestigious Philosopher still dominates the scene in most moral textbooks of the sixteenth and early seventeenth centuries or at least hovers in the wings; the familiar list of virtues is unavoidable and there is usually a discussion of justice in exchange on the pattern of *EN*, V, 5, tied to one or other of the mediaeval branch traditions. No clear distinction between regular commentaries and semi-Aristotelian textbooks is required for our purpose. Of the two types taken together, some seventy different works are to be quoted in this study.[8]

This naturally constitutes the body of our material, but the value analysis inspired by *EN*, V, 5 soon spread to other types of scholastic literature as well: collections of questions, theological and moral

direction under the influence of classical humanism and other different ideas." (Kristeller 47). Burke 40 makes the same point ("Humanism did not destroy interest in scholastic philosophy"), citing Lorenzo de' Medici's search for a copy of Buridan's *Ethics* commentary as an example.

8 The informed mediaeval scholar will miss some well-known names among the *Ethics* commentators. For each item included here, at least one more was studied and discarded. These are authors who either pass over our locus or else fail to make a quote-worthy comment. I have chosen to save the space needed to record these rejects.

summae, lexical works, and not least the many commentaries on the *Sentences* of Petrus Lombardus, the twelfth century compilation of patristic texts which became such an important vehicle of dispute on almost any moral and social issue in the late Middle Ages. Authors of more independent treatises *de contractibus*, *de usuris*, *de emptionibus et venditionibus* etc., also frequently quoted Aristotle or his commentators on economic value. Most of this can safely be ignored; it is usually brief and non-committal. But in between are a few items, without which the pictures of some of the Aristotelian branch traditions would have been incomplete. As the differentiation of professions and academic disciplines, aided by the printing press, gave birth to new media of literary expression, the channels of Aristotelian influence also changed. Commutative justice naturally established itself as a technical term in legal literature, which for a period became a major outlet for economic analysis until its place was yielded to professional economic literature proper. But now a new critical tone was also spreading, eventually to erase the Aristotelian quotations.

*

Gradually cut off from its textual toots by the switch to a humanistic type of *Ethics* commentary, the Aristotelian economic tradition was no doubt partly kept alive by transplantation into moral textbooks and various other kinds of professional literature until partly fading out and partly merging into the implicit premises of the new economics. But the importance of such secondary literature for this process of transition should not be overestimated. Aristotelian elements in economic texts proper of the sixteenth and seventeenth centuries indicate that the scholastic results were being assimilated earlier and under more direct influence of the regular commentaries than might be expected. In tracing the connection between mediaeval and modern economics, I would suggest that closer attention be paid to regional differences. By a small coincidence, of the founders of our six branch traditions, two are German (Albertus Magnus and Henricus de Frimaria), two French (Buridan and Odonis), while one is British (Grosseteste — but there should have been two if the immensely influential commentary by Burlaeus had broken some new ground). Thomas of course was an Italian — by birth. In the universal community of scholarship where nationality by birth made no great difference, the contribution made by Italians after Thomas to Aristotelian economics was not remarkable. But in the long years of scholastic decline when national barriers — political, religious, linguistic — break up the intellectual community, Italy becomes a bridgehead of historical communication.

By contrast, and to start where the classical tradition was born, consider Britain. The late Aristotelian tradition was rather weak there, at least as far as domestic work is concerned. While there are obvious Aristotelian echoes not only in an early author like Barbon, but also for instance in Smith, as pointed out already by Senior, and in Malthus, it is not possible to trace a convincing line of influence.[9] Before long, England became the country of the triumphantly rediscovered Aristotle. In 1797 John Gillies published in London the first (very free) translation of the *Nicomachean Ethics* into English. In an annotated preface he refers to Aristotelian "discoveries of science, unjustly claimed by the vanity of modern writers" and refers in a footnote to, among other loci, *EN*, V, 5, which he compares favourably with "the works of the modern oeconomists, not excepting those of Hume and Smith". But all praise is for the Greek thinker; there is something positively Hobbesian about Gillies's brief account of the scholastic tradition, Averroes, Albert and Thomas, among others: "This vast and cold mass of Gothic and Saracenic dulness is now consigned to just oblivion".[10] It was, too. When Senior a generation later presents Aristotle the economist in his *Lectures*, he does not realize that he is restating a

9 Adam Smith owned a four-volume Greek and Latin edition of Aristotle's *Works*, presumably including the *Nicomachean Ethics* (Yanaihara 95). His shelves also contained the six volumes of Du Hamel's *Philosophia vetus et nova* (ibid. 108), a set of Aristotelian commentaries in the late scholastic style; it does include the *Ethics* but passes over the economic material. (Cp. ed. Nürnberg 1682, Tom. I, pp. 683–4 — probably not Smith's edition). Since Adam Smith owned a copy of Samuel Pufendorf's treatise on Natural Law (in a French translation, cp. Yanaihara 122), it is possible that some of his knowledge of scholastic economics reached him through this source. On Pufendorf as a transmitter of Aristotelian value theory, see below, pp. 104–5 and note 3,50 (note 50 to Chapter 3).

10 *Aristotle's Ethics and Politics*, Vol. I, London 1797. References are to p. viii, text and note e, and to p. 2, note a.

scholastic theory. There is also a school of historians who see a connection between Aristotelian and Marxist labour theory. But Marx also worked in England in an intellectual climate which barred his conscious access to scholastic sources; when he discusses *EN*, V, 5, restating another scholastic theory, he quotes a modern Greek edition.

"Gothic dulness" having been laid to rest in England, it was stirring for some time on the Continent. We can pass rapidly over the German language area, where Protestant Aristotelianism had produced a vast moral literature of mostly poor quality; nothing much was stirring there now as far as economics is concerned. When the Austrians later brought Aristotle into the argument over value again, their conscious attitude was negative, while there is the same vague hint of a hidden scholastic influence. The situation was decidedly different in France, where the scholastic tradition had its strongest roots and much of its nourishment. Aristotelian study, though decreasingly analytical in character, continued in spite of a growing anti-scholastic sentiment, and the seventeenth and eighteenth century economists still quoted Aristotle openly. The vivid correspondence between French and English writers, sometimes over points of value theory, speaks of a close connection, and partly accounts for the second thoughts which finally enabled some classical authors of the early nineteenth century to give a balanced explanation of value. But this influence is partly an Italian one, via French authors.

We must pass beyond the Alps to find the freest access to scholastic economics in the eighteenth century. The continued growth of Aristotelianism in the heartland of the Renaissance was ensured for another century or two by the decrees of Trent. There was no economist of note among the late Italian *Ethics* commentators; the humanist approach was taking over as elsewhere. But Bernardo Segni had translated the *Ethics* into the *lingua vulgare Fiorentina* in 1550, with a long explanation, and his work was followed by paraphrases, dialogues and many ethical texts with an Aristotelian leaning. Moreover, the copious references to the *Etica* in all types of Italian literature in the two centuries between Segni and Galiani are generally free of the paralyzing hostility which was spreading among transalpine writers in the same period. Though some of this ran outside the mediaeval traditions, education at the hands of the clergy preserved important scholastic elements, for theorists in the new fields, including economics, to take what they found worth using. There is hardly an Italian economist from this period who did not take something. In the end it was this soil which produced Ferdinando Galiani, to whom all roads in the development of economic value theory seem to go back, first from France, later from all Europe. Galiani is an enigma only to those who fail to realize that he was, among other things, a scholastic philosopher. He may argue with this or that point in the *Ethics,* and even with *gli Aristotelici,* but it is still a scholastic Aristotle, not a newly discovered Greek Aristotle, who is to him *uomo per altro d'ingegno grandissimo e maraviglioso.*[11]

*

It goes without saying that comments on *EN,* V, 5 and texts derived from this commentary tradition do not exhaust the source material of mediaeval value theory. There are other traditions which will not be discussed here except in so far as they interact with the Aristotelian one. A number of recent critical editions of early texts and commentaries and some excellent bibliographical surveys[12] particularly call for and greatly facilitate a reexamination of the Aristotelian contribution, whose general importance and special significance have not, in my judgment, been adequately appreciated. Several factors combine to make of that brief locus in the *Ethics* a uniquely constructive vehicle of value analysis. The

11 *Della moneta,* I, ii; cp. *Scrittori classici italiani di economia politica* (ed. Pietro Custodi; 50 vols., Milan 1803–1816), Parte moderna, Tom. III, p. 55.
12 Definite critical editions of St Thomas Aquinas's commentary and of the all-important *First Commentary* by St Albertus Magnus have recently been published; an edition of the Latin translations of Greek commentaries by Grosseteste is under way. In particular, the model offered by Father Gauthier's Thomas edition can hardly be overpraised. This work also comes with an excellent preface, supplementing the wealth of bio-bibliographical information to be found in the commentary history of the *Ethics* attached to the French translation and commentary by Gauthier and Jolif, in Lohr's catalogue of Latin Aristotelian commentaries to the year 1500 and in Cranz's list of sixteenth century Aristotle editions based on the *Index Aureliensis.*

23

first concerns *identification* of the problem at hand. Aristotle has been much praised for his pioneering venture into monetary theory in *EN*, V, 5, but in point of fact his interest in money is only an indirect one; he is concerned primarily with price not with credit. Hence his monetary remarks will not as a rule lead immediately to a discussion of usury, the one topic which otherwise overwhelmingly dominates mediaeval economic literature. We thus have here one of the really quite few central scholastic loci which call upon the commentator to consider the problem of balancing exchange values while disregarding the time factor.

There are some others in scriptural and patristic sources, but they lack the high degree of *abstraction* of *EN*, V, 5, which prevented the mediaeval commentator from indulging his bent for casuistry. This second point is no less important. The casuistic economic literature of the Middle Ages contains much wisdom, but to the student of general theory it raises serious problems of interpretation, since the discussion tends to get involved in a mass of circumstantial detail. The description of the exchange situation in *EN*, V, 5 is devoid of such detail. All we are presented with are the exchangers as bare types: the builder, the shoemaker, and their products. If one is to say anything at all relevant to their situation, it must also assume an abstract character, must relate to principles of exchange. This very much increases the generalizing potential of comments on the text. To these I must add a third and no doubt surprising point, since it concerns the *obscurity* of the text. Gibbon described the philosophy of the Stagirite as "alike intelligible or alike obscure for the readers of every age". But each century, says Mauthner, taught "seinen eigenen Geist im Namen des Aristoteles".[13] The more obscure the text, the more room, presumably, for the *Zeitgeist*, and there is no doubt that our short section is one of the Philosopher's murkiest passages. On the other hand, the text is highly suggestive. If one assumes that it must mean something, it could be a number of things. The schoolmen certainly looked for meaning in Aristotle; sometimes obscurity signalled profundity. It is a commonplace of scholastic research that interpretation of the ancient authorities to some extent mirrored the commentators'

13 Gibbon, *Decline and Fall*, Chapter LII; Mauthner 3.

times and environments, but this effect is probably particularly strong in the present instance. Interpreters have had to draw on the best insights available at any given time, and many fruitful suggestions have been made in the attempt to explain what in the world Aristotle could mean at *EN*, V, 5.

The *continuity* of a tradition referring to the same basic locus for several centuries is also a point worth mentioning, though in comparison with modern economics rather than with other scholastic traditions. The development of the modern theory of value has been characterized by the playing out against each other of a series of partial explanations, each being built on one of the several elements that must in the end go into a full explanation. But each of these partial theories has been born and reborn in changed historical and ideological settings, thus endlessly confusing the polemics between them. In mediaeval economics the Aristotelian reference spares the theorist, and the historian, some of this confusion. The elements which define the different main theories of value soon appeared in the commentary literature. It was to no small extent the fact that they continually referred to the same model, reinforced by the ever-present text of Aristotle, which made possible the gradual maturing of these complementary explanations towards the composite theory of a later date. In scholastic thought, however, this type of continuity is nothing exclusive to the Aristotelian tradition. It is shared to some extent by all commentary literature and thus by a considerable part of all scholastic literature. It is in fact necessary in order to grasp the nature of mediaeval economics to realize how much of it had to be written in comment on a limited number of suitable loci in the standard texts upon which university instruction in philosophy and theology was mainly based. In all this literature, despite the ingenuity of the commentators, the invocation of the locus must to some extent condition the nature and direction of comments. This brings us to the fifth and most important point in the evaluation of Aristotle as an analytical medium. It is related to several of those made above but lies deeper.

Each literary task invites its own attitude. It takes a feeling for mediaeval intellectual temper too often missing in economic historians if one is properly to compare two authors' — or even the

25

same author's[14] — different statements about just price made in comments on Aristotle and Augustine. If there happens to be, in a certain basic text, a locus which states a specific economic problem in a manner conducive to thinking along analytically fruitful lines, it is obvious that this would tend to further theoretical development more readily than if the mediaeval master had to wring a dubious license to discuss this problem from a reluctant text. But such *contextual influences* may come from beyond this single locus and reflect the moral and psychological frame of the work as a whole. I can think of no better way to illustrate this than by comparing Aristotle's *Ethics* with the *Sentences* of Petrus Lombardus, which drew a volume of economic comment quite as large, mostly concerning usury but often about just pricing as well. There are three standard loci for such comments, two in Book III, namely Distinctio 33 (about the Cardinal Virtues, including Justice) and Distinctio 37 (about the Ten Commandments, with a chapter about Theft) and one in Book IV, namely Distinctiones 14–16 (about Penitence, where restitution for sinful economic gains is frequently discussed by the commentators). Two frames of reference rest heavily on these loci. The very notion of economic exchange as bordering on theft, suggested at *Sent.* III, 37 and none too foreign to a certain strain of ideas running into scholastic social analysis from patristic sources, involves both these references: a reference to *Sin*, calling for restitution under a reference to divine *Justice*. The emphasis will not naturally shift, in commentary made on these references, from the concern of the individual soul cleansing himself, the more the better, under the Law. The economics of pricing and exchange value, i.e. the balancing of productive and market requirements in view of the common good, cannot emerge except by forceful and deliberate emancipation from these contextual influences. It does so emerge sometimes, but not often, in commentaries on the *Sentences*. The context of justice as such does not, as we shall have every chance to ascertain, necessarily impede economic analysis, but then the frame of reference would not be Biblical justice but rather Aristotelian justice.

14 This point is made in the case of a related discipline by Gilby 248–9. On the other hand, attitudes determined by a major work can sometimes influence a simultaneous, minor work; cp. below, p. 88.

For it is not the ethical intent as such which makes the difference. There used to be a tendency to dismiss all scholastic economics on account of its moral basis, but I trust it is no longer necessary to go all out to meet such objections, which reflect both a lack of historical perspective and, more specifically, a confusion of analytical terms with analytical motivation. If a certain general moral code is to find expression in consistent rules of conduct in a specific area, for instance in terms of economic variables, the working of the economic system on which these variables operate must be to some extent understood. The ethical motive then reverts to the immediate intellectual need of all positive analysis, the terms of which may well be similar — difference of motivation notwithstanding — to that, say, of the latter-day "objective" economist. They may be similar; they are not necessarily so. It is all a question of the analytical challenge both of the basic moral code and of the type and circumstances of the behaviour it is called upon to advise. It is obvious that a morality which involves condemnation of the profit motive will not get us far in the analysis of monopoly pricing, for instance. Distinctions of this type do occur in the Aristotelian material; a certain narrow view of "respectable" economic areas apparent in the early commentaries being broadened in later branches. But all branches had to respond to the challenge of Aristotle's juridical system.

The commentator found an invitation to constructive analysis in the *contrapassum* equation. Granted that they are both moralists, there is a great difference between the preacher who admonishes his flock against fraud and cupidity in business dealings for the sakes of their individual souls and the master who, commenting on Aristotle, has to say something relevant about just exchange between two honest craftsmen. To preach about greed may serve as an introduction but does not really get to the core of the problem since, after all, the less greedy the shoemaker is, the more the builder will line his pockets. So here is a problem of equilibrium, of balancing the "dues" of the one against those of the other, and there really is no way of doing this except by looking into the economic consequences of their acts, so as to determine what norms of pricing will benefit the Community of Christians as a whole. Thus the individuals placed in opposition by Aristotle become truly economic agents; before telling any individual what is right for him to do, the Aristotelian must sit down and reason out the economic relations involved. The notion of equilibrium is not one to be taken lightly here, but there is in the equation of *contrapassum* a primitive idea of value as *equilibrium value*. It is this basic conception which enables some of the authors to be quoted here to push their insights into the problem so far ahead. This is not a conventional assessment of the Aristotelians. Rather, it is one which this book has to argue for, against a historical judgment which has improved somewhat of late but which is still one-sided and rather less flattering. To state the ultimate thesis of this study, it is best to approach it through a review of these previous interpretations.

*

The authors on whom previous interpretations have been almost exclusively based, are Albertus Magnus and Thomas Aquinas, the first two great regular commentators. Johannes Buridanus was also discovered early and has received much praise, but he has been correctly classified as somewhat atypical. It is regrettable that historians have been content to judge a long period of analytical development on the basis of a few initial works, but as far as the question now to be raised is concerned, it may well be discussed, at least for the time being, with reference to them. The attempts which were made, early in this century, to recapture mediaeval value theory, got off to a wrong start on account of the unfortunate distinction then current between so-called *subjective* and *objective* theories. Looking back with some of the anti-scholastic sentiment still lingering, historians in a period when subjective explanations were on the upswing, readily found evidence of objective thinking in the leading schoolmen. Thus Kaulla and Schreiber:

... Albertus Magnus (scheint) derjenige gewesen zu sein, der die Reihe der "*objektiven*" *Werttheorien* einleitete.

Man kann in Thomas immerhin einen characteristischen Vertreter der objektiven Wertlehre des Mittelalters sehen.[15]

15 Kaulla (2) 53; Schreiber 120.

Seeking to explain the nature of such objective value, some authors took an extremely bleak view of the common sense of mediaeval philosophers, suggesting some kind of inherent value divorced from economic realities. But this was, in all fairness, not the dominant interpretation of Albert and Thomas. For one thing it would be difficult, even by the most unscrupulously selective reading, to find textual support for it. For another thing there is a much less far-fetched interpretation of objective value which can be established on the basis of the texts — always read selectively. This is one which finds the basis of objective value in objective cost of production; it is based on Albert's frequent reference, once or twice repeated by Thomas, to *labor et expensae*. Such is the interpretation of objective value by Kaulla and Schreiber:

> Entsprechend erklärte Albertus Magnus das . . . aristotelische Beispiel . . . so, dass eine justa commutatio dann vorliege, wenn jeder der beiden Vertragsgegner an Arbeit und Kosten ebensoviel auf sein Produkt verwendet habe wie der andere. Thomas von Aquino . . . folgt in seinem Kommentar zur Nikomachischen Ethik seinem Lehrer Albertus Magnus in fast wortgetreuer Uebereinstimmung.

> Albertus Magnus und Thomas von Aquin sehen die Gerechtigkeit des Preises in der Wiedervergeltung von Arbeit und Kosten.[16]

This sounded very much like a more recent labour theory of value of which most economists were at this time rather weary, and so interest in the Aristotelian tradition fell to a low ebb, while the labour interpretation persisted since there seemed to be no other reasonable way to construe the Aristotelian principle on which the supposition about an objective theory rested, namely the principle of reciprocity, of *giving equal for equal*. Menger, principal spokesman for the Austrian subjective value theorists, made Aristotle top his list of authors chasing a non-existent "Gleichheit im objektiven Sinne";[17] it was through Mengerian glasses that German-speaking historians of the following generation reread the early schoolmen and came up with the labour explanation. Now the principle of reciprocity or equivalence is a central one in Aristotle's juridical model and the schoolmen never argued with it. Thomas, who stated

16 Kaulla, ibid.; Schreiber 227.
17 *Grundsätze*, Vienna 1871, pp. 173–4.

it repeatedly, says in his *Ethics* commentary that *contrapassum* requires *aequalitatem rei ad rem*.[18] Does not that imply objective measures, by which goods in exchange between different persons can be compared? Maybe so, but not in the sense in which the proponents of a subjective theory understood these categories. The points at issue here are brought out very clearly in a statement of the principle of equivalence by a somewhat later Aristotelian, Johannes Maior. An important *Ethics* commentator, he is quoted here in his commentary on the *Sentences*:

> ... si mercem excedat pretium aut contra, non servatur haec aequalitas, et istud perspicuum est secundum doctrinam Aristotelis V. Ethicorum. Si unus habet de lucro in fine contractus, et alter de damno, oportet resecare lucrum unius et addere damno alterius quousque redeant ad aequalitatem. ... [19]

A basic principle of modern analytical economics is that one man's gain is *not*, as Montaigne has it[20], another man's loss. There is a *lucrum* to both parties in an economic exchange. It was the fate of the Aristotelians for a long time to be judged an obstacle in the path to this insight. But the judgment was based on a misconception of the quantities involved in the equation.

The first to have pointed this out may be Eugène Daire, the French economist who, a quarter of a century before Menger, edited Quesnay's *Dialogue sur les travaux des artisans*. Quesnay was, like other leading Physiocrats, influenced by the Aristotelian tradition; he states the principle in the mouth of one of his dialogists: "... le commerce n'est qu'un échange de valeur pour valeur égale, ... relativement à ces valeurs il n'y a ni perte ni gain entre les contractants". To counter this, the editor quotes (in a footnote) Condillac, voicing new ideas: "Il est faux que, dans les échanges, on donne valeur égale pour valeur égale. Au contraire, chacun des contractants en donne toujours une moindre pour une plus grande." In different senses, both are right, says Daire, one in the sense that taking less for more is against the laws of our moral nature, the other in the sense that exchange of equal for equal would be (in a memorable phrase) like a movement "de deux forces en parfait état

18 V, 8; cp. also *Sum. theol.*, II–II, 77, 1, c and *Quodl.* II, V, 10.
19 *Sent.* IV, 15, 40; ed. Paris 1519, f. 151rb.
20 *Essais*, I, 22; cp. note 1,6.

30

d'équilibre". But there is no real contradiction. Employing Adam Smith's distinction, one of these authors refers to *value in exchange*, in terms of which the proposition is true, the other to *value in use*, in terms of which it is false.[21] And the first step to an understanding of the Aristotelian contribution, difficult as it has proved to be historically, is really as simple as that. The Austrians, rightly emphasizing the importance of subjective valuation, mistook the notion of equivalence for an expression of some alternative, objective criterion, at best associated with labour input, by which the real worth of goods could be compared. But there is no warrant for this. One cannot read a violation of the hard-earned principle of utility in the gallant struggle of an early school to understand value in exchange, and there is no evidence that the Aristotelians ever used equivalence otherwise than to express a condition in exchange values as such. If this made their theory an objective one, it was only in the sense in which any theory of exchange value can be said to be objective, namely in that it describes a social phenomenon seemingly emerging as a result of forces beyond the control of the individual. It is only by keeping this firmly in mind that one can begin to see what equivalence really meant.

The significance of Aristotle is primarily methodological. It took us a long time to assemble an appropriate set of tools of value analysis. Assessing any school, the historian should be keenly aware of the suggestive potential inherent in its proper vehicle of analysis, working — apart from the theoretical results reached at any time — to further this search for better tools. For the modern ear, equivalence ought to ring a bell. The theory of value as we now accept it is *a theory of equilibrium value*; its deductive search is not for this or that single value basis but for a fuller picture of the several forces which produce, in mutual balance, the price towards which the market tends. How was this "balanced" view of value brought about? Eugène Daire's lucky — or uniquely perceptive — expression is a clue. My thesis is that the Aristotelian model helped decisively in this process, and did so exactly by posing the problem of just pricing

21 *Collection des Principaux Économistes*, Vol. 2, Paris 1846, pp. 185–212 at p. 196, with note. Condillac is quoted by Daire from *Le commerce et le gouvernement*, later to be edited in the same series, Vol. 14, pp. 247–448, cp. p. 267.

as one of equivalence, *because equivalence bred the idea of equilibrium.* We may approach this inference through another school of historians.

*

A reinterpretation of Aristotle's value theory was one of the shrewd proposals made by Schumpeter in his *History of Economic Analysis*; unfortunately, the theory has tended to deteriorate at the hands of his followers and has not provided the insight it promised. The gist of Schumpeter's analysis is as follows. Since both parties to an exchange must normally profit from it, there can be no question of an equivalence of subjective values; on the other hand it does not follow that Aristotle entertained some notion of a mysterious objective or absolute value inherent in the goods themselves. There is one manner of valuation which is in a sense objective to the individual, namely the valuation of the competitive market under normal conditions; normal competitive price is objective in the sense that the individual buyer and seller can do nothing to influence it; it is given to them. And this normal or natural price is the Aristotelian just price, for with Aristotle and his followers, the "natural" is the "just". Proceeding to mediaeval economics, Schumpeter applies this interpretation with strict analogy to St Thomas Aquinas:

St. Thomas was as far as was Aristotle from postulating the existence of a metaphysical or immutable "objective value". His *quantitas valoris* is not something different from price but is simply normal competitive price.[22]

This new way of looking at Aristotelian value theory must have seemed highly convincing, both in view of the speculations which it replaced and in view of its ability to make sense of controversial statements like the one quoted from Maior above. *Lucrum* and *damnum* could now simply be defined in relation to normal competitive price. If one party can influence price, by monopolistic manoeuvres, which the schools condemned, or by other fraudulent practices, he makes a profit which is unjust because it is unnatural, etc. Following Schumpeter, there is now a strong tendency,

22 Schumpeter 62, 93. *Quantitas valoris* is an expression used by Thomas in the *Summa theologiae*, not in the *Ethics* commentary.

particularly among American historians, to read the mediaeval just price as exclusively determined by the market. It was "nothing more mysterious than the competitive price", says De Roover.[23] It would be difficult to find support for this interpretation in the *thics* commentaries of Albertus Magnus, who tends in consequence ' recede into the background, Thomas Aquinas now taking all the)otlight. Read selectively, Thomas provides some support for the ew theory, though not without qualms to the conscientious his-)rian. Baldwin's conclusion is significant:

'rom the total perspective of the writings of Thomas Aquinas there is a suggestion f an evolution within the doctrine of the just price. In his *Commentary to the Ethics*, Thomas considered both the cost of production and the current price as)ossible bases for the just price. When, however, he wrote the *Secunda-secundae* of :he *Summa theologica* five or six years later he definitely decided for the current price.[24]

St Thomas's *Ethics* commentary used to be placed earlier; we now know that it was written simultaneously with the *secunda secundae*.[25] So there is no evolution of thought, only a diversity of response to different literary tasks. This is interesting enough, since Baldwin does point out that it is the *Ethics* which draws the balanced picture. But he does not himself make anything of this fact, and the reason is clearly that Baldwin, like most other historians, of the present "current price" conviction or of the earlier "labour and cost" conviction, believes that the mediaeval commentators would tend to "decide for" one or another partial theory of value. This belief correspondingly divides historians into groups holding contrasting views as to what theory the schoolmen did in fact decide for. Unfortunately, Schumpeter's otherwise remarkable analysis failed to ease off this polarization.

However, it is clear from the examples quoted above that the presently prevailing interpretation is a distortion of Schumpeter's on an important point. The latter was careful to explain Aristotelian just prices as "the *competitive* prices that emerge in free market *under normal conditions*".[26] The first emphasis is his, the second is

23 De Roover (1) 496.
24 Baldwin 78.
25 See below, p. 86.
26 Schumpeter 61.

mine. Schumpeter does not explain what he means here by normal conditions. But one would of course usually think of it as conditions under which price covers cost. If that is what Schumpeter had in mind, his whole argument could have been restated in terms of a cost theory. It would run something like this: Both parties do of course usually profit from mutual exchange in terms of individual utility, otherwise they would not exchange. But there is a certain valuation, objective in the sense that it is made by superpersonal economic forces, in terms of which goods exchanged must be equalized, namely normal cost, otherwise exchange will break down. Hence the individual buyer and seller should do nothing, even when this happens to be in their power, to keep price artificially below or above this just and normal level. To my mind this is an eminently congenial interpretation of one broad strain of ideas running through the mediaeval texts. It is obvious that a restatement of the older cost theory in these terms would make it seem much less in conflict with the more recent competitive price theory than it appears today. More important, we should be able to see their essential relation better, even if we had to renounce the specific condition under which the two theories exactly converge.

They would have been identical if the just price idea had expressed exactly what we now call long-run equilibrium price. But that is a preposterous suggestion; not because we can quote Albert and Thomas among the numerous schoolmen who contradict it by allowing short-run market fluctuations to influence the just price calculus and permitting cost above the normal to be covered under certain conditions.[27] It is not in their *Ethics* commentaries that Albert and Thomas make these concessions, and one of my points has been that remarks made in other contexts do not fully apply. But I am far from suggesting even that the *Ethics* could have inspired anything like this complex modern idea to these primitive economists. It is only a question of a general drift of ideas towards a unified explanation. Given the problem posed at *EN*, V, 5, the commentator is called upon to reflect on cost and market, not in order to "decide for" one or another partial just price theory, but to understand a composite field of causation. In the end this did bring

27 For instance, Albert, *Sent.* IV, 16, 46; Thomas, II–II, 77, 1, c.

some of them closer to grasping the conditions of long-run equilibrium, as this book will show. In the long intermediate process many statements about pricing and value were made in comment on Aristotle, showing different degrees of insight and sometimes hitting each other on the head. But this should not be permitted to rob us of a basic principle of interpretation, according to which these apparently conflicting statements are rather meant to be tentative, mutually supporting criteria of an underlying, unifying principle which the authors did not yet fully master. I do believe that the historical development of our science, at least in the scholastic age, is best understood when looked upon as a gradual realization of how different economic forces work together, not as the changing fortunes of a conflict between them. The conflict is of a more recent date and in the eye of the historian.

Being an equation involving opposing "dues", as I said above, Aristotelian justice in exchange appears as a problem of equilibrium in an immediate, logical sense; the deeper significance of this for economics is a matter of moral emphasis. As Aristotle saw it and as his commentators were led to think of it, the problem is not just a limited interpersonal one but a social one in a broader sense — the frame of reference is Plato's theory of the State. This basic orientation is spelled out clearly in *EN*, V, 5: if justice were not maintained, "arts would have been destroyed", "there will be no exchange and no intercourse". Specifically, just terms of exchange must be such as ensure that the different arts subsist to produce what society needs; this is in modern terms a general equilibrium condition of industries. The commentators of course could not explain it like that and would not in any case have been content to state it in generalities; they sought to specify what justice meant in terms of everyday variables, and so their value theory became a set of criteria by which to estimate a vaguely sensed, basic condition. In this search for criteria, Aristotle is of little help, but there are certain clues in *EN*, V, 5, and on the basis of these, two broad criteria developed. Albertus Magnus reasoned that the normal level of price must have something to do with cost; unless the artisan has his costs covered, he will not continue to produce. This is a reasonable criterion; Thomas and many others repeated it. But Thomas also reasoned that the

35

normal price must reflect human wants; many later authors repeated this and developed it into a demand theory. As a matter of fact, each of the original commentators suggested both criteria, but circumstances caused their emphases to differ, hence a cost theory has come to be associated with Albert, a market (supply-demand) theory with Thomas Aquinas.

Now, as we know, a comprehensive theory of value, like the one shakily assembled by the second or third generation of classical economists, is in the nature of a *synthesis*, it is a statement of the cost explanation and the supply-demand explanation simultaneously and in terms of one another. My overall conception of the Aristotelian exchange model as used by the mediaeval economists is this, that it indicated the nature of the just price as that of an equilibrium price, and that it was supplied, through the works of the first two great commentators, with one suggestion which led later commentators to reflect on the nature and role of cost and one suggestion which led them to reflect on the nature and role of supply and demand. Thus were placed in this narrow context two rigid matrices of thought, which most historians have interpreted as producing conflicting partial theories, but which actually brought to the study of economics in the Aristotelian tradition a heavy intellectual tension calling for release. Over the centuries, as we shall see, each line of explanation was developed — sometimes one and the same author contributed materially to both, sometimes mostly to one, sometimes mostly to the other — until the continual rubbing of these matrices against each other brought off the flash of insight which is the *Aristotelian synthesis*, a comprehensive theory of value anticipating the one which the classical economists offered several centuries later. This synthesis, the end product of Aristotelian value analysis, is documented on pages not studied by the many who have expressed opinions about the value theories of Albert and Thomas. In proper perspective, the thirteenth century Dominicans are mainly of interest as initiators of the analytical development towards a final synthesis which it is the task of this book to record.

1. Context

The tradition of Robert Grosseteste

The date at which Aristotle could begin to influence Western economic thought can be estimated both fairly closely and with a fair degree of confidence. Lottin[1] demonstrated the total ignorance of Aristotle's juridical system in authors ante-dating the mid-thirteenth century translations. There was no reason to expect economic justice to be a special case, and I have found nothing to indicate that it was. It is true that fragments of an *antiquior translatio* of the *Ethics* have been found and that it originally included Book V, but most of this book is lost and no application of it is known. Nor does the exchange model in *EN*, V, 5 seem to have filtered into Latin thought through indirect channels. The extant translation of the *Magna Moralia*, which does sketch the model, was not made until 1258 at the earliest, i.e. several years after Albertus Magnus's *First Commentary*. There may have been another translation of this work also.[2] This is worth noting because of a curious allusion to labour in the *Magna Moralia*,[3] in which some interpreters have read an explanation akin to Albert's.[4] But there is no valid basis for assuming an influence. As for other ancient texts, I can find no mention of the exchange model. It is omitted in the outline by Arius Didymus which found its way into the *Eclogae* of Stobaios,[5] and if it

1 Lottin (2) III 283–299.
2 AL, *Codices*, I, 71–2.
3 Mediaeval translation (Bartholomaeus de Messana) at 1194a3–4 (I, xxxiii, 9), just before the presentation of the builder and shoemaker and other agents: *Sicut autem laborans habet ad non laborantem, ita multa ad pauca.* (Vat. Palat. lat. 1011, ff. 138vb–139ra). But the *Magna Moralia* does not properly subdivide particular justice.
4 See the discussion in Hardie 191.
5 Particular justice is touched upon briefly: "... nor is he just who allots to himself too much or too little, but equally", i.e. *secundum proportionem, non*

did after all travel to the Latin West through some late Peripatetic influence, it left no trace in positive analysis either in Roman writers or in the Church Fathers.[6] This means that the early Latin commentators had to rely on limited and quite recent material for direct hints on how to interpret Aristotle at *EN*, V, 5. Their main source of inspiration was the great codex which issued from the work group at Lincoln, but we must go back a few years and start with Averroes. It was in 1240, shortly after joining the school of translators at Toledo, that Hermannus Alemannus initiated our tradition by presenting in Latin dress, later to be known as the *Liber Nicomachiae*, the commentary to the *Ethics* by the great twelfth century Arabian philosopher. A few years later he also translated another work derived from the *Ethics*, the so-called *Summa Alexandrinorum*, which was to create a tradition of its own, but it is brief and of little interest at *EN*, V, 5.[7]

While Averroes came to play a decisive part in the development of Aristotelianism in more central fields of philosophical study, his

secundum numerum in the translation of Canterus, Antwerp 1575, p. 193. The original is also in Tom. II, p. 86 of Meineke's edition, Leipzig 1860–4.

6 The shoemaker and the farmer do make an appearance in St Augustine's commentary on the 70th Psalm (PL, Tom. 36, 886–7), whence they were transferred to the *Decretum* (Dist. 88, c. 12), but this is most likely a Platonic rather than an Aristotelian remnant. In Plato's account of the foundation of the perfect state in *Republic*, II the agents mentioned are a farmer, a builder, a shoemaker and a weaver. But to illustrate the elusiveness of influences, consider the essay (I, 22) where Montaigne uses the examples of a farmer, a builder, a doctor (as well as a priest, a merchant and a lawyer) to reflect on the sad thought than one man's profit is another's loss. As pointed out by Villey (*Sources*, I, 215, cp. I, 343), Montaigne here plagiarizes Seneca (*De beneficiis*, VI, xxxviii). But has Seneca transmitted something from Aristotle? Fortunately, we can let this kind of question rest. It is sufficient here to establish that Aristotle's analytical exchange model, where these agents appear, is untraceable in Latin literature antedating the mid-thirteenth century translations.

7 Justice is discussed twice, first in its normal position, then even more briefly in Book VII. The longer section explains the introduction of money: *Oportet igitur ut aliquid statuatur quod coaequans sit inter eos, ipsorum conservans in debita consistentia participationem et connegotiationem. Huius itaque causa statutus est denarius* .... (Paris BN lat. 12954, f.14v). There is nothing about the role of human need. The summary appeared in French as part of Brunetto Latini's *Livres dou Trésor* (Italian versions: *Tesoro*, *Tesoretto*) and in adaptions by Manente (Venice 1538) and Wilkinson (London 1547), the lines on economics becoming wholly corrupt in some retranslations. See also note 1,33.

importance to Aristotelian economics is less easily demonstrable. The numerous commentators, from the thirteenth century "Averroists" to Buridan and his many imitators, who discussed whether human want, or demand, is a measure of goods in exchange, regularly referred part of their argument to Averroes's theory of measurement in his *Metaphysics* commentary. I can find no one referring to his *Ethics* commentary at V, 5. But there are one or two minor points in it to be noted below and one point of potentially very great interest to the ensuing tradition. Here is how Averroes, in Herman's translation, explains the introduction of money:

> Cum itaque connegotiatio sit propter indigentiam et quorundam indigentium non semper conveniant in eadem hora indigentiae, verbi gratia carpentarius interdum indiget agricola qui illa hora non indiget carpentario sed medico vel aliquo alio et sic de aliis in aliis, posuerunt inter se homines per modum convenientiae aliquid quod sit instrumentum connegotiandi in omnibus, et hoc est nummisma.[8]

The reader will find as he proceeds along the line of later commentators, that one ever visible thread in the web of tradition is the meaning and role of *indigentia*. Averroes's commentary having been lost in the original, we cannot know what Arabic word was in fact translated like that in the *Liber Nicomachiae*.[9] Nor can we be sure to what extent Herman's choice influenced Grosseteste in his search for an appropriate term in his notes or in the commentaries translated from Greek or to what extent it influenced the revisor of Grosseteste who established *indigentia* in the text of the *Ethics* itself. Proceeding at once to these developments, we may at least remember Herman the German as the one who first used that suggestive word.

Robertus Grosseteste was born in Suffolk about 1168. He studied and taught at Paris and Oxford, to which latter university his name is forever tied as that of a great scholar and administrator. After several decades of academic work, in theology as well as in physics,

---

8 Manuscripts consulted (quoted sections in parentheses): Vat. Borghes. 57 (f.12r-v); Florence BLaur Plut. 89 sup. 49 (f.17rb); Erfurt Amplon. F.23 (f.36va-b); Saint-Omer BMun 623 (f.55r-v). Early editions are faulty, cp. Venice 1483 (f.f$_6$rb); Venice 1562 (f.72ra-b); no critical edition.

9 An early Arabic translation of *EN*, V itself is preserved, but we cannot be sure that this is the version Averroes used.

39

he was elected bishop of Lincoln in 1235. The mediaeval diocese of Lincoln was very large and included the University of Oxford, and Grosseteste retained his academic connections until his death in 1253.[10] Having acquired a knowledge of Greek unusual for his time, though working with specialist *adiutores*, he now set about translating and commenting on a number of mainly theological works. And it was here at Lincoln, at an advanced age, that he conceived the idea of composing a Latin corpus of Aristotle's *Ethics*. Greek manuscripts were brought home and the work, Robert Grosseteste's last finished work of translation, was completed "not later than 1246–7".[11]

The typical early codex of the *Translatio Lincolniensis* consists of a translation of Aristotle's text interspaced with a translation of a Greek commentary, in the case of Book V an early anonymous one (perhaps dating from the sixth century) and supplied with marginal and interlinear notes by Grosseteste, sometimes initiated by the ascription *Epc* (*Episcopus*). Receiving special attention, Book V is the subject of yet another commentary, added at the end of the triple exposition of that book, by Michael Ephesinus, an eleventh century Byzantine professor, who appears to know the anonymous commentary and sometimes follows it closely.[12] Only seven manuscripts containing all four elements have been located; about twice as many have the text and commentaries but no significant notes. The seven are important: **RG1**: Oxford All Souls 84, **RG2**: Cambridge Peterhouse 116, **RG3**: Eton College 122, **RG4**: Florence BN I. v. 21, **RG5**: Vat. lat. 2171, **RG6**: Paris Arsenal 698, **RG7**:

10 On Grosseteste, see Callus (2), as well as Emden II 830–3; Tanner 345–6; Chevalier 3995–6; DNB VIII 718–721; EF V 832–5; DTC VI 1885–7; LTK VIII 1339; Wulf II 40–3, 88–93; Ueberweg 358–9, 371–7, 731–2; Fabricius VI 403–5; Gilson 261–5, 662–5; Lohr XXIX 100–7.

11 Callus (2) 67. On the *Translatio Lincolniensis*, see also Callus (1); Pelzer (1) at 378–404; as well as Powicke; Thomson; Francheschini (1); Dunbabin (2).

12 Michael also commented on Books IX and X, our Anonymous covered Books II–IV in addition to V. Both are rather obscure figures; some scholars hold that the Anonymous paraphrases Michael rather than vice versa. Anyhow, they entered the Latin tradition together. Commentators on the remaining books were Eustratius, Aspasius and a more recent anonymous. Greek readings are occasionally quoted from CAG; the Anonymous on *EN*, V is in Vol. XX, Berlin 1892; Michael on *EN*, V is in Vol. XXII, Pars III, Berlin 1901.

Stockholm KB V. a. 3.[13] Michael's commentary, but not the anonymous one, was retranslated by Felicianus and printed in several editions from 1541.[14] The mediaeval translations of the Greek commentaries have not yet been printed,[15] nor is there as yet any complete, critical edition of Grosseteste's *notulae*. These enigmatic notes, which lie at the root of the entire Latin tradition, are of varying length and character. Most of them are to the text of Aristotle; there are some to the translated commentaries as well, but none to the sections of the commentaries which concern us here. To the relevant section of Aristotle there are seven common notes, i.e. notes occurring in at least two of the seven manuscripts listed above; only **RG7** has them all, while **RG2**, **RG3** and **RG4** have six each. Some are only brief philological notes; the others are of an exegetical character, but only three of the notes have a bearing on the value analysis; each of these has a main and a variant reading. In **RG1** there are also some important singular notes.

The history of Grosseteste's translation of the *Nicomachean Ethics* itself is quite complicated. Albertus Magnus knew the *Translatio Lincolniensis* only in its original version, but even before Thomas Aquinas composed his commentary, a revision had been made of the text. This was long thought to have been undertaken at Thomas's request by a fellow Dominican, Guillelmus de Moerbeke, but doubts as to this have been voiced and the question is not settled.[16] The recent edition of the *Nicomachean Ethics* in *Aristoteles Latinus* includes the *textus purus*, **L¹**, as well as the "Moerbekan" *textus*

13 Locations of relevant sections of text with anonymous commentary, and of Michael's commentary: **RG1**: ff.90ra–91ra, ff.107va–108vb; **RG2**: ff.85vb–87ra, ff.105va–107rb; **RG3**: ff.71ra–72ra, ff.89ra–90rb; **RG4**: ff.84ra–85rb, ff.102vb–103vb; **RG5**: ff.67vb–68vb, ff.86va–88ra; **RG6**: ff.55rb–56ra, f.67ra–vb; **RG7**: ff.72vb–74ra, ff.90rb–91rb. (Author's initials prefixed to numbers will be used to identify manuscripts; an **X** inserted will indicate a printed edition.)

14 Venice 1541 (IA 108.025 — rare copy in Cambridge UL), Basel 1542, Paris 1543, and later editions by Samuel Rachelius at Helmstedt.

15 A critical edition is in preparation as No. 6 in *Corpus latinum commentariorum in Aristotelem graecorum*, of which Vol. I, Leiden 1973, contains commentaries to *EN*, I–IV, with an Introductory Study by H.P.F. Mercken. Vol. II is yet to appear.

16 The fact of the revision was discovered by Francheschini, who attributed it to Moerbeke. Doubt as to Moerbeke's authorship was raised by Gauthier.

recognitus, **R**. It seems that **R** was not made directly on **L^1** but on an intermediate, minor edition, **L^2**, of the *Lincolniensis* without notes and commentaries. The revisor, whoever he was, can be seen to have compared Grosseteste's readings with two Greek manuscripts as well as with the *antiquior translatio* when available. The archetype of **R** is lost; it must be deduced from derived manuscripts in two traditions, namely an Italian tradition, documented by a single manuscript now at Toledo, **Rt**, and a Paris tradition, **Rp**, copiously documented. R. A. Gauthier, who edited the AL texts, has also established the revised version **T**, which served as a basis for St Thomas's commentary. It is somewhat related to **Rp**, but is fortunately quite clean in our section, while the Paris recension is badly corrupted in some lines.[17] The all-important element of the revision at *EN*, V, 5, changing one of Grosseteste's key words, is touched by this corruption. However, it was soon to be rectified, and there is no evidence of its having spoiled any branch of the economic commentary tradition. Choice of textual version (and subsequently choice of translation) may sometimes indicate other influences on a commentator, and we shall have occasion to point out such cases in what follows. Both the pure and the revised versions of Grosseteste remained in use, but most commentators after Thomas found their ways to some variant of **R**. (See Appendix for Aristotle's exchange model in the *Translatio Lincolniensis*, with variants.)

*

The reception of Aristotle's exchange model was influenced by all elements in the Grossetestan corpus: text, commentaries and notes, and they cannot be separated in our analysis. But all comments are necessarily shaped by a peculiarity in the text as received by the translator, and this requires some preliminary remarks. Any reader of *EN*, V, 5 must be struck by the obtrusive repetitiousness of Aristotle's discussion. The clue to the whole section may be, as suggested by Jolif,[18] to read it as three successive redactions of the

---

17 I refer to Gauthier's own work for more detailed accounts of this complicated process of revision. There is a summary in (3) 125–9. For the recension **T**, see (4) 203*–234* and 289ff. The *antiquior translatio*, the *textus purus* and the *textus recognitus* are all in AL, XXVI (*Ethica Nicomachea*), Leiden/Brussels 1972–4.

18 Gauthier/Jolif, II, 1, pp. 380–5.

same argument, starting, respectively, at (1) 1133a19, (2) 1133a25, (3) 1133b14, and prefaced by a general presentation of the operation of justice in exchange in terms of a proportion involving two producers and two products. The first and last redactions can then be seen as less complete variants of the middle redaction. Using one of Grosseteste's key terms, (2) states that economic exchange requires a common measure; *opus* is what holds society together in the sense that without *opus* there is no exchange; money is introduced to effect this measurement of goods for which there is *opus*; an example is given in terms of shoes and food, to explain reciprocal exchange of goods thus evaluated. By comparison, (1) is a much shorter redaction. *Opus* is not mentioned; commodities must be measured; the measure is money; an example is stated in terms of shoes and a house (the one already used in the preface). The final redaction (3) again has all elements. Jolif suggests a transposition of lines which preserves the order as it is in (2): need for a common measure, *opus*, money, and an example: beds and a house. If resort is had to transposing lines, other hypotheses may suggest themselves,[19] but the basic theory of the triple redactions remains inviolate. Omitting sections about money, it explains why *EN*, V, 5 comes to treat intermittently and repeatedly of two elementary topics, namely the operation of proportionate justice in exchange between artisans (builder and shoemaker, shoemaker and farmer, builder and carpenter), and the role of *opus* in economic intercourse. From these elements were shaped the two blades of the Aristotelian scissors of value theory.

Opus is Grosseteste's translation of Aristotle's χρεία. Of the multiple meanings of this Greek noun, there are several, more or less clearly distinguishable, of interest to economic analysis, viz. *usus* (= advantage, service, use; cp. *utilitas*); *opus* (= need, in the somewhat passive sense of necessity; cp. *necessitas*); and *indigentia* (= need, in the rather more active sense of craving, perhaps demand).[20] Forms of χρεία occur five times in *EN*, V, 5. Grosseteste translates *opus* at 1133a27, b6, b20, *necessitas* at 1133a29, b7. These

---

19 See note 1,29.
20 *opportunitas* is also among alternatives used in Latin Aristotle translations; see AL, XXVI, p. CCXLV and p. 734.

are pertinent translations; they might have stood, and so perhaps steered value theory in other directions, were it not for one of those linguistic coincidences which sometimes interfere with the course of intellectual history. In his explanation of proportionate exchange, Aristotle employs the word ἔργον four times, at 1133a9, a13, a33, b5. It means "work", and Grosseteste correctly translates — *opus*, a very different meaning of *opus*. Hence this word comes to occur seven times in the brief space of *EN*, V, 5, now in one, now in the other of these senses. This may not have caused all that much confusion as far as Aristotle's own text is concerned (though there are at least two important instances to be recorded.[21]) But the translated commentaries, whose style is much less concise, are another thing. If Grosseteste were to have kept strictly to that one translation, *opus* would have had to be used so frequently in shifting senses as to make pure nonsense of some sections of the commentaries.

So he starts varying his translation. *Opus* is sometimes used alone for χρεία in the commentaries; so is *necessitas* a few times, as well as the combination, *opus et* (or *seu*) *necessitas*. But we also find the longer forms, *opus seu necessitas sive utilitas*, and frequently *opus sive necessitas sive indigentia*, even the full string, *opus sive necessitas sive utilitas sive indigentia* (or *id est* or *et* or *seu* or *vel* instead of *sive* in the latter two forms). Judging by the translated commentaries, *necessitas* would seem to be Grosseteste's preferred substitute for *opus*; *indigentia* and *utilitas* are at best third choices. But the translator has also deemed it requisite to distinguish the two meanings of *opus* as occurring in the text of Aristotle; he does so by adding notes to *opus* at 1133a27 and 1133b6. The first of these notes is in **RG2, 4, 7** with a variant in **RG1** and reads, *id* (*hoc* **RG1**) *est necessitas et indigentia*.[22] The second note is in **RG2, 3, 4, 7** and reads, *id est indigentia mutua*. Again, **RG1** has a variant, *id est indigentia. et utilitas*. Occurring in both notes, *indigentia* now moves up as the

21 See note 1,23 and pp. 67–8.
22 **RG6** has *id est indigentia* in a later hand; this variant is also recorded in Kues BHosp. 181, as noted in AL, XXVI, p. 237n, but this evidence is of doubtful value since some of the longer marginal notes in the Cusanus manuscript are of obvious Thomist inspiration, including a note on the same page (f.68v) reproducing Thomas's *superabundantias* explanation. (see below, p. 55).

leading suggestion at the cost of *necessitas*. This is strikingly confirmed by the fact that in some copies of the *Translatio Lincolniensis*, *indigentia* has come into the text at 1133b6, not indeed to replace but to supplement *opus*.[23] In **R** (including **T**), *indigentia* replaces *opus* at 1133a27, b6, b20. Since **L**² still reads *opus*, we can only guess at what caused the revisor to make this switch, but it is hard to avoid the thought that it is Grosseteste's *indigentia* which now, through some channel or another, moves permanently into the text.

It is tempting to ask whether *opus* may have been the word used in the *antiquior translatio*, the notes suggesting *indigentia* being in a true sense, Grosseteste's translation. However, since he frequently writes *opus* himself in the commentaries, there is no valid basis for this conjecture. As for the prominence of *indigentia* in the *notulae*, it may of course have been little more than accidental, Grosseteste picking from his list of equivalents without much forethought. But we do not have to believe this. Deciding for *indigentia* as against *necessitas* is deciding for one interpretation of need as against another. The change is a subtle one, but its importance can hardly be overestimated. We are dealing here with a string of terms which play very close to the core of Aristotelian value theory at a crucial stage of its early growth, and (at least as they sound to my ear) none of the associations which *necessitas* calls up could have helped along the interpretational sliding of Aristotle's concept towards the modern concept of demand the way *indigentia* did. That word does not necessarily signify an active state, an operative force, but it has this associative potential, which *necessitas* has not. The scholar who put *indigentia* into *EN*, V, 5, really triggered that line of theory which reasons about value from the force of market demand.

The new interpretation was destined to remain with the Latin Aristotle. Except Turnebus (1555) who has *usus* and Camerarius (1578) who paraphrases, *id quo usus indiget*, all subsequent, published Latin translations of the *Nicomachean Ethics* retain *indigentia* at 1133a27: Aretinus (1469), Argyropulus (c.1480), Melanchthon (1532), Perionius (1540), Felicianus (1541), Lambinus (1558),

---

23 Paris BN lat. 17832 (f.94r, f.95r); Reims BMun 876 (f.50vb, f.51ra); Vienna NB CVP 2327 (f.54ra, va). Note that these manuscripts read *opus indigentia* not only at 1133b6 but also, confusing the two meanings of *opus*, at 1133a33.

Muretus (1565), Victorius (1584: *usus, et indigentia*), Bergius (1591: *usus, seu indigentia*), and Riccobonus (1596).[24] It is hardly a coincidence that the three who suggest *usus* (not counting Camerarius) edited combined Greek and Latin texts; of the others, only Riccobonus did so. The translations surveyed here usually recur at 1133b6, but several translators (Perionius, Lambinus, Muretus) suggest *usus* or *utilitas* at 1133b20, recalling a forgotten Grossetestan alternative. It is interesting to ask what would have become of Aristotelian value theory had *utilitas* won through originally. However, *indigentia* won through and survived, obviously not because it would be the consistent first choice of the Greek scholar, but as a virtually unavoidable inheritance in the tradition of the Latin Aristotle, going back to the mediaeval translation in the revised version, soon generally adopted and frequently commented upon, and beyond it to the *notulae* of bishop Robert of Lincoln.

*

Greek scholars still disagree about the best translation of χρεία in *EN*, V, 5.[25] I prefer not to cast a vote but would suggest that the

24 Editions quoted: Aretinus, Strasbourg 1469 (Uppsala UB), s.f., cp. Paris 1497 (ed. Lefèvre d'Étaples — London BL), f.b$_8$v; Argyropulus, Florence c.1480 (Vienna NB), f.g$_6$r, cp. Paris 1497, f.g$_6$r; Melanchthon, Wittenberg 1532 (Lübeck SB), f.L$_7$v; Perionius, Paris 1540 (Munich SB), p.90; Felicianus, Venice 1541 (Cambridge UL), p. 231; Turnebus, Paris 1555 (Cambridge UL), p. 110; Lambinus, Venice 1558 (London BL), p. 121; Muretus, Rome 1565 (Milan BTrivulz.), f.B$_3$v; Camerarius, Frankfurt 1578 (Marburg UB), p. 217; Victorius, Florence 1584 (Oslo UB), p. 283; Bergius, Frankfurt 1591 (London BL), p. 208; Riccobonus, Frankfurt 1596 (Oslo UB), p. 208.

25 In the vernacular languages, different traditions developed regarding the translation of χρεία at 1133a27. There is a strong Grossetestan flavour to Oresme's fourteenth century French translation (from Latin): *indigence humaine ou neccessité et besoing*. The fifteenth century version by Don Carlos de Aragon, based on Aretinus and published posthumously in 1509, reads *menester*, an excellent choice of word and still the logical translation into Spanish. In Italy, Segni in 1550 translates *mancamento*, the modern edition by Plebe (1957) has *bisogno*. In France, similarly, Le Plessis (1553) still retains *indigence*, but Catel (1644) has switched to *besoin*, which is retained by Thurot (1830), Barthélemy Saint-Hilaire (1856) and more recently Voilquin (1940), Tricot (1959) and Gauthier/Jolif. Tricot has *demande* in a footnote, but this alternative has no real tradition on the Continent; it was the English who insisted on reading Aristotle like that. Gillies, in his 1797 paraphrase, has in fact *wants*, but the anonymous translation published in 1819 has *demand*, and

role assigned to χϱεία in the moral analysis is a useful clue to its meaning. We must say something about the role probably assigned by Aristotle, to introduce a discussion of this point in the Latin tradition. Since Thomas Aquinas, most interpreters take the role of χϱεία to be that of a "measure" of goods in exchange; there are in fact two measures, an institutional one, money, derived from a natural one, *indigentia* (in Thomas's terminology). The theory is to some extent anticipated in the Grossetestan material. But does Aristotle say this? He states repeatedly (1133a20–21, b16, b22) that money measures economic goods; what he says about χϱεία is less clear. Measurement is mentioned twice in connection with χϱεία, once in redaction (2) at 1133a25–27:

Oportet ergo uno aliquo (ἑνί τινι) omnia mensurari, quemadmodum dictum est prius. Hoc (τοῦτο) autem est secundum veritatem quidem, opus quod (indigentia quae — χϱεία ἥ) omnia continet.

and once in redaction (3) at 1133b18–20:

Secundum veritatem quidem igitur impossibile tantum differentia, commensurata fieri. Ad opus (indigentiam) autem (πϱὸς δὲ τὴν χϱείαν), contingit sufficienter.

The latter redaction goes on immediately to introduce money, and I would see the reference *ad indigentiam* as no more than a general orientation to measurement in a specifically economic sense, suggesting a distinction, later to be picked up by the schoolmen and tied variously to Averroes's *Metaphysics* commentary and to St Augustine, between an economic and a non-economic order of measurement. It is when we consider goods in terms of the fulfilment of human wants, that we can measure them by money,

so have Chase (1847), Browne (1850), Williams (1869), Hatch (1879), Welldon (1892), Ross (1925), Rackham (1926), Thomson (1953), Warrington (1963). The exception is Peters (1881), who prefers *need*, and this choice has reappeared of late in Ostwald (1962) and Apostle (1975), but these English versions were published in the United States and in the Netherlands, respectively. The German translations are true to the Continental alternative. Garve (1801), Stahr (1863), von Kirchmann (1876), Lasson (1909), Rolfes (1911) and Gigon (1951) all follow Jenisch's (1791) *Bedürfnis*. Dirlmeyer (1957) makes a small but distinct change to *Bedarf*, indicating need in the economic sense as underlying demand= *Nachfrage*, but the latter translation itself does not appear in German.

47

otherwise not. To the modern mind, the immediate corollary is that wants determine value, but Aristotle does not say this; nor could he be expected to, if he just followed the obvious source of this analysis, the *Republic* of Plato. In the foundation of the perfect state, χρεία (the word is used repeatedly) is the *cause of exchange*, while exchange, in the next instance, creates a need for money.[26] When Aristotle himself speaks of the introduction of money in the *Politics*, the role of *indigentia* (in the mediaeval translation) is essentially the same, primitive one.[27] If we had only redaction (3) of *EN*, *V*, 5, it would be easy to argue that Aristotle was simply voicing these ideas once more.

It is harder to get around redaction (2) that way. It is true that the reference to what "is said before" can only be to 1133a20–21, where money is said to be a measure, but τοῦτο, referring back, would seem to tie measurement directly to χρεία: "That something (i.e. that which measures) is in fact χρεία, which holds everything together"; one can hardly read, though the whole context asks for it: "That which holds everything together, is in fact χρεία".[28] Let it only be realized that the interpretation of this important point in Aristotle rests on those two lines alone, or rather on their connection. It is tempting to suggest that they may have become thus connected by a transposition of lines different from that indicated by Jolif.[29] But that is to speculate about the Greek Aristotle. As it has

26 *Republic*, II, xi–xii.
27 *Politics*, I, iii, 12–3.
28 While most translators after Grosseteste make need a measure at least by referring back to the preceding sentence and sometimes by a repetition which is not in Aristotle (". . . *this unit* is in truth demand . . ." (Ross), ". . . *this standard* is in reality demand . . ." (Rackham), etc., etc.), there are in fact a few, starting with Nicole Oresme, who break the crucial relation at 1133a26: *Donques convient il teles choses mesurer par une autre chose quelle que elle soit, si comme il est dit devant. Et selon verité, indigence humaine ou neccessité et besoing, c'est ce qui contient teles choses.* (ed. Menut, p.295). Much later, Thurot: *Il doit donc y avoir . . . une commune mesure; et, dans le vrai, c'est le besoin qui est le lien commun . . . .* (Paris 1830, p. 216). Similarly, Browne (London 1850, p. 130); Barthélemy Saint-Hilaire (Paris 1856, pp. 155–6); Lasson (Jena 1909, pp. 105–6).
29 Jolif's suggestion that the statement about money now in lines 1133b16–18 properly belongs after the mention of *indigentia* as a measure is presumably made on the evidence of a similar arrangement in redaction (2). I might suggest a reverse solution. Money measures value in a certain sense, as stated immediately in (1) and (3) on the present arrangement; it is only (2) that

come down to us, there is in the end no denying that the *Nicomachean Ethics* at this one point states that need is a "measure" of commutables. But the reader interested in economic not grammatical analysis is left where he was, for in the immediate continuation of our quotation Aristotle explains it by stating that in the absence of need there is no exchange, thus arguing from the role of cause to the role of measure. If that is all that "measure" means, it really makes little difference whether Aristotle can be made out, grammatically, to have stated that need is a measure. The whole point is trivial until a commentator comes out and explains measurement by human need in terms of a scale of values. That is what Thomas Aquinas did; it is his main contribution to value theory. But he had a forerunner.

It was not Averroes. According to the *Liber Nicomachiae* as quoted above, it is money which is *instrumentum connegotiandi*; while it is true that exchange is *propter indigentiam*, this is the typically vague statement recalling Aristotle in redaction (3). The two Greek commentators translated by Grosseteste refer to money as *mensura* or *medium et mensura*, while, according to Michael Ephesinus, *causa* (αἴτιον) *ad invicem communicationis est opus seu necessitas sive utilitas*. The phrase, *communicationis causa*, is also in the Anonymous, copied repeatedly by Michael, but the Byzantine professor seems to have missed his ancient model's much more interesting observation, where need is a measure in a sense transcending cause:[30]

inserts a mention of *indigentia* between the need for a measure and the use of money, inviting by a treacherous pronoun the current theory. Is it not possible that it is this section (1133a26–28) that is misplaced? If it is moved one line up to conclude redaction (1), the reference from *indigentia* to that which measures, is broken, and Aristotle comes to say, in all three redactions, exactly what Plato says, namely that need ties citizens together in exchange, causing them to invent money for value measurement. But one would of course be wary of this or any interpretation which depends on shuffling the text.

30 Michael only paraphrases 1133a28–29 where Aristotle's meaning is in doubt. Most modern translators take him to say that money is introduced to represent need, thus, by implication, making need a measure also, and that is how Felicianus retranslated Michael (ed. 1541, p. 231). But Grosseteste says that money is introduced *propter commutationem necessitatis* (*id est rerum necessariarum*, explains Thomas), and this locus did not originally support the theory of the double measure.

... oportet et comparabilia aliqualiter esse quae commutantur et habere aliquam communem mensuram, et hanc mensuram ipsorum secundum quam comparata fiunt dicens proprie quidem opus id est necessitatem sive indigentiam esse.

This is still a vague statement, but *hanc mensuram ipsorum secundum quam comparata fiunt* is the first pointer to a scale of value measurement. Thus, according to the Anonymous, there are two measures of exchange value, both conceived in a non-trivial sense, money and need. This is the Thomist *theory of the double measure* in embryo. It is proper to name it after Thomas because he stated it more explicitly and because it was in the Thomist version that measurement by *indigentia* became the frame of subsequent value analysis. But Thomas Aquinas had also consulted the ancient commentary.

*

This is as far as we can get here in explaining the background of the Aristotelian demand theory. There is something to say also about the background of the labour theory in the Grossetestan material. Turning to the alternate topic of the value analysis in *EN*, V, 5, we must face Aristotle's main riddle. It is a formula stated twice, for different pairs of producers and products: ... *quod aedificator ad coriarium, tanta calciamenta ad domum vel cibum* (1133a22–24); ... *quod agricola ad coriarium, hoc opus coriarii ad quod agricolae* (1133a32–33). Since this is clearly some kind of valuation, and to avoid the more specific term "value", let us say that the formula states a relation between relative "producer worth" and relative "product worth" in some sense or another. The riddle then turns on the first term of the analogy: what kind of valuation should be understood as lying at the basis of this comparison between two producers? The question still invites new answers. To clear the ground for a sensible discussion, we can rule out one answer, occasionally voiced by modern interpreters, namely that exchange rates of products depend on personal worth or dignity or "status" of producers. From the point of view of economic theory the idea is preposterous, and it was further ruled out in scholastic Aristotelianism by a subdivision which placed exchange within the confines of commutative justice, where there is "no respect of persons". It may be that this modern interpretation can be traced to a post-Renaissance degeneration of the

Odonis tradition, and so we shall have to deal with it at a much later stage of this study.[31] At the present stage I can only say that I never encountered it in a pre-Renaissance text. Those who read the schoolmen — for instance St Thomas — like that, are simply wrong. Their mistake is chiefly due to a mix-up of what the commentators say about distributive and commutative justice.

Needless to say, the ability to command a favourable exchange rate for his products may often add to a man's status, but that is a sociological and not an economic observation. It is inappropriate to argue (or interpret Aristotle) in the reverse order, deducing exchange rates from status.[32] Any economically relevant interpretation of "producer worth" in Aristotle's formula must relate in some way or other to these persons' roles as producers, and so to the second term of the formula, the products. The early commentators acknowledged this in various ways. Averroes was the first to state the formula in terms of arts, not artisans, a clear sign of this way of thinking:

Nisi . . . esset arti domificatoris ad artem artificis calciamentorum proportio eadem quae est operi domificatoris scilicet domui ad opus calcificis scilicet ad calceum, non posset comprehendi notitia aequalitatis inter illa duo opera. . . .

Michael Ephesinus seems to state right out that relative "producer worth" is to be determined in the first instance by relative "product worth": . . . *propter domus ad calciamenta superexcellentiam dictus est aedificator superexcellere coriarium* . . . . This does emphasize the nature of "producer worth", but it seems to lead to a circular argument since it is, after all, the exchange rates of products which are to be determined in the end. So this sounds all very confusing, but that is how Aristotle and the translated commentators left it. In fact, some of the commentators added to the confusion by juggling with the terms of the analogy.

It is stated in the text of the *Ethics* itself in what may be called a *reverse form*, referring then to the order of products, which is reversed compared to the order of producers: Builder to shoemaker as shoes to a house. It is by this arrangement that the formula can be

31 See pp. 150–3.
32 Cp. for instance Hagenauer 21.

appropriately called, as is sometimes done, a *cross-conjunction* of producers and products. Six manuscripts of the *Translatio Lincolniensis* (**RG2, 4, 5, 6, 7** with a variant in **RG3**) have a marginal note at 1133a33, changing the order of the products so as to make it conform to the order of the producers (the *direct form*). As to the books mentioned in the note as having this form, Grosseteste may perhaps mean the Greek commentaries which also employ it, though they use the reverse form in quotations from Aristotle. Or could it be that Grosseteste had manuscripts of the *Ethics* itself in the direct form? It is remarkable that we find it in both of Herman the German's translations.[33] Now the formula makes no more sense if we switch the order of products, as long as we do not know how to define "producer worth". If we knew that, it would make sense, technically, either way: "As producer A is to producer B, so is (direct form:) A's product to B's product (i.e. the exchange rate of A's to B's) or (reverse form:) B's product to A's product (i.e. the number of units of B's in exchange for one unit of A's)" — the latter is of course exactly what Aristotle does say at 1133a23. There is a difference in that the reverse form involves the minimum of arithmetic needed to divide the number of units of one product into the other. Considering that Aristotle was concerned with the technicalities of proportionate *contrapassum*, I may perhaps suggest that that operation was mainly what he had in mind, taking the economics as given — or uninteresting. But the schoolmen from Albertus Magnus would not have it that way.

Assuming that there must be some economic sense to the cross-conjunction formula, there are at least two reasonable solutions, not unrelated, close at hand. Let us first note that what looks like a circular argument, may sometimes be a logical system. Joachim, whose judgment I put above that of most other modern commentators, having confessed that the determination of the "values of the producers" is "in the end unintelligible" to him, proceeds to suggest that their ratio may express the producers' "demand respectively

---

33 Repeatedly in the *Liber Nicomachiae*, for instance as quoted immediately above. The *Summa Alexandrinorum* requires *proportio fabricatoris ad artificem calciamentorum tamquam proportio domus ad calceum*. (Paris BN lat. 12954, loc. cit.).

for one another's services".[34] When demand finds expression in markets, this suggestion can solve the riddle by uniting the two textual elements in *EN*, V, 5, and the pivot of synthesis is the word "services", which means both product and productive factor. In the equilibrium of interrelated markets, factor value and product value, "producer worth" and "product worth", explain one another. This solution may well be regarded as a modern restatement of a scholastic one, first indicated by Geraldus Odonis, who found a road to synthesis in the analysis of certain rare productive skills which will be in demand and so command a higher price in the product market. Relative "producer worth", then, to Odonis meant *relative productive skill*. But he belonged to the third generation of commentators and there is no anticipation of such ideas in the pre-Albertian texts.

Albertus Magnus, however, had made a suggestion which Odonis argued against (in Thomas's version), but which preconditioned his own theory: the first term of the formula, says Albert, is *relative cost of production — labor et expensae*. This is "producer worth" in an important new functional sense. It does not contradict Odonis's explanation, rather it includes it along with other explanations, depending on how cost of production itself is evaluated. For Albert's suggestion is of a different kind, its significance is not basically analytical at all but ideational, at once opening a whole new field of approach to Aristotle. It is the possible background of the Albertian labour theory in the Grossetestan material which remains to be investigated in this chapter. To this end, we must turn from the cross-conjunction formula (to which Albert repeatedly applied the labour argument) to another riddle which he also solved that way.

*

It occurs at the top of 1133b and describes the consequence of unequal exchange as conditioned in the preceding lines: *Si autem non, utrasque habebit superabundantias alterum extremum*. The interpretational history of this locus is further confused by the fact that the conditioning statement in 1133b1 omits a negation in the *Translatio*

34 Joachim 150–1.

Lincolniensis; it was restored in the revision and retained by Bekker, but the omission is still noted by some editors of the Greek text. There is a variety of modern interpretations, most of which underestimate the economic sense in Aristotle. The current majority view, which also comes in several variants, seems to be that Aristotle simply employs a figure of speech according to which a gain (or loss) from unequal exchange can in a sense be counted twice. For example, giving you four pounds' worth in exchange for five, I was one pound behind you and am one pound ahead of you; one and one makes two. This idea seems rather obvious, and it is in fact the only modern interpretation which recalls a mediaeval one.[35] With utmost economy, it is expressed thus by the fifteenth century Spanish commentator, Pedro de Osma: ... *alterum extremum haberet utrumque excessum, scilicet plus in bono et minus in malo.*[36] This author here deviates from his normal Alberto-Thomist adherence; it was in another version, defining as it were *malum* in terms of labour, that this explanation was most common in the scholastic texts. But Albert originally took his inspiration from the translated Greek commentaries.

The Anonymous can be made out to express the same idea about an adding of gains and losses, except that he insists on generalizing the notion of excess so as to be taken both ways and applied with different signs to both parties in turn; this gives four terms, gains and losses, *bonum*'s and *malum*'s to both parties. Lacking such simple descriptive words, his explanation gets extremely involved. Michael's paraphrase, with a numerical example, is not much clearer,[37] but Albertus Magnus's explanation in his *First Commentary*

35 Historically, they are probably not unrelated, one connecting link being Felicianus's influential translation of Michael Ephesinus, another possibly Acciaiolus (see note 6,12), though he did more to invite the quasi-Odonian "status" interpretation. Those two Renaissance traditions would occasionally mix, as in Riccobonus's comment (p. 618) to his 1596 *Ethics* translation.

36 *Super VI libros Ethicorum*, Salamanca 1496, f.n$_4$r. On Pedro de Osma, see below, p. 73.

37 The anonymous comment is repetitive; this is part of the conclusion: *Existente enim superabundantia hac quidem secundum superexcessum, hac autem secundum defectum. Si commutent agricola et coriarius propria opera ante quam in proportionalitate assumantur, alterum comparatorum ad invicem utrasque habebit superabundantias. Agricola enim cum calciamentis et secundum superexcessum superabundantiam habebit, superexcessit enim agricola coriarium, et secundum defectum, superexcessus est enim*

is a definite improvement; the idea is exactly the same, but the phrasing is much stricter: . . . *tunc esset apud* (*coriarium*) *abundantia defectus operantis et abundantia excessus operis et e contrario apud agricolam.*[38] However, having hit upon the labour explanation, it was to be expected that Albert would restate the interpretation in terms of labour, and this is what he does in his *Second Commentary*:

> Agricola . . . superabundantiam habebit in laboribus et expensis in quantum est agricola: defectum autem habebit in contrapasso propter calciamenta quae minus valent. Rursus coriarius accipiens cibum, ambas habebit excellentias: propter cibum quidem enim superabundat, quia plus accipit quam redonet: agricola enim et opus agricolae in laboribus et expensis excedit coriarium et opus illius. Unde coriarius accipiens opus agricolae excedit: reddens autem calciamentum, deficit.

So now there are double gains and losses, one pair in terms of *labour and expenses,* the other in terms of what is *given* in exchange. What Thomas Aquinas brought to this explanation was, to permit an anachronism, Ockham's Razor. There is no need, in order to make Albert's point, to encumber the explanation with the heavy apparatus brought down from the Anonymous, taking the excesses both ways and for both parties. If the labour explanation is adopted, it suffices to say that since you have first *laboured more* and then *given more,* you have a double loss (compared to the other party); the reader should be able to generalize from there and should really have a better chance, unhedged by superfluous terms, to get the point. So this may be Thomas at his best, cutting away to the bone: (*agricola*) *haberet superabundantiam laboris in opere et haberet etiam superabundantiam doni, quia scilicet plus daret quam acciperet.*[39]

A comparison of these quotations would seem immediately to strengthten the hypothesis that Thomas knew Albert's *Second Commentary* when he wrote his own,[40] since he is more likely to have

---

propter calciamenta a cibo. Rursus autem et alterum extremum et idem utrasque habebit superabundantias, et eam quae secundum defectum, minor enim coriarius agricola, et eam secundum superabundantiam, superexcedit enim proprius cibus calciamenta. Michael Ephesinus: *Si enim accipiat aedificator duo calciamenta, erit quidem superexcedens ut aedificator, superexcessus autem et deficiens ut duo calciamenta habens, et coriarius similiter ut coriarius quidem deficiens et superexcessus, ut autem habens domum superexcedens.*

38 For references to Albertus Magnus's two commentaries, see notes 2,6 and 2,7.
39 For references to Thomas Aquinas, see note 3,9 as well as note 1,43.
40 See below, p. 67, p. 89.

taken the labour explanation from the context of the *superabundantias* discussion itself in Albert's *Second Commentary* than from somewhere else in the *First Commentary*. But there is another possibility. The intriguing question is what caused Thomas to use the rather unexpected noun, *donum* to express what is being supplied in economic exchange; can it be explained only as a reflection of Albertus Magnus's verbal forms?[41] There is no doubt that the word met with some difficulty of reception. Henricus de Frimaria, who repeated the *superabundantias* analysis after Thomas Aquinas, simply rejected it at wrote *superabundantiam damni*,[42] thus reverting to the more general notion of a "loss" rather than a "gift". When Thomas's *Ethics* commentary came to be printed, only the first and third editions (1478, 1505) read correctly *doni*. The second edition (1482) actually reads *domi*, a printing error which speaks eloquently of the trouble inherent in the original expression. The fourth edition (1519) switched to Henricus de Frimaria's *damni*, which is retained in all later editions of St Thomas until corrected from manuscript in the recent Leonine edition.[43] Numerous commentators, old and new, who adopt this version, are in the paradoxical situation of quoting Henricus through St Thomas.[44] The *superabun-*

41 Grosseteste translates *donum* for δώρημα at 1099b11 and for δῶρον at 1123a5, a15 (AL, XXVI, p. 617); both Greek words mean more or less straightforwardly a "gift".

42 For references to Henricus de Frimaria, see note 4,7.

43 References to the first four editions of St Thomas: Barcelona 1478 (New York Hispanic Society), f.I$_8$vb; Vicenza 1482 (Uppsala UB), f.g$_4$rb; Venice 1505 (Besançon BMun), f.57ra; Venice 1519 (Rome BN), f.79vb. The following also read *damni*: Venice 1539 (Rome BN), f.79vb; Venice 1563 (Paris BMaz), f.88va; Rome 1570, f.66r; Paris 1644, p. 187; Paris 1660, p. 187 (all in Paris BN), and editions dependent on these, as well as the Parma edition of the *Opera* (Vol. 21, 1867, p. 173) and numerous editions derived from it. Litzinger's English translation of Thomas is in this tradition: ". . . a surplus of labor in his product and . . . also an excess of loss . . .". (Chicago 1964, p. 427).

44 Henricus de Frimaria's commentary was not printed. Direct influence through the manuscript tradition can hardly have extended to Bernardo Segni, the first Italian translator, who explains, in his companion commentary: . . . *piu nella fatica, & piu nel danno* . . . . (Florence 1550, p. 246). Reflecting other influences elsewhere (cp. note 4,26), Laelius Peregrinus, another Italian commentator, also follows the printed Thomas half a century later: . . . *utramque exuperantiam habebit, laboris scilicet, et damni* . . . . (pp. 197–8). North of the Alps, the formula reappears in the notes to the *Ethics* edition of

dantias analysis was omitted by the summarists of Thomas and by all those who imitated him through Burlaeus. As a matter of fact, I have not come across his *donum* again except in arguments against it in the Odonis tradition. Odonis has several objections to Thomas's analysis; the most important concerns labour. About *superabundantiam doni* he says that it does not make sense since *non dator sed acceptor doni dicitur habere donum.*[45] It seems a little strange that Odonis should actually have misunderstood St Thomas. Perhaps he is only picking a fight over words. But it must be admitted that the use of *donum* is unfortunate. It does sound as though the party in question (the "giver") has gained since he "has" the "gift". Albert's verbal forms leave room for no such misunderstanding.

But Aristotle does say that "one extreme will have both excesses", and a reader asking himself, "What both excesses?", hitting upon a labour explanation, would naturally answer, "Well, first an excess of labour and then an excess of what you give out", i.e. excesses *in labore et dono.* As a gloss on these words, St Thomas's form of expression would follow. Why did he in fact choose that form? Perhaps he for once let slip in an unhappy phrase, giving occasion for criticism, rare in the case of the *doctor angelicus,* for lack of lucidity. The issue might have rested there, but for one additional piece of evidence. In one of the few really early annotated copies of the *Translatio Lincolniensis,* written just outside and above the line containing *superabundantias* at 1133b2, and apparently in the hand which ascribed 105 notes to *Episcopus,* there is a brief note reading, *in labore et dono.* The note is either copied in from St Thomas, or else Thomas has read something like it in his own manuscript copy and based his analysis on it. The first of these alternative hypotheses would not cause us to readjust historical interpretation significantly, though we should have to make a note of how rapidly the Thomist influence (or really the Albertian influence, through St Thomas) was able to take hold. The alternative hypothesis would

Wilkinson (Oxford 1716), who suggests two explanations of *superabundantias,* one based on Acciaiolus through Lambinus (see below, p. 152), the other on Thomas: . . . *plus laboris,* . . . *et plus damni* . . . . (p. 215). To modern exegesis, this explanation has spread mainly through the influential German edition of Rolfes. (Leipzig 1911, p. 253).

45 Full text on p. 148. For references to Odonis, see note 6,3.

take the Aristotelian labour theory of value out of the hands of Albert of Cologne and put it into the hands of Robert of Lincoln, and that would be to the historian of economic ideas a readjustment of some import. The remaining pages of this chapter deal with the evidence bearing on these hypotheses.

*

RG1, in which the enigmatic note occurs on f.90r, is described by Thomson, who considered this codex, along with **RG2** and **RG3**, to be the most important for critical research into Grosseteste's notes. This judgment is only partially confirmed by later studies; it now seems clear that the group **RG2, 4, (5)** will provide the best clue to this material.[46] But **RG1** stands apart from the other manuscripts on account of the many singular notes, of which ours is one of several in the chapter about exchange. Thomson counted four different note hands in **RG1**; two are more recent and easily eliminated; there remain "the earliest, a neat English chancery hand almost contemporary with the text; the second a chancery hand at the end of the century which disappears after Bk. II —."[47] Let us call them (a) and (b). The ascribed *notulae* are in (a); in (b) — as well as in one of the later hands — there are a number of Thomist notes. In the first few books, where long notes in both hands can be compared side by side, (a) and (b) are readily distinguishable. Hence Dunbabin surely makes a mistake, as pointed out by Gauthier,[48] in attributing to Grosseteste a note in Book I, clearly in (b) and borrowed from St Thomas. What we must avoid first of all is making a similar mistake here. If we could believe Thomson on two points, namely that there are only four note hands at work and that (b) disappears after Book II, this part of the problem would be solved. The long notes in (b) soon disappear, but it is more than common for a reader to start enthusiastically to annotate a manuscript and then lose interest but still go on jotting down a briefer note here and there while working through the rest of the volume. A chancery hand, cramped and uncomfortable in

---

46 AL, XXVI, p. CC.
47 Thomson 198. See also Gauthier (4) 24*.
48 Dunbabin (2) 468; AL, XXVI, p. CC, note 1.

margin or between lines, is not easily identified. I would not rule out the possibility that some of the early notes in Book V are in other hands; however, *in labore et dono* looks very much like (a) and there is really no good reason to reject it.[49] But proving the note to be written in (a) does not mean proving its Grossetestan origin. Depending on the precise date when he wrote, this annotater could have known both Aquinas and Grosseteste, taking some inspiration from each. Variant readings of other notes in **RG1** may offer some clue as to influences. We have already noted a variant at 1133b6, where the note in **RG1** reads, *id est indigentia. et utilitas* as against *id est indigentia mutua* in four other manuscripts. Now *mutua* does not sound as much like Grosseteste as *utilitas* does, and *utilitas* does *not* sound like Thomas, who adhered closely to the terms of the revised version, *necessitas* alternating with *indigentia*. On direct paleographical evidence, it is impossible to believe that *et utilitas* and *et dono* were written in different hands. This piece of evidence may lose some weight by the suspicion that *et utilitas* has been added to *id est indigentia* afterwards. There is what could be a punctuation mark before the conjunction sign to suggest this. Now suppose *the same* annotator, having first finished the note in its briefer variant, adds *et utilitas* on a Grossetestan inspiration, is he likely to have had a Thomist inspiration for *in labore et dono* just overleaf? In the final reckoning, there is of course no gainsaying the heavy numerical evidence against the note. Counting **RG2, 4, 5** for one and the other, less related codices for one each, there are still four counts against the one which records it.

While **RG1** is alone among extant manuscripts to have this note, a later work hints vaguely at a tradition. When Nicole Oresme in 1370 translated the *Nicomachean Ethics* into French, he supplied it with a note material which in some aspects recalls that of Grosseteste; though the notes are fuller and more frequent, each refers to a point in the text. At 1133b2, to explain *les .ii. superhabundances*, Oresme notes: *C'est a savoir, une de labeur et de poine et l'autre de*

49 The editor of AL, XXVI indirectly supports this by quoting another singular note, concerning which much the same argument could be made, namely a philological note at 1133a19 explaining *comparata: id est appretiabilia*. True to its intention, the AL would not cite an exegetical note like ours.

damage.[50] Is this *in labore et dono* copied from Grosseteste? Henricus de Frimaria was one of Oresme's main sources; his *damage* is obviously Henricus's *damnum*. Since the latter in fact copies the whole superabundantias analysis from St Thomas, Oresme might well have had no other source for his note at all. If he had another source, it would in any case have to be conceded that he changed the wording on the basis of the later commentator. Oresme's notes have not been studied closely. We do know that he used the recension **Rp** as a basis for his translation;[51] on this evidence it seems unlikely that he should have used the pure *Lincolniensis* as a model for his edition and copied some of its notes. But it certainly is strange that Thomas Aquinas and Henricus de Frimaria, independently of one another and in different translations of the *Ethics*, should insert at the same locus what looks very much like the same note.

Perhaps the best test as to the origin of the labour theory is in the commentaries by Albertus Magnus himself. It hardly seems likely that two authors got that idea independently. The hypothesis that the note in **RG1** is original must therefore imply that Albert and Thomas both knew it at first hand, since the latter could not have reconstructed it in his own text through those of the former. We should also have to accept that Albert in his *First Commentary*, having already got the labour idea from the note since he uses it elsewhere, fails to apply it to the *superabundantias* analysis which inspired the note, though he does so apply it in his *Second Commentary* but in a different verbal form, while Thomas, who had the labour explanation from Albert as well, chose to use the note much more literally. This sequence of events, though possible, leaves the hypothesis a little uncomfortable. It seems safer to settle for the alternative, namely that Thomas took his labour explanation only from Albert and that the note in **RG1** is based on Thomas. At least until the full sets of *notulae* have been studied in depth, we cannot rob Albertus Magnus of the Aristotelian labour theory of value.

50 Ed. Menut, p. 296. Menut, following Brussels BR 2902, spells *damage*. I confirm this from Paris Arsenal 2668 (f.154v) and BN franç. 541 (f.93r), 542 (f.151v). But other manuscripts now in Paris BN have *domage* (franç. 204 (f.448r) — an early copy, before 1380) or *dommage* (franç. 205 (f.91r), 206 (f.78v).). On Oresme's sources, see also note 4,16.
51 AL, XXVI, p. CCXLVII, with note 2.

2. Labour and expenses

The tradition of Albertus Magnus

Albertus Magnus was born at Lauingen, a village on the Danube below Ulm, and joined the recently founded Dominican Order while studying at Padova. He was for short periods German Provincial of his Order and bishop of Regensburg, but most of his adult life he spent studying and teaching, at Paris (where he left a lasting mark) and at a number of Dominican schools in Germany, notably in Cologne which he made his second home and where he died in 1280 at an advanced age.[1] St Albert was *doctor universalis* and the first great Latin Aristotelian; the new Cologne edition of his *Opera* is to comprise 40 large volumes, 17 of which will consist of commentaries on Aristotelian works. On some of these works he was the first Western commentator, on one at least, the one that concerns us, he remained the most important. His impact on economics is enormous. For all subsequent thought on exchange and value there are points of departure in the sections of his two commentaries on the *Nicomachean Ethics* where Albert pours the old Greek ideas on these subjects into a mould shaped by the economic structure of late mediaeval society. Less in this field than in most others has he deserved to fade into the shadow of his pupil, St Thomas Aquinas,

1 On Albert's life and works, his *Ethics* commentaries, and his economics, see Scheeben; Grabmann (2), (4) at 39–42; Wulf II 127–150; Ueberweg 401–416, 739–742; Gilson 277–294, 666–673; Jöcher I 203–5; Chevalier 105–7; Fabricius I 42–5; Glorieux I 62–77; Quétif I 162–183; EF I 151–8; DTC I 666–675; LTK I 285–7; NDB I 144–8; Lohr XXIII 338–345; Pelzer (2); Lottin (1); Dunbabin (1); Gauthier (3) 109, 115, 122–5; Jourdain 44; Graziani 14–5; Brants 193–5; Sewall 13; Kaulla (1) 455–6, (2) 52–3, (3) 22–4; Tarde 27–31; Schreiber 17, 45–53, 62, 71, 76; Gelesnoff (1) 205; Dempsey (2) 476–8; Soudek 64–5; De Roover (3) 421–2; Baldwin 10–2, 61–5, 67, 71, 73–7, 82; Mandel II 388–392.

whose improvements on the Albertian economic analysis were not all that remarkable.

Some of the works where Albertus Magnus might have used the Aristotelian exchange model were already written when he got his hands on an early copy of the *Translatio Lincolniensis*. With one such work, his *Summa de bono*, he had been occupied until quite recently; another one, his commentary on the *Sentences* of Petrus Lombardus, was in fact in progress at that very time. So his first use of the new source seems to have been in supplementing and completing these works. Albert read the *Sentences* at Paris, finishing Book III there without having seen anything but the earlier fragmentary translation of the *Ethics*. In 1248 he moved to Cologne and may have brought a copy of the new translation with him; at any rate, the following year he refers to the full text of Aristotle in his commentary to the last book of the Lombard. While the best *loci* of economic teaching in the Sentences are in Book III, Albert used Dist. 16 of the final book to good advantage. In Article 46 he discusses conditions under which certain activities, including trade, are licit.[2] The locus is well-known to students of mediaeval just price doctrine; it is here that Albert states what looks out of context like an uncompromising "current price" definition, disturbing the usual picture of him as a labour theory purist: *Iustum autem pretium est, quod secundum aestimationem fori illius temporis potest valere res vendita.* However, I must emphasize again that the conflict is not historically valid. The context is an injunction against fraudulent market practices and not against cost pricing. For that matter, cost is mentioned elsewhere in the article; it is interesting here to note the wording, . . . *negotiationem omnium in labore et expensis.* The bricks for the Albertian structure are being gathered.

But even more interesting to us is a third locus, with a reference to *EN*, V. Concerning trade, Albert argues:

Nihil eorum sine quibus dissolvitur civilitas, et cum quibus optime conservatur, est peccatum: sed negotiatio est aliquid tale: ergo ipsa non est peccatum. Prima patet ex hoc quod omnis moralitatis laudabile studium est circa conservantia civilitatem. Secunda autem accipitur ex libro V Ethicorum, ubi loquitur de iustitia commutativa. . . .

2 Ed. Borgnet, Vol. 29, pp. 636–8.

This may not seem like a very exciting use of Aristotle, but it signals a recurrent theme, to be developed in the other works from which we are to quote Albert on exchange. One of these is the *De bono* mentioned above, a recent discovery, printed for the first time in the Cologne edition of the *Opera*.[3] The work seems to have been put aside unfinished before the author had knowledge of the *Translatio Lincolniensis*, but to the last of its five treatises, which deals with Justice, Albert later added a final Quaestio IV, *De iustitia speciali*, based on *EN*, V. In terms of the development of economic ideas (even if not in chronology), this addition to the *De bono* belongs between *Sent.* IV and the *First Commentary* to the *Ethics* itself. The builder and the shoemaker here make their entrance in the Latin commentary tradition:

Item, dicit Philosophus, quod iustitia consideratur in quattuor minimis. Verbi gratia aedificator habet domum, quae valet quinque mnas, calcifex habet calceum, qui valet unam. Si voluit commutare ad hoc, ut servetur iustitia inter eos, oportet, quod ille qui habet calceum, superaddat alii quattuor mnas, et sic erunt illa quattuor reducta ad aequalitatem; alioquin enim periret civilitas quantum ad aedificationem, si non plus acciperet quam calceum.

Now that also looks like a rather ordinary statement, except for three words. When referring to Aristotle in *Sent.* IV as quoted above, Albertus Magnus states society's need for exchange; his point is now, if we take it in its most general sense, the need for justice, otherwise *periret civilitas*. These are certainly in themselves commonplace ideas. Society based on exchange is the familiar Platonic concept; it spread to the Latin West long before Aristotle. Society based on justice is a commonplace of Latin legal thought itself, and the combination of these ideas is rather obvious. Cicero, for instance, whom Albert knew well, said that with people robbing each other for their own profit, *disrumpi necesse est . . . societatem*.[4] But Albert says something more precise than this, namely, in effect, that if there is not just exchange in the builder's market, society will perish *quantum ad aedificationem*. That is a much more advanced idea, suggesting a basic condition of competitive equilibrium. He was to express it more succinctly in both of his *Ethics* commentaries, and

3 Vol. 28; quoted p. 306.
4 *De officiis*, III, v, 21.

I shall return to this development later on. But the idea is already there in the *De bono*, and the birth of that idea put economic science on the road to the Law of Cost.

*

The first of Albertus Magnus's commentaries on the *Nicomachean Ethics* was based on lectures given at Cologne between 1248 and 1252. In the following decade, official duties of various kinds interfered with his teaching, but when he could again devote himself to what was surely his main interest, he also took up the *Ethics* again, composing about 1263–7, a second commentary. For the lack of good distinguishing titles, I shall continue to call these works St Albert's *First* and *Second Commentaries*. One is a close textual exposition with questions, the other a rather freer paraphrase. In the sources for the present study, the *First Commentary* of Albertus Magnus occupies a position of unique importance, for three reasons. Firstly, because it became the model of all subsequent Latin commentary, in conception, design and detail. Secondly, because it is in a sense not only Albert's first commentary, but also Thomas Aquinas's. According to the old biographical tradition, it was Thomas, then in his twenties and Albert's student at Cologne, who *collegit et redegit* his master's lectures on the *Ethics*.[5] Thirdly, because it has not been studied before. Incredible as it may seem in view of its influence, this commentary was not among those which found their ways to the early printing press; the new *Opera* edition is in fact its *editio princeps*.[6] Hence it is only at a date when St Albert's contribution to economics has already been the subject of extensive and often controversial discussion for almost a century, that we can seek it in its prime source. Albert's *Second Commentary*, on which this discussion has then been based (in addition to *Sent.* IV), is yet to appear in the new edition and must still be used in the Borgnet edition, a rather uncritical reprint of the Jammy edition which dates from the seventeenth century.[7]

5 So reported by both Petrus Calo and Guillelmus de Tocco; cp. *Fontes vitae* (ed. Prümmer) 27, 79.

6 Albert's *First Commentary* to the *Ethics* is in Vol. 14. Lectio V, 7, which contains the exchange analysis, is on pp. 341–6.

7 In the *Second Commentary*, the exchange analysis is in V, ii, 9–10. It is in

secundum quod unumquodque in sua natura accipitur: secundum hoc enim mensuratur unumquodque sui generis numero (read: minimo). Sed sicut paulo ante diximus, oportet hoc accipere secundum relationem ad usum, hoc est, secundum quod valet in usu supplere indigentiam. . . .

There is a natural and an economic order, in which things are graded differently; introduced by Albertus Magnus, this came to serve for the Aristotelians as an opening to a discussion of the nature of economic value. Thomas Aquinas also made this distinction, and some later commentators (for instance Henricus de Frimaria) took it both from the "Averroists" and from Thomas; the source is easily recognized, since Thomas chose to refer the first order of measurement to St Augustine's scale of natural perfection rather than to Averroist metaphysics.[13] If this is a conscious effort on his part to play down the Averroist elements in Albert's Aristotelian analysis, which does not sound improbable, it would go to support the conjecture that Thomas did know his old master's *Second Commentary*, since what Albert says in his *First Commentary* is rather different.

This difference takes us back to the confusion involved in some of the terms of the pure *Lincolniensis*. The following are the two instances where Albert in his *First Commentary* distinguishes the orders of measurement:

Possunt enim opera artificiata mensurari secundum veritatem suae speciei, inquantum scilicet sunt artificiata quaedam, et sic mensurat omnia opus, quod continet omnia, quod est simplicissimum in genere illo. Et hoc potest accipi vel secundum rationem, et sic opus, quod omnia continet, est ipsa ratio operis; vel opus primum et simplicissimum secundum esse, ad quod omnia opera ordinantur accidentium, et hoc est opus civilis.

Et dicit, quod cum opera artium sint tam diversa, secundum veritatem suae speciei non possunt uno mensurari, sed secundum quod sunt ad opus, idest ad operositatem communitatis, sufficienter mensurantur per unum, et unum hoc est mensurans per suppositionem, idest per institutionem a civilitate, quae instituit nummismata.

In the economic order, goods are measured in relation to *opus*, and in Albert's *Second Commentary* this is clearly distinguished from measurement *sui generis minimo*. But in the *First Commentary* this distinction is not clear; the only way I can read the first section

13 See below, p. 87.

67

quoted above is to make *opera artificiata* measurable by *opus* in both orders. If this reading is correct, it can only mean that Albertus Magnus takes *opus* rendering χρεία to be *simplicissimum in genere* of *opus* rendering ἔργον.[14] When he turns again to economic measurement, as he does in our last section quoted, this confusion of the two meanings of *opus* takes Albert precariously close to suggesting that the *opus* which contains everything in the economic sense has something to do with labour and not, as intended by the translator, with need or wants. For *operositas* cannot be taken otherwise. It means labour — in a very basic sense familiar to the economist. When Smith says, in the *Wealth of Nations*, that the real price of everything is the *toil and trouble* of acquiring it, that is exactly *operositas*. I should not be surprised if we have here uncovered one active root of the Albertian labour explanation of *EN*, V, 5. What he says about labour and expenses comes very natural in the context of *operositas*.

In his *Second Commentary*, as we have seen, Albert changes his mind, drawing on Grosseteste's (notes? and) translations of the Greek commentaries in expressions like the one quoted, *opus diximus esse usum vel utilitatem vel indigentiam*. Elsewhere, economic measurement is taken *ad indigentiam, ad opus autem indigentiae*. But these *ad*'s do not tell us precisely what Albert now considers the role of human need to be in economic exchange; we are back with the problem of interpretation encountered in redaction (3) of Aristotle's own text. Thus one of the references above is taken from a context which actually states that goods should be exchanged *secundum proportionem valoris rei unius ad valorem rei alterius, proportione habita ad indigentiam quae causa commutationis est*. Whether or not Jammy/Borgnet here misread for *communicationis*, this is quite obviously the old Platonic idea as transmitted by the Anonymous.[15] As for the important lines 1133a25–27 of redaction (2), Albert's comment is extremely obscure but apparently cannot be made out to mean that *opus sive indigentia* is a measure at all. On the basis of such statements it is difficult to assess Albert's role in the foundation of the *indigentia* theory soon to be developed by Thomas Aquinas and

14 See above, pp. 43–4.
15 See above, p. 49.

the Paris "Averroists". That the latter group was inspired by Albert's arguments concerning measurement is clear, but Albert asked the question only as regards money; when the "Averroists" asked the twin question about *nummisma* and *indigentia*, their reference was equally clearly the *theory of the double measure* as stated by St Thomas. Perhaps, in the end, Albert's most interesting remarks about need and utility occur in the other half of the value analysis of *EN*, V, 5, where he ties these phenomena to the cross-conjunction formula and thus to his labour analysis, to which we must now turn.

*

. . . *quantum aedificator superat coriarium in labore et expensis, quas ponit in suo opere, tantum domus superat calceum;* . . . *sicut aedificator se habet ad coriarium in laboribus et expensis sui operis secundum excessum, tot et tanta calciamenta per additionem nummismatis commutentur ad domum* . . . . At *EN*, V, 5 in his *First Commentary*, Albertus Magnus refers to labour four times, always along with expenses and always in the singular. In his *Second Commentary*, for some unexplained reason, he switches to the plural, referring to labour(s) and expenses no less than six times. This means that Albert, who may have based his original labour explanation partly on an error of interpretation, confirmed this interpretation even when the error had been corrected; hence, while we have not until recently had him on primary evidence as to labour, we have had his considered opinion in the matter. If he intended a subtle change of meaning by the switch to the plural, I am at a loss to account for it, but since the tradition did not take him up on this point, I think we can safely let it rest.

But the characteristic pair, "labour and expenses", is significant. Albertus Magnus speaks of the two cost elements in one breath, later commentators often do the same, but some (like St Thomas) occasionally mention one factor only, occasionally only the other, as though the selection makes no great difference, nor does it, as long as the emphasis is, as with Albert, on productive input as such and *not* on this or that specific factor *nor* on labour as contrasted with other factors. Both distinctions are important. Let us first note that the absence of specification of the cost elements in Albert's commentaries is in the spirit of the *Ethics* itself, discouraging casuistry[16] and concentrating on the question of how cost as such influences value. Next, as to labour in contrast to other factors of production, it is clear that a theory of value at some point needs a theory of distribution. We shall have something to say about this both in the present chapter when we come to a group of commentators with whom the labour theory degenerated and later in connection with the Odonis tradition. But it is also clear that the problem of distribution as we now think of it, requiring an explicit distinction between labour and capital inputs, was less important to mediaeval value theory, and Albert himself never raised the issue. (This ought to refute any alleged association between Albert — or Thomas as representing Albert — and the nineteenth century labour theory is so far as it was a theory of distribution.)

No sooner had Albert introduced labour and expenses to explain cross-conjunction, than commentators began to speak as though this was what the Philosopher had actually said. The "Averroists" took no great interest in the cost factors, but one of them, Aegidius Aurelianensis, could state, as a matter of course, that *nisi esset illud contrapassum, tunc perirent artifices et destruerentur, ut tantum scilicet reciperent quantum ponunt et expendunt in operibus suis, ut declarat Aristoteles de aedificatore et coriario*.[17] Aristotle, as we know, declared nothing of the sort, but the view prevailed. Two and a half centuries later, when Philip Melanchthon, the enormously influential first teacher of the Protestant moralists, translated Book V of the *Ethics* once more, he wrote (and this is not a comment on 1133a22–24, but a translation): *Tot igitur pro domo aut frumento calceos dari oportebit quantum aedificationis impensae superant calcearii impensas*.[18] Such quotations will help explain the nature of what I propose to call the tradition of Albertus Magnus. All commentators spoke of labour, or any commentator might; the question is not whether he did, but what he made of it. Some branches can be distinguished in the Albertian labour theory also, but they cut across those of the *indigentia* theory, on the basis of which the chapter division of this

16 See above, p. 24.
17 Paris BN lat. 16089, ff.215vb–216ra.
18 Ed. Wittenberg 1532, f.L₇v.

book has mainly been designed. Two authors who otherwise follow Thomas Aquinas, say, or Henricus de Frimaria, may say quite different things about labour. Hence, to account for the labour theory I shall record here statements by a number of commentators whom we shall meet again in different chapters as well as by some who had nothing else of interest to contribute. I shall stop short of some authors in the Odonis tradition, since their contributions to demand theory and to labour theory must be seen in relation to one another and on the basis of all the other Aristotelian branch traditions.

Up until Odonis, we can account for the development of the Albertian labour theory without going outside Aristotelian sources. The other mediaeval traditions in this area, developed in patristic and Canonist texts, generally lacked an analytical nerve. At the time when Albert commented on the *Ethics*, the Biblical principle that "the labourer is worthy of his hire"[19] and related influences had long since worked to inspire legal and moral precepts justifying a price which, free of fraud and cupidity, covered labour and various expenses in an extending catalogue, such as transportation, care, risk, etc., all discussed with enthusiasm by the casuists. But these discussions were not the stuff of which value theory is made. Hence, while even Albert's terminology proves that he knew these earlier traditions,[20] there is no need to search them for elements to explain the development of his theory once it was set up in the analytically more fruitful scheme of the *Ethics*. With every second author repeating some Albertian labour statement, it is also clear that we should needlessly encumber the following survey by quoting everything that the Aristotelians said about this subject. A case in point is the Thomist tradition. Besides the *superabundantiam laboris* discussed at length above, Thomas employs the literal Albertian form, *in labore et expensis*, once, and once explains just exchange between builder and shoemaker in terms of *quot plures expensas facit aedificator*. The latter phrase caught on; it was repeated by at least six

19 Luc. X, 7; cp. 1. Tim. V, 18.
20 "Since the middle of the twelfth century the two factors of *labores* and *expensae* were of crucial importance in the Canonist justification of all kinds of economic increment and profit." (Baldwin 49).

Thomists.[21] But it never embodied any relevant analysis. A different case is Henricus de Frimaria, who also passed on a number of labour statements of no analytical interest but also, unlike Thomas, caught on to each of the significant aspects of Albert's theory. However, as we now proceed to a brief selection of authors to illustrate some analytical uses of Albert, let us not forget to read these quotations against the background of a mass of less reflective imitations of the original commentaries; without issuing in any theories, these echoes of Albert continued, throughout the scholastic period, to hammer into the Aristotelian audience a persistent reminder that value in exchange must comply with cost of production. Those statements which do have some analytical content must weigh all the more heavily given this background, because we must assume that the theories which they express have often been applied to these simple statements as well.

*

One branch of the labour theory can be traced no further back than to the middle of the fifteenth century, when Johannes Versoris, a Paris master, composed a commentary to the *Ethics* in question form, printed posthumously at Cologne in 1491 and 1494. Most of it is lifted uncritically from the pages of St Thomas, but when he comes to the bed/house example in redaction (3) of *EN*, V, 5, Versor makes a contribution of his own, explaining it in terms of *relative production time*. This is something neither Albert nor Thomas had done; until now this example had in fact remained largely untouched by the commentators. It is therefore remarkable, since it looks like a coincidence, that it should now also appear in another early printed commentary, even more influential than Versor's. The other author is Donatus Acciaiolus (1429–1478), of Florence, a man under many influences, some of which will be discussed in Chapter 6. He wrote after Versor, but I can detect no similarity except for the fact that they both extend an Albertian solution to Aristotle's final example about exchange. If we read the two explanations in succession, however, the striking thing is not their

21 Guido Vernani, Gualterus Burlaeus, Albertus de Saxonia, Petrus de Castrovol, Chrysostomus Javelli, Tarquinius Gallutius.

similarity, but the difference of expression, founding in Versor's commentary a retrograde quasi-Albertian theory but permitting in the case of Acciaiolus another, more constructive, interpretation as well, thus revealing both the danger and the importance of tying value to productive labour. Here, then, are Versor and Acciaiolus on the exchange of a house for beds:

> ... ante quam inventum esset nummisma fiebat commutatio rerum ad invicem sic quod adaequabantur operationes diversorum artificum (diversarum artium **JVX**), ut puta si domificator per quinque dies fecisset domum et alius in una die lectum, dabantur quinque lecti pro una domo.[22]

> Dicit post haec Philosophus quod ante inventionem nummi erat permutatio rerum et indigentia mensurabat res et pretium mutabatur ut requirebat indigentia, ut quinque lecticas pro domo permutassent, quia mensurassent labores domus cum lectica, et sic vidissent quod valebat quinque.[23]

A later variant is that of Tarquinius Gallutius, professor at Rome, whom we shall meet again in the following chapter; he suggests that *labores insumpti in aedificanda domo (fuissent) comparandi cum iis, qui adhibiti sunt ad lecti structuram* ....[24] Similarly, Joseph Saenz de Aguirre, at the very close of our period: ... *mensurabatur sumptus, et labor necessarius in extruenda domo cum labore et sumptu in faciendis quinque lecticis* ....[25] Both sound very much like Acciaiolus, but Versor's interpretation may well lurk behind these phrases, as it may indeed behind those of Acciaiolus himself. Anyway, it now soon started to appear in comments elsewhere in *EN*, V, 5.

A few examples must suffice. Petrus Osmensis (de Osma), whose *superabundantias* remark was quoted in Chapter 1, was a professor at Salamanca who died about 1480 and left an *Ethics* commentary, to be printed in 1496. In some other respects a conventional Thomist, he adds another note to his labour explanation of exchange between

---

22 Eds. 1491, 1494 (Hain 16053–4=**JVX**), f.44vb. A third entry in Hain (16055, Cologne 1497) is a mistake for the *Politics* commentary. To manuscripts in Lohr and Gauthier (3), I can add Vienna NB CVP 5214, ff.1–141, dated 1465. On Versor, see EF III 209; Jöcher IV 1547; Chevalier 4651; Wulf III 191; Ueberweg 627, 788–9; Gilson 319; Lohr XXVII 290–9; Gauthier (3) 140–3. See also below, p. 97.
23 Ed. 1478, f.q$_3$r. See also notes 1,33 and 6,12.
24 Ed. 1632, p. 939. On Gallutius, see below, p. 103.
25 *Philosophia moralis*, Salamanca 1675, p. 260.

builder and shoemaker, suggesting that one consider *tempus laborem simul et impensas fabri cum unicam domum fabricaverit, tempus quoque laborem et impensas sutoris cum unum par calceorum fecerit* . . . .[26] Two famous sixteenth century humanists and Aristotelians, who commented on their own translations of *EN*, V, 5, took the same line. Petrus Victorius (Vettori, 1499–1585), the great Florentine humanist and teacher, added a Latin translation and a commentary to his previously published Greek text, when he reedited it at Florence in 1584. Equality implies that *calcei, opus sutoris, pares sint labori, quem longum sustinuit faber in domo aedificanda.*[27] Marcus Antonius Muretus (1526–1585), the French humanist who found refuge and fame in Italy, published a translation of Book V of the *Ethics* in 1565 and later wrote a commentary to the whole work, which I know only in the posthumous edition, Ingolstadt 1602. In it, Muretus states the relation between builder and shoemaker in terms of *quo plus laboris, temporis, pecuniae consumit in faciendo opere suo, quam sutor* . . . .[28] When these commentaries appeared, the definite version of Alessandro Piccolomini's *Della institutione morale* was already out — one of the most influential Aristotle-inspired ethical texts in the vernacular. Born in 1508 into the famous Sienese family, he taught Moral Philosophy at Padova and Rome and as early as 1542 expressed his Aristotelian reflections in another work; the better known version appeared at Venice in 1560 and at least four times more and was translated into French. Here is a final expression of one line of labour theory, with an addition which points beyond it:

Ordinarono adunque le monete, & secondo questa misura posero il pregio à ciascheduna cosa: osservando nel por questo pregio, che nessun de gli artefici fusse piu dannificato dell'altro; ilche facilmente fecero, considerando le fatiche, le spese, e'l tempo dell'opere di ciascheduno, contrapesando, & ben computando

26 f.n₃v. Rare copies of this book (Salamanca 1496; Hain 12122, Haebler 504) are in Paris BN and Trinity College, Dublin. Text commented on is Aretinus. On the author, see Stegmüller; Elías de Tejada 710–1; DTC XII 2032–3; LTK VIII 374; Chevalier 3733; Fabricius V 271–2; Lohr XXVIII 363–4; Gauthier (3) 152–3.

27 Ed. Florence 1584, p. 282. On Petrus Victorius, see EF VI 900–1; NBG XLVI 69–70; Jöcher IV 1583–4; Gauthier (3) 160, 182–3.

28 Ed. Ingolstadt 1602, p. 416. Copies of this edition abound; I cannot locate an alleged edition, Venice 1583. On Muretus, see NBG XXXVI 997–1000; Jöcher III 762–4; Gauthier (3) 182.

ogni cosa, à fine, che ciascheduno potesse nell'arte sua, usando diligentia, & non stando in otio, sostenar se stesso, & la sua famiglia.[29]

*

In the history of knowledge one danger of hindsight is to read into early expressions of important ideas a degree of sophistication which was not yet there. I would suggest a crude model according to which many early authors can be assumed to have had an inkling of a functional relationship between productive labour and the market value of products, but where the important distinctions between levels of insight are the varying conceptions of the causal relations involved. According to this model, there would be one line of value theory, running from mediaeval thought straight through to the nineteenth century, which sees value as simply caused by labour. The origin of this way of thinking is evidently not in the Aristotelian tradition alone, but when Albert's labour statements were left to themselves, they invited it, as our quotations show. Two points are to be noted about this corruption of Albert as it occurs in the Aristotelian texts, Versoris being the prototype. One is the emphasis on *labour time*. It is in the nature of this primitive type of labour theory to seek descriptive characteristics, independent of value and value-related phenomena, by which "quantity of labour" (to quote Smith, or Ricardo) can be expressed. It does not have to be time spent labouring; other physio-technical measures of exertion will do, but labour time often suggests itself. Secondly, it is interesting to note that the labour time interpretation first appeared in the context of the bed/house model. The fact that Albertus Magnus failed to explain this example in terms of labour and so failed to pave the way for a different labour interpretation is probably not the reason for this; I suggest that the peculiar condition stated, *ante quam nummisma erat* (which is how the *Translatio Lincolniensis* puts it in 1133b26–27), was decisive. This is not exactly Smith's "early and rude state of society" in which a day's labour

29 Ed. 1560, pp. 350–1. See also *Della institutione di tutta la vita*, Venice 1542, f.163r. This book is in London BL and Venice BMarc. The quoted 1560 edition is also in these libraries as well as in Hannover LB, Vienna NB, Oxford BodL, B Vat, Siena BCom. There are editions 1569, 1575, 1594 and a French edition, Paris 1581. On Piccolomini, see EF IV 1577; Jöcher III 1545; NBG XL 66–8; LTK VIII 492; Gauthier (3) 180.

exchanges for a day's labour, but the parallel is evident. However, there is an even more striking one in store for Versor.

In view of the attempts that have been made to tie Marxist value theory to a scholastic tradition,[30] it is fascinating to note here that the only use of Aristotle's *Ethics* in Volume I of *Das Kapital* is a discussion of the bed/house model in *EN*, V, 5.[31] Quoting 1133b18–19 to the effect that it is "in Wahrheit" impossible for "so verschiedenartige Dinge" to be commeasurable, Marx proceeds to point out "die gemeinschaftliche Substanz" which solves this problem of measurement: "Das Haus stellt dem Polster gegenüber *ein Gleiches vor*, soweit es das in beiden, dem Polster und dem Haus, wirklich *Gleiche* vorstellt. Und das ist — *menschliche Arbeit*". Aristotle did not understand this, says Marx, because he lived under social conditions which obscured "*die Gleichheit* und *gleiche Gültigkeit aller Arbeiten*". It is a matter of historical irony that the Age of Reason had cut Marx off from a scholastic tradition which had long since found its way to a type of labour explanation of the precise textual locus from which he argues against Aristotle, an explanation which, by a kind of lowest common denominator, can be compared to Marx's own. In that sense he is, if not "the last of the Schoolmen", at least of a mind with certain schoolmen. But in another sense, and in the final analysis of Marxism and Scholasticism, Marx's "gemeinschaftliche Substanz" is of a kind with those principles of measurement which the schoolmen wisely eliminated

---

30 Cp. for instance statements such as these: "Alles, was der heilige Thomas über die *Preis*bestimmung sagt, kann und muss auch von dem Anhänger der sogenannten Arbeitstheorie oder der Ricardo-Marx'schen Wertlehre vollständig unterschrieben werden." (Hohoff 475). ". . . tatsächlich weist bei näherer Betrachtung die thomistische Wertlehre in der weiteren Ausgestaltung der Analyse des Arbeitswertes eine grosse Ähnlichkeit mit der Marxschen Wertlehre auf . . . ." (Hagenauer 15). "The true descendant of the doctrines of Aquinas is the labour theory of value. The last of the Schoolmen was Karl Marx." (Tawney 36). On precise textual evidence, Thomas Aquinas personally did very little to further (or indeed to retard) a labour explanation of value; besides a rather passive acceptance of Albert's interpretation of Aristotle, his contribution is limited to a conventional justification of a *stipendium laboris* in pricing. (II–II, 77, 4, c). But it has been the fate of Thomas to be taken to represent a whole genre too vaguely known to most students for discriminating hypotheses to be formulated.
31 *Das Kapital*, I, I, 3, A, 3.

from economic analysis proper, whether they derived from the Christian scale of natural perfection or from the metaphysics of Averroes.

The point is that "die gleiche Gültigkeit aller Arbeiten" is a moral not an economic proposition. To demonstrate that labour causes value, as Marx himself and others who tried it discovered, it is necessary to modify the simple labour time explanation by distinguishing different classes of labour, and this argument sooner or later gets involved in the problem of wage differentials as determined by the market, i.e. by variables related to what labour itself was supposed to determine; which means that the explanation has run into a circle, and this is historically the reason why some schools and authors dropped it and started to rethink the problem of labour and value. It can hardly be said that this is what happened in the Aristotelian tradition, but it is a fact that one of its most fruitful lines of analysis started with a rejection of the labour time theory as empirically false. From that point there is an irresistible next step, namely to argue in the opposite direction, from the fact of market value to the fact of differentiated labour remuneration and to ask why. In early economics this seems to be the most feasible opening to a simultaneous explanation of product and factor value and thus to approaching a synthesis of the market and cost explanations. The reason for this is exactly that it introduces the notion of distribution into pre-capitalistic value analysis, not indeed between labour and capital (except in so far as it concerns capital invested in acquiring productive skills, which in fact does enter explicitly into some mediaeval value discussions) but between different classes of labour. However, in the Aristotelian tradition this development belongs in the Odonis branch. What remains to do here is connect it with the original labour theory.

Did Albertus Magnus intend a labour quantity explanation? He does not say so and the chances are that he did not. But the problem is that an Aristotelian "cross-conjunction", by which the works of the exchangers are to be "equalized", involves two operations which are not properly distinguished in Albert's statements — or in those of most later proponents of the labour theory. There is a scaling operation; since a house is obviously a larger piece of work than a pair of shoes, it has to be reduced to a comparable unit. In addition there is normally an interoccupational comparison: a unit of housebuilding compared to a unit of shoemaking. To choose an hour's labour or some other period of time as a unit, as Sir David Ross suggests, does not, as his analysis demonstrates,[32] imply a labour time theory of value, as long as these units are not assumed to yield equal product value. To assume this is really to do violence to Aristotle's elaborate argument; though its precise meaning does not get across to us any more, it is clear enough that he has in mind some comparison of work units in addition to the scaling. I am sure Albert read him like that. The nature of this comparison still makes room for different kinds of value theory. A labour quantity (as opposed to a *simple* labour time) theory is possible if some relation between "producer worths" per unit independent of the market is postulated, but this involves a type of "status" thinking which Aristotle's juridical system proscribes and of which I would not suspect Albert. The alternative is to turn the problem around, as I said above, and take the work units as compared by the market. In Aristotle's limited model this is arguing in a circle, but to make sense of the circle is to reach a fuller understanding of value.

Reading scholastic commentaries, it may be difficult to know which alternative applies. Taking Acciaiolus, quoted as saying that *mensurassent labores domus cum lectica*, there is no way of saying for sure what kind of measurement is intended. There may be a crude comparison of labour time as in Versor, or there may be a comparison of work unit value (of wages, actually) by the market. The fact that Acciaiolus mentions labour only after twice referring to *indigentia* in the same breath, strongly indicates that demand measures the value of labour rather than labour the value of products:[33] in fact, having probably read Odonis, Acciaiolus may

---

32 Footnote to translation at 1133a7.
33 While most manuscripts of Acciaiolus (Florence BN II. I. 80, f.111v; Magl. VI 162, f.86r; Conv. Soppr. J. III. 26, f.136; Bologna BU 7, f.112v; Venice BMarc lat. VI 78, f.110r; Paris BN lat. 6461, f.108r) read, *ut requirebat indigentia*, as in the printed version quoted on p. 73, there is one (Urbin. lat. 200, f.124r) which reads, *et requirebat indigentia, ut quinque . . .* ; another (Florence BLaur Strozzi 53, f.75v) omits the first *ut*. These variants pose *indigentia* unmistakably as the determinant.

have been closer to grasping the true role of labour than any commentator yet quoted. However, faced with formulations like his, interpretation remains in the end a guess, and this problem is ever present in the scholastic commentaries; since the labour time theory became explicit in some, I suspect that it lies hidden in many others. As for Albertus Magnus himself, he was read both ways. Henricus de Frimaria, early on in his comments on *EN*, V, 5 has a builder and a smith — perhaps to stress "producer worth" difference — work one day for one another, concluding, *tunc non esset aequalitas rei datae et acceptae, puta domus et cultelli, esto quod quilibet suum artificium una die compleret.* This is as clear a rejection of labour time as can be found. But Henricus never quarrelled with Albert; we must assume that he here explains the labour theory as he read it in Albert. It is possible that Odonis had read these lines in Henricus and was influenced by them; he pretended to read Albert (through Thomas Aquinas) differently. Perhaps he did, perhaps again he only wanted to quarrel with the Dominicans. Anyhow, one effect of Albert's labour theory was to inspire fruitful counter-arguments against a naive interpretation.

*

But a truer development of Albert's theory starts where the commentator asks himself *why* value in exchange must comply with cost of production. Prices should cover costs, says Piccolomini in effect in the line which concludes our quotation above, so that an artisan can live decently by his art. This is no more than a reasonable social norm; it can lead to interesting analysis only if one asks what will happen to the arts if it is broken. This logical next step was taken by some commentators in the Albertian tradition, invited by a repeated hint in Aristotle: *Destruerentur enim* .... A quotation from the *De bono* on one of the first pages of this chapter shows that Albert himself caught on early to *destruerentur*. In each of his *Ethics* commentaries he commented on it not once, but twice, for again a peculiarity in the inherited text interfered with the commentary history. In the *Nicomachean Ethics* as we have received it, the lines 1133a14–16 with the statement that arts would have been destroyed in the absence of equivalence, occur also as 1132b9–11. This is an obvious interpolation which many editors now omit, but Grosseteste duly translated it. Consequently, Latin commentators who explained the running text came upon it twice, once in and once out of context.[34] The Greek commentators took it up only at 1132b9–11. The explanation of Michael Ephesinus, echoing the Anonymous, includes the following statement: *Non enim utique operarentur non futuri aequale accipere.* This may have put Albert in a constructive frame of mind. His own five successive comments make a study in the gradual maturing of an idea. *De bono:* ... *periret civilitas quantum ad aedificationem, si non plus acciperet quam calceum. First Commentary* at 1132b9–11: ... *destruerentur artes per hoc quod nullus vellet exercere eas, si* ... *pretium non est* ... *quantum valet* ... *opus. First Commentary* at 1133a14–16: ... *artes destruerentur, secundum quod nullus vellet uti eis, si non faciet* ... *quantum ad expensas et quantum ad laborem* .... *Second Commentary* at 1132b9–11: *Si enim lectorum factor pro lecto non tantum et tale accipiat, quantum et quale posuit in expensis, lectum de caetero non faciet: et sic destruetur ars quae lectorum factrix est.* And so only a brief textual paraphrase at 1133a14–16; the point has been made.

The "destruction of arts" in the absence of just exchange, stated in general terms is, as I said, a commonplace. The Greek commentators would seem to point to the agent who may bring this destruction about, namely the artisan himself on being unjustly treated. The allusion, Albert explains, is to the artisan who does not have his costs covered, because then production will be suspended. On the whole, his pupils must be said to have responded less than brightly to this really remarkable observation. Thomas Aquinas was quite deaf to it. Henricus de Frimaria caught on at 1132b9–11: *Numquam enim artifex faceret archam vel lectum nisi tantum pro ipso reciperet quod sibi satisfieret in laboribus et expensis.* In the context of the value analysis itself at 1133a14–16 he repeats this in different words: *Nullus enim vellet intendere alicui operi in quo pateretur dispendium tam laboris quam sumptuum.* Buridan's attitude should also be touched upon, since he evidently knew Albert and has been taken in support of Albert's interpretation of *destruerentur* in a passing reference to the builder and the shoemaker in his Quaestio V, 15 to the *Ethics*, where he notes that if the builder *dabit unam domum pulchram pro uno calciamento*

34 Unless it is foreign to both loci; cp. Ross in note to 1133a16.

. . . , *domificator non posset vivere, quoniam ipse annum apponit in construendo unam domum.*[35] This is typically Buridan, dramatizing a point for emphasis, but it is hardly an analytical use of the labour theory; there is in fact no evidence that Buridan intended to support this line of value theory in any of his questions. But he lends himself to an interpretation along this line in V, 15 and it is of interest to note that he was thus interpreted even in the early scholastic tradition. Conradus de Susato, professor at Heidelberg, who wrote an *Ethics* commentary in question form, paraphrasing and explaining Buridan, sometimes brought in labour arguments from Henricus de Frimaria, who was his second important source. In V, 15 he brings together our quotation from Buridan and our last quotation from Henricus above, thus explaining Buridan in terms of labour.[36]

It clearly makes quite a lot of difference whether you say that production will be suspended if value is not received or say that it will be suspended if costs are not covered; the latter statement provides an opening for reflection on the role of cost in the value forming circle. Some years before Buridan, Petrus Cornethi (or de Corveheda), a *magister* and probably a native of the Midi but otherwise an obscure figure, composed a textual exposition of the *Ethics* which is still preserved in three manuscripts, one at Bordeaux and two in Italy.[37] He comments on *destruerentur* in words reminiscent of Albertus Magnus: . . . *si faber de gladio non reciperet tantum de pellibus a pellipario sicut valet gladius, nullus vellet esse faber.* Labour is not mentioned, but in the lines leading up to this conclusion, where the other manuscripts read *valoris* rather than *laboris*, the Bordeaux manuscript says, that though works exchanged are different, *tamen fiet aequatio ut quamvis maioris laboris sit domus quam sotulares, cum tot poterunt dari sotulares qui aequipollebunt domui.* Cornethi may have meant it like that or a scribe may have read him like that; anyhow, at some stage, *destruerentur* elicited this interpretation. It was occa-

35 **JB8**, f.118va. On the Buridanian manuscripts, see note 5,2.
36 **CS1**, f.295ra-b; **CS2**, f.310v; **CS3**, f.75va-b. On this author, and the manuscripts, see below, p. 111, pp. 129–130 and note 5,14.
37 Bordeaux BMun 169 (quoted on f.47va); BLaur S. Marco 452 (f.19vb); Urbin. lat. 222 (f.256ra). On this commentary, see Pelzer (1) 380–2; Grabmann (4) 89–90; Lohr XXVIII 350; Gauthier (3) 135.

sionally commented on in the later tradition. In 1620, Robert Balfour, a Scot who had come from St Andrews via Paris to Bordeaux, published there a regular *Ethics* commentary in the old style. The ways of scholastic influence are sometimes inscrutable. Had he seen the Bordeaux copy of Cornethi before writing the following?: ... *si enim non pluris aestimares operam fabri in aedificanda domo, quam sutoris, in suendo calceo: nemo est qui faber aut architectus esse volet.*[38] Some years earlier, Johannes Magirus, like Balfour in some respects a faithful Thomist, but working in the very different academic milieu of Marburg, made a similar inference, explicitly in terms of cost: ... *si sutor semper deberet minus accipere pro calceis, quam ipsi constitisset corium, non posset diu suum officium exercere.*[39]

At some point on the scale of deepening insight marked by these comments, there emerges a concept which looks very much like Mill's "necessary price". But if another question were to have been asked at that extreme point of the scale where Petrus Cornethi says that *nullus vellet esse faber*, it becomes evident how close we might have been to something like Wieser's *Kostengesetz*: When the carpenter stops making beds since they do not pay him back his costs in exchange for a house, what will he in fact do, rather than go idle? Perhaps build a house? Albertus Magnus did not enter upon this line of inquiry, the Aristotelian *Expositio* did not invite it. And looking back, we can of course now see that scholastic economics was entirely unequipped for a successful approach to the "circle of value" along this route, which involves the notion of adjustment of productive resources towards an equilibrium of industries. It can hardly be done in a mediaeval economic setting — nor has anybody done it properly without the aid of differential calculus. So the Aristotelians, following Odonis, found another way and emerged perhaps where Senior came to stand, still in the premarginal world. On the eve of Senior's synthesis, Malthus wrote:

... the cost of production itself only influences the prices of these commodities, as the payment of this cost is the necessary condition of their continued supply ....

38 p. 280. Copies of the book are in Paris BN, B Vat, Basel UB. On Balfour (c.1550–c.1625), see DNB I 997–8; NBG IV 284; Jöcher I 742; Gauthier (3) 210–1. See also below, p. 99.
39 Ed. Frankfurt 1601, p. 476. On this author, see below, p. 101.

. . . the labour expended upon it should be so remunerated in the quantity of desirable objects given in exchange for it, as to encourage the exertion of a sufficient quantity of industry in the direction required, as without such adequate remuneration, the supply of the commodity must necessarily fail.[40]

Schumpeter says that this "points far ahead toward Jevonian teaching".[41] So do the words of our unknown master of the Bordeaux manuscript half a millennium before, expressing in cruder language but with equal poignancy, an Albertian idea.

*

Cost imputed to products as necessary price is not conceived of as autonomously causing value; there is here rather a notion of the inverse causal relation. In a comprehensive explanation of factor and product value the notion of causality recedes, but it is hardly possible to point to a familiar, leading economist before, say, Senior, who got further than enumerating causal factors, labour being one, utility, demand, scarcity representing the traditional alternative. Sometimes the occurrence of broad and intelligent demand and cost explanations side by side in the same treatise can lead critics to hail it as a synthesis. A case in point is Galiani.[42] It is true that Galiani treats brilliantly of utility, scarcity and labour, but hardly as an integrated system. He takes them one by one. This distinction should not be taken lightly. On the other hand, the constant rubbing together of alternative causal factors in early Italian economics was undoubtedly influential in bringing about the true synthesis of a later generation. Coincidence demands correlation. To conclude this account of Albertian labour theory it is fitting to make the same point in this case. By bringing labour into the context of *EN*, V, 5, where Grosseteste had prepared the ground for a demand theory soon to spring out in other traditions, Albertus Magnus was instrumental in juxtaposing the two factors whose rubbing together produced in the end the Aristotelian synthesis. From this point of view his most interesting use of the Grossetestan *opus* equivalents may be where he once varies the

40 *Principles of Political Economy*, II, 3; ed. 2 (1836), p. 71, p. 74.
41 Schumpeter 602.
42 Cp. for instance, Gonnard II 158; Arias 352.

usual cost reference to explain cross-conjunction in terms of *urbanitatis indigentiam* in his *Second Commentary* or where he combines the factors to an equalization *in expensis et labore et utilitate operis* in his *First Commentary*. Henricus de Frimaria, always alert to Albert's finer notes, catches this one too; we may take this basic theme of Albertian value theory as stated in his words: ... *valor mensuratur secundum proportionem humanae indigentiae et etiam sumptuum illius rei* ....
As long as economists referred some of their ideas to Aristotle, this coincidence was maintained. We can see how it helped work the correlation which shall be recorded in a later chapter of this book. But Aristotelian remnants in modern economics prove that it was active much later than that.

3. Human wants

The tradition of Thomas Aquinas

Thomas Aquinas was born at Roccasecca in Lazio and died less than fifty years old in 1274 while travelling through the same region of Italy. The story of the life that lies between and the work he crammed into it belongs to our common intellectual and spiritual heritage. Only a small part of it touches upon the subject matter of the present study.[1] I think in fact it would be wise, in view of all that has been written about his comments on *EN*, V, 5, to point out two sober facts: first, that economics probably would range far down on St Thomas's own list of favourite subjects; secondly, that to the extent that he did write to explain and advise on economic exchange, Aristotle was not at all his prime reference. The all-important locus of just price teaching in St Thomas Aquinas is the *Summa theologiae*, II–II, 77. The *Ethics* is quoted there, but the main analysis is in older Latin traditions. It does not follow, however, that we can relegate the angelic doctor to a position of minor or even medium importance to this study. Once he set himself the task of explaining the *Ethics*, some murky corners in the young Aristotelian tradition became much clearer. Thus also in the field of Aristotelian economics, Aquinas slides into a pivotal position on account of this

---

1 A recent addition to the bio-bibliographical literature, with useful references, is Weisheipl, supplementing Grabmann (5). The Aristotelian works are in Lohr XXIX 159–172. See Gauthier (2), (4), (5) on the *Ethics* commentary. On Thomas's economic ideas, see Jourdain 44; Endemann II 32–48; Graziani 15–9; Brants 68–9, 74, 194, 197–9, 207; Žmavc; Rambaud 26–33; Sewall 13–20; Kaulla (1) 455–6, (2) 53, (3) 22–3; Tarde 28–31, 36–7, 47–50; Schreiber 16–121; Gelesnoff (1) 205, (2) 33; O'Brien 111–9, 131–6; Ashley (2) 500; Tawney 36, 40, 152; Nègre; Hagenauer; Dempsey (2) 478–482; Sandoz 286–8, 299; Whittaker 410–2; Soudek 65; Schumpeter 93; De Roover (1) 495–8, (2) 163, (3) 421–3, (4) 7–8, 17–18; Dognin; Baldwin 9–12, 15, 61–80; Mandel I 100, II 388–393.

analytical and expositional brilliance and not, as I see it, on account of any keen interest or insight into the economic issues involved, nor indeed because of any determinate or decisive standpoints on these issues. Keeping these points in mind we should be better prepared to evaluate St Thomas's commentary on the *Nicomachean Ethics* as one link — important but not exceptional — in the long scholastic chain.

It may be added that arguments over Thomas's economic views are to be expected, considering how his often brief and passing remarks on the subject are scattered throughout his numerous works. It is tempting in the case of an author of such great general importance to try to reconstruct a comprehensive theoretical system from these patches; but far-reaching conclusions drawn from this kind of patch-work theory are often doubtful and sometimes ridiculous. Undertaking a more limited task here, we shall be spared the full *Opera* search. Our interest being limited to Thomas's contribution to Aristotelian value theory, works other than the *Ethics* commentary are relevant only in so far as they help us understand it or else if they also quote *EN*, V, 5. The *Summa theologiae* does both, and so I shall refer to it occasionally, but there is really no other work of St Thomas that does either.[2] The rest of the corpus is therefore left out and whatever inconsistencies with the Aristotelian analysis may be hidden there we shall ignore. When Thomas commented on the *Ethics*, his aim was to explain in simple terms what he thought Aristotle meant, not to adjust each remark to all he had previously said about the facts and morals of economic endeavour.

According to recent research,[3] the *Sententia libri Ethicorum* was composed in Paris during the years 1271–2, that is, more or less simultaneously with the economic questions of the *Summa theologiae*. There is one particular point of view applied to value in both works which is best understood with reference to the *Summa*, where its source is quoted. Following his early teacher, St Thomas defines the area of economic measurement by posing a contrast to grading of a more essential nature. The specifically economic aspect of goods is

2 Thomas's use of Aristotelian justice at *Sent*. III, 33 is limited to simple definitions. His comments on the economics of *Politics*, I stop short of the role of *indigentia*. The economics of the *De regimine principum ad regem Cypri* is spurious, see below, p. 93.

3 Cp. Gauthier (2), with comments in (3) 128, note 135.

that which emerges when they *veniunt in usum et utilitatem communitatis*, says Albertus Magnus in a catching phrase which Thomas and many others adopted, but while Albert contrasts this to *mensuratio artificialium secundum esse suae speciei*, calling in the metaphysical categories of Averroes, Thomas, in a characteristic switch of reference, embraces St Augustine. Men will not always rank things according to the natural order, says the latter; who would not rather have bread in his house than mice? Even a servant girl, a human being, is often valued less than a jewel. *Ita libertate iudicandi plurimum distat ratio considerantis a necessitate indigentis seu voluptate cupientis . . . .*[4] A basic model in Thomas's thought as well,[5] the scale of natural perfection would be to him an obvious choice to illustrate, by contrast, the scale of valuation in economics. Quoting St Augustine in the *Summa theologiae* in a question about defects in commodities, he uses the two scales to distinguish *occultas rei venditae qualitates*, which are irrelevant in exchange, from those *per quas redditur humanis usibus apta.*[6] In his *Ethics* commentary Thomas chooses for his example the Augustinian mouse compared to a pearl (clearly a pendant to the original *gemma*); later commentators drew from the fauna as their fancies took them, to embellish this distinction between the natural and the economic order, which became a fixture of the Aristotelian tradition as well as the tradition which developed from the *Summa*.[7] In view of this a difference of viewpoint, and hence of emphasis, between Thomas and his patristic source ought to be pointed out.

In both works where he uses that source, Thomas treats of economic exchange and brings in the natural order for contrast; St Augustine does the opposite. Exchange is not in fact mentioned by him at all, it is at most implied when the natural order is contrasted to the valuation of man, whether in need or in search of pleasure. But the point is that in this formula, need and pleasure are not distinguished, they serve the same purpose of illustration.

4 *De civitate Dei*, XI, 16; PL, Tom. 41, 331.
5 Cp. for instance, *Sum. theol.*, I, 72, ad 1; I–II, 3, 2, ad 4.
6 II–II, 77, 2, ad 3.
7 Additional authority was provided by Duns Scotus's use of this source in his important economic discussion at *Sent.* IV, 15, 2 (*Opera*, Tom. 9, Lyon 1639, p. 166); economic goods are taken *in comparatione ad usum humanum, propter quem fit commutatio ista.*

This would seem to be a fruitful approach to economic demand theory and Aristotelians were to find it later, but Thomas let it rest. For when shifting the viewpoint to that of economics, Thomas also brings to it a purpose of moral instruction essentially alien to the *Ethics*, namely that of the *Summa theologiae*; this work, which must have occupied much more of his mind in these years, reflects also on his use of adopted material in his Aristotelian comments. And the purpose of moral instruction will tend to discount pleasure; the emphasis in Thomas is squarely on the human usefulness of commodities as contrasted to their place in the natural order of creation. In the Aristotelian tradition, the concept of *indigentia*, having recently come into the revised text of the *Ethics*, was in a process of formation; while Thomas developed it decisively in other respects, he never really took it beyond basic need at least in this moral sense. Following Thomas, many authors in his immediate tradition and in the dependent one of Henricus de Frimaria used *necessitas* and *indigentia* alternately and synonymously. No analytical use was made of the Augustinian pearl until Buridan (who inherited the formula in the shape of a fly compared to gold) rectified this bias in the earlier traditions by embracing in his market model any willingness to buy which springs from desire, whether the object sought is "necessary" or not. To point out the bias and indicate a reason for it is not to accuse St Thomas of harbouring notions of intrinsic values — that accusation will hardly stick to an author who makes a point of excluding *occultas rei venditae qualitates* — or of confusing use value and exchange value. The point is rather that markets in necessaries usually provide less instructive pictures of price formation than some of those where *voluptas cupientis* runs unbridled. This theme is a recurrent one in the Aristotelian tradition.[8]

*

8 There is one direct reference to *EN*, V, 5 from II–II; it is at 77, 1, c, where Thomas says that *Quantitas autem rerum quae in usum hominis veniunt mensuratur secundum pretium datum: ad quod est inventum nummisma* . . . . This has given rise to speculation as to what *pretium datum* is. (Hagenauer 53). The whole issue rests on an overinterpretation of a syntactic detail; *pretium datum* is simply *pretium* as paid; the Fathers of the English Dominican Province translate, "measured by the price given for it". Except for the usual mis-dating, I agree with Baldwin (77, note 204) that the passage is "a greatly condensed summary of ideas already elaborated in the *Commentary to the Ethics*".

Some eighty mediaeval manuscripts of Thomas Aquinas's *Sententia* are extant; it was printed at least twelve times before 1650. For scholarly purposes, the text of the 1867 Parma edition of the *Opera* and versions derived from it have only recently been replaced by the definite text of the Leonine edition.[9] Thomas was the first commentator to use a revised text of the *Translatio Lincolniensis*. Reading him at *EN*, V, 5 it is difficult to believe that he did not also know Albertus Magnus's *Second Commentary* or at least that there had not been some kind of exchange of material between them since their days together in the Dominican auditorium in Cologne.[10] However, the point is not essential here. The *indigentia* analysis in St Thomas's commentary was probably inspired elsewhere. As for his labour analysis, it is interesting to note that he uses the singular form of *labor*; whether or not he knew the *Second Commentary* and whatever other inspiration he may have had, it is the form which his teacher impressed upon him in his youth which comes through in his own commentary. The point does not seem trivial to me. Enough has been said about the contents of Thomas's labour analysis and about its possible sources and its limited influence.[11] But since this chapter is to deal with human wants and not with labour, a few words may be needed about the ideas which structured St Thomas's remarks on these subjects.

First, to repeat the point once more: The confrontation of opposing partial theories, a cost theory and a market theory, is historically unfounded. There is no favouring, either in Albert or in Thomas, of either of these explanations over the other. But secondly, since Albert had set the labour theory on foot and devoted quite a lot of space to it, there was little for Thomas to do but repeat some of this (and little for us to do but note that he repeated it). While his statements about labour and expenses are fewer and less inspired than those of Albert, they are explicit and unambiguous; one should read into them just as much (and as little) as one would normally do when some commentator is found to be voicing the

---

9 Tom. 47, Rome 1969. The comments on economics are in Lectures 8 and 9 to Book V (pp. 289–296). See also note 1,43.
10 See above, pp. 55–6, p. 67.
11 See pp. 55–60, pp. 71–2, p. 76 with note 2,30.

theories of his acknowledged master. There is a corollary to this, regarding the *indigentia* theory. Albertus Magnus had no argument against human need as a value determinant, and Thomas could not have understood him that way. So far their explanations are again in harmony. But Albert's explanation of the role of human need is less happy than his labour explanation. I suggest that Thomas realized that he must improve on this and knew how to do it. This is essentially the relation between the value theories of the two great Dominican commentators.

The conflict with Albert, then, is imaginary and can be forgotten. But there is another element which enters and plays havoc with the Thomist tradition and for which the reader should be prepared before turning to an examination of Thomas's own contribution. The fact is that Thomas as an Aristotelian economist had an *alter ego*. He is Gualterus Burlaeus (Walter Burley), the fourteenth century author of a highly influential work which is superficially a somewhat abbreviated version of the *Sententia* of St Thomas, but into which are mixed elements from another source which garbled Thomas's message. A number of schoolmen who have been routinely classified as Thomists, actually read Thomas through Burlaeus and got the message wrong. The history of the Thomist branch of the Aristotelian tradition is therefore to a large extent the history of different interpretations of Thomas fighting one another and attaining some measure of reconciliation in the seventeenth century.

The man who caused this confusion was born about 1275 in Yorkshire. He was a secular cleric who had studied at Oxford and for an extended period at Paris but returned to England to serve as a clerk to King Edward III and later to write a number of philosophical commentaries under the patronage of the bishop of Durham, to whom his *Expositio super libros Ethicorum*, completed after 1338, is dedicated. The philosophical doctrines of Burlaeus, *doctor planus et perspicuus*, are little known today, most of his works remain in manuscript. But his exposition of the *Nicomachean Ethics* became one of the most popular textbooks in this field, meeting as it did the need for something handier than the expansive commentaries of previous generations and the more recent collections of questions. Cutting out what seemed difficult or unnecessary in Thomas and stringently editing the rest in a system of minute textual subdivisions, Burley as a "plain and perspicuous" pedagogue is hardly matched in the scholastic age. He came to exert a particular influence in Italy, where his book was later to be printed three times in Venice.[12] One can only regret that the editing of Thomas introduced a corruption at *EN*, V, 5. Following the original almost verbatim in long sequences, Burlaeus occasionally skips significant sections, for instance both sections where Thomas mentions labour (including the *superabundantias* analysis), and less frequently inserts alien material. One of these instances occurs just when Thomas has stated what is the crux of his whole explanation of *EN*, V, 5. Burlaeus repeats this but then adds something which obscures and negates it, and this is what many students came to read in lieu of the true Thomas and were mislead by.

The formal contribution of Thomas Aquinas to Aristotelian value theory consists of two elements, one conditioning the other. The first element is his *theory of the double measure* of commutables; the second is his *price formula*, explaining what it means to say that *indigentia* is a measure. While Aristotle states that money was

12 **GBX1**: 1481 (economic comments: ff.p$_1$va–p$_3$ra); **GBX2**: 1500 (ff.83ra–84rb); **GBX3**: 1521 (ff.91va–92vb). The latter improves somewhat on the first two. For locations of **GBX1–2**, cp. GW 5778–9; they are also in Hain 4143–4. **GBX3** is in B Vat, Siena BCom, Venice BMarc, Vienna NB, Paris BN, BMaz. I cannot locate an edition, Venice 1536 indicated by Bolduanus 465. Our brief section indicates a preference for these four manuscripts: **GB1**: Cambridge Pembroke College 157 (XIV, ff.84ra–85ra); **GB2**: Gonville and Caius College 490 (XIV, ff.161va–162va); **GB3**: Oxford BodL Can. misc. 251 (1424, ff.77ra–78ra); **GB4**: Padova BU 1452 (XV, ff.88va–89vb). Another loose group: **GB5**: Cambridge Peterhouse 93 (XIV, f.24ra–va); **GB6**: Oxford Magdalen College 205 (XIV, ff.68rb–69ra); **GB7**: New College 242 (XIV, ff.87vb–88vb); **GB8**: Oriel College 57 (XIV, ff.100va–101va); **GB9**: Vat. Urbin. lat. 1396 (XIV/XV, ff.125v–126v). A third group: **GB10**: Paris BN lat. 6459 (1401, ff.83rb–84ra); **GB11**: Brugge SB 502 (XIV, ff.108ra–109va); **GB12**: Venice BMarc lat. VI 88 (XIV, ff.117ra–118rb). Individual relations within groups: **5–8** (close), **6–9, 11–12**. Copies in the Biblioteca Laurenziana and in the Biblioteca Angelica, lack Book V. Many catalogue items prove to be only brief *Conclusiones* to the *Ethics*. On Burlaeus, see Martin; Tanner 141–2; Emden I 312–4; Fabricius I 283; Grabmann (3) 70; Heidingsfelder 86–102; Jourdain 44; Schreiber 172; EF I 1133–4; LTK II 794; DNB III 374–6; Jöcher I 1500–1; Chevalier 734; Wulf III 164–6, 174; Ueberweg 619, 621–2, 788; Gilson 769–770, Lohr XXIV 171–187; Gauthier (3) 136.

introduced to serve as a measure of value in exchange and some of
the early commentators hinted at the role of human need, it was
Thomas who cut through these ambiguities by stating repeatedly
and directly that there are two measures: . . . *omnia mensurantur per
indigentiam naturaliter et per denarium secundum condictum hominum* . . . ;
. . . *primo ostendit quod necessitas sit mensura secundum rei veritatem;
secundo quomodo denarius sit mensura secundum legis positionem* . . . . The
term I have used to describe this theory can be found in Guido
Vernani, the first summarist of Thomas, who says that value *potest
sciri duplici mensura*, and in Albertus de Saxonia, who wrote a little
later: . . . *duplex est mensura commutabilium, una scilicet naturalis
quemadmodum est indigentia humana, alia autem est inventa quemadmodum
est nummisma.*[13] From now on all commentators said that human
need is a measure of goods in exchange along with money; this
interpretation has become universal, even to such a point that I
suppose it will be met with surprise when I insist that Aristotle
himself perhaps did not hold any such views. To paraphrase what I
said in the last chapter about the Albertian labour theory: The
question after Thomas is not whether a commentator says that
human need is a measure of commutables, but what he makes of it.

For granted that *indigentia* is *mensura*, it clearly is not so in the
sense in which money is *mensura*.[14] The word as applied to human
need is vague and permits of many interpretations. Since Aristotle
himself seems to argue that way,[15] it is not surprising that some
commentators, even after Thomas, fell back on an interpretation
which makes measure in exchange mean no more than cause of
exchange, the more so since the idea that human need causes
exchange and society is a genuine ancient one which still found
expression. As a matter of fact it found expression very close to
Thomas himself, in a spurious addition to a work later to be in-

13 On these commentators, see below, pp. 95–6.
14 Money has a number of functions; Aristotle was the first to point out so
   many of them. The way he uses the word μέτρον, translated by Grosseteste as
   mensura, it corresponds well to what we now mean by money's role as a
   measure of value, viz. as something by reference to which values of different
   goods can be compared, although his use of the word also indicates the
   functions of a medium of exchange and a store of value.
15 See above, p. 49.

cluded in his published *Opera*. Discussing the constitution of states, the author who completed Thomas's *De regimine principum* in the early years of the fourteenth century refers to *humana indigentia, per quam cogitur homo in societate vivere*.[16] Remarks like that may have influenced *Ethics* commentators. Besides, the composite *Translatio Lincolniensis* with the Greek commentators was still in circulation, most commonly, no doubt, in England. There is reason to believe that Burlaeus had access to a copy when he revised St Thomas's commentary. His references to "Eustratius" are not significant, since these would normally be, at this time, only indirect ones through Albertus Magnus. But Burlaeus also quotes Grosseteste's notes,[17] though unfortunately not in the economic section of the *Expositio*. He might have had a separate collection of the note material. In my judgment, however, the fact that he knew the notes, seen in conjunction with his interpretation of *EN*, V, 5, strongly indicates that he had studied a regular copy of the annotated text interspaced with the anonymous commentary and that the latter is the source of his revision of St Thomas.

Burlaeus does not say in so many words that *mensura* means *communicationis causa*, but in the fatal section inserted just after Thomas has explained whāt *he* means by need as measure (copied by Burlaeus), he implies it very strongly. Thomas, in comment to 1133a28–29, explains the second element of his double measure, money, as representing human need: *Et quod secundum rei veritatem indigentia omnia mensurat, manifestum est per hoc quod nummisma factum est* .... Burlaeus, in his long substitution, adds another idea:

Et hoc est signum quod indigentia est secundum veritatem mensura omnium commutabilium, quia, si non esset indigentia, non esset commutatio, et ad variationem indigentiae sequitur variatio commutationis. Et quia indigentia mensurat omnia commutabilia, propter hoc est nummisma factum. ...

It is a remark entirely uncalled for by Thomas and expressing most graphically the ancient idea of *mensura* as *causa*. Variation in need

16 *Opera*, ed. Parma, Vol. 16, Opusculum LX at p. 271. In the printed version the treatise consists of four books. Scholars now believe that Thomas's contribution ends in II, 4; quotation is from IV, 2. Author of the addition is Tholomaeus de Lucca. (cp. Grabmann (5) 330–6; Weisheipl 189–190, 388–9).
17 Rose 66, 109–110; cp. Grabmann (1); Pelzer (1); Powicke; Thomson.

causes *exchange* to vary. It is not what Thomas has just said in comment upon 1133a25–27:

Et dicit quod ideo possunt omnia adaequari, quia omnia possunt commensurari per aliquid unum, ut dictum est. Hoc autem unum quod omnia mensurat, secundum rei veritatem est indigentia, quae continet omnia commutabilia, in quantum scilicet omnia referuntur ad humanam indigentiam; non enim appretiantur res secundum dignitatem naturae ipsorum; alioquin unus mus, quod est animal sensibile, maioris pretii esset quam una margarita, quae est res inanimata; sed rebus pretia imponuntur secundum quod homines indigent eis ad suum usum.

Price varies with human need; that is the important economic relation and the significant definition of *indigentia* as *mensura*. But Burlaeus was to obscure it to Thomists for centuries.

Historically, the price formula of Thomas Aquinas is important because it marks the beginning of an analytical demand theory of value. His own contribution was a formal one because he does not explain the terms, he just makes the connection. But it was the Thomist formula linking *indigentia* to price which invited Aristotelians of the following generations to work out a theory of value, for what they did was precisely to seek a definition of *indigentia* which would make economic sense of the formula. The development of the Aristotelian demand theory of value consists exactly in the gradual maturing of the concept expressed by the argument-variable of the price formula of St Thomas. Not only must his rather narrow concept of *indigentia* be broadened to comprise any desire backed by the power to influence the market: *necessitas* must move over to accommodate *utilitas* and eventually *voluptas*. Equally important, *indigentia* must be transformed from a concept denoting personal urges and motivations of these various kinds to one denoting aggregate, quantitative market demand. I have tentatively suggested the words "wants" or "need" to translate Thomas's *indigentia*; since he does not develop the concept further in his *Ethics* commentary, and since his successors had to argue their ways through the following steps, we cannot credit Thomas with having anticipated these steps. It is true that some passages in the *Summa theologiae* suggest more advanced ideas, but *indigentia* is not actually mentioned there, and this Thomist inspiration only entered the *Ethics* tradition at a later stage, when some commentators interpreted what Thomas said about *copia et inopia* in terms of Aristotelian *indigentia*. It was only then, when tied to the price formula, that these ideas became elements of constructive value theory; I shall discuss them at that point.[18]

As a matter of fact, in the tradition of the *Ethics*, *indigentia* as a quantitative expression of aggregate wants bounded by scarcity (which may be what Thomas hints at in II–II, 77) came first, in the tradition of Henricus de Frimaria; ability to pay, defining effective demand, came later, in the tradition of Johannes Buridanus, as a natural consequence of the extension of *indigentia* to include *voluptas* — "the needs of the rich". The authors who assembled this increasingly accomplished model were truly Thomists, not mainly in the sense that some of them used the *Summa theologiae*, but in the sense that their contributions cannot be envisaged except as a superstructure on the basic Thomist price formula in the *Ethics* commentary. We cannot turn to them just yet. An adequate picture of the historical conditions under which they wrote requires an account of a number of other Thomists, struggling to clear the price formula of the tangles of older and vaguer notions of *indigentia* as *mensura*. The theme is Thomas Aquinas versus Gualterus Burlaeus. I shall briefly review eight authors, scattered over two centuries, who used one or the other or both of these authorities directly, then trace some independent and mostly later developments.

*

Guido Vernani (of Vergnano), a Dominican who lectured at Bologna in the 1320's, summarized St Thomas's *Sententia*. Like Burlaeus, he leaves out the labour references at *EN*, V, 5, but there is no extraneous material. The price formula is intact.[19] Albertus de Saxonia, who was rector of the University of Paris in 1353 and the first rector of the University of Vienna in 1365 (becoming thus also the first in a line of interesting *Ethics* commentators associated with

18 See below, pp. 117–9.
19 Vat. lat. 1172 (economic comments: f.35rb–va); Venice BMarc lat. VI 94 (f.23va-b); complete list of manuscripts in Gauthier (4), 37*–43*. On Vernani, see Wulf III 66–7; Quétif I 726; Fabricius III 127; Chevalier 4649; EF III 417; LTK IV 1270; Grabmann (3) 65, (4) 84–9; Lohr XXIV 191–2; Gauthier (3) 135–6.

that university), composed an *Expositio* which at first glance appears to be only an abbreviation of Burlaeus but proves on closer inspection to be something more than this. Composed in the 1350's, the work is preserved in some twenty manuscripts, more than any other post-Thomist commentary except for the *Quaestiones* of Buridan. Its popularity may have been due to its form; preserving Burlaeus's editorial frame, Albert has rephrased and simplified many sections. Moreover, he has evidently been consulting Thomas Aquinas directly with the intention of taking the imitation back to the original without spoiling its form. Most significantly, he omits the unfortunate section quoted from Burlaeus above. Albert states the price formula, or rather the value formula, for a new feature is added: ... *pretium et valor imponitur rebus in commutationibus secundum quod homines indigent de eis* ....[20]

Another commentary built on Burlaeus's editorial frame is that of Henricus Totting de Oyta, preserved in a single manuscript at Leipzig and probably composed before 1371. Henricus later befriended the great Langenstein and worked with him in Vienna and even wrote a *Tractatus de contractibus*, but that work is a disappointment and so is his *Ethics* commentary. It is probable that Henricus had consulted pre-Thomist material; at any rate, *indigentia humana est causa commutationis rerum*.[21] A more obvious disciple of Burlaeus is Paulus Venetus, who taught in North Italian universities in the

---

20 Heidingsfelder attempted a classification of manuscripts; the list has since been more than doubled. The best tradition is represented by these almost identical copies: Oxford BodL Can. misc. 304 (1365, economic comments: ff.47vb–48rb); Innsbruck UB 159 (1365, f.31ra–va); Erfurt Amplon. F. 365 (1371, f.35ra–va). In the same group belongs BMarc Z. lat. 262, ff.16–83, attributed by Lohr to Buridanus. So is Vat. lat. 6384, but this copy belongs to an inferior tradition also known to Heidingsfelder in Paris BMaz and elsewhere. In Vienna NB I found a fifteenth century manuscript, CVP 5401, of the *Ethics* with Henricus de Frimaria's commentary (without the "Averroist" material — see following chapter) and with Albert's exposition in the bottom margin — a most serviceable combination. Besides biographies by Dyroff and Heidingsfelder, see Ueberweg 596, 600–2, 784; Wulf III 135–8; Gilson 516–7, 520, 795; Quétif I 735; Fabricius I 47; Chevalier 107; EF I 158; NDB I 135; Grabmann (6) 224; Aschbach 359–366; Lohr XXIII 348–352; Gauthier (3) 136–7.

21 Leipzig UB 1413, f.194vb; see Lohr XXIV 229–232. Oyta's treatise on contracts is on ff.224r–253v, following that of Langenstein, in Vol. IV of Gerson's *Opera*, see below, p. 127.

early years of the fifteenth century. Before that, he had studied for a time at Oxford; we must assume that that is where he got the material for his *Conclusiones morales*, based on lectures at Padova and preserved in a Vatican manuscript. At *EN*, V, 5 this is no more than a collection of Burlaean quotes, with a tendency: the price formula is omitted, and *ad variationem indigentiae sequitur variatio commutationis.*[22] None of these four commentaries was printed. Among those later to be printed we encounter again that of Johannes Versoris, whose ideas about labour were quoted in Chapter 2.[23] That would seem to be the only part of his value analysis not copied from St Thomas. The double measure is stated, as well as the price formula, in a section otherwise littered with errors in the printed editions. An approximate contemporary of Versor at Paris is Nicolaus de Orbellis, a Franciscan. Among his works is a *Compendium ethicae*, published posthumously at Basel in 1494 and a second time in 1503. There are traces of Odonis and of Henricus de Frimaria, but the main analysis of value is pure Thomism, apparently copied from the *Summa* of Guido Vernani.[24]

While the unadulterated Thomas held sway at Paris, Burlaeus reigned in the South. A disciple of his was Petrus de Castrovol, of Mayorga in Spain, also a Franciscan. In the last decades of the century, commentaries on no less than ten of Aristotle's works were edited in his name; among them is a *Commentum super libros Ethicorum secundum novam translationem Aretini*, Lerida 1489, the first commentary to be printed with that textual basis. It is not a distinction which Castrovol did much to deserve, however, for his commentary is only a lightly worked over copy of Burlaeus. Thus, at *EN*, V, 5, variation in exchange follows from variation in need, and other sections are also borrowed, sometimes quite uncritically.[25]

---

22 Vat. lat. 2125, f.35vb. On this author, see Wulf III 103–5, 180, 183; Ueberweg 618, 787; Gilson 527, 798; Fabricius V 209; Chevalier 3547; Emden III 1944–5; EF IV 1321; Zumkeller 244–6; Lohr XXVIII 314–320; Gauthier (3) 138–9.

23 p. 73.

24 Ed. 1494, f.x$_3$va; ed. 1503, f.v$_3$va. The first edition is Part 3 (in Vol. 2 = Hain 5864) of his *Cursus philosophiae*. An influence of Albertus de Saxonia on Orbellis, as suggested by Heidingsfelder 147, is not evident at *EN*, V, 5.

25 There is a copy of this very rare book (Copinger 1481) in the Biblioteca Comunale in Perugia. The economic comments are on ff.m$_3$vb–m$_4$vb. The model used must have been a copy of Burlaeus related to **GB11–12**, where

There is of course some up-dating of terminology, and one is worth mentioning. Towards the end of his comments on exchange, Burlaeus says that *indigentia est regula (et mensura) commutationum et rerum commutabilium*; some manuscripts have only *regula*, and this may well be the original.[26] Castrovol rewrites this as *regula et ratio*, and the latter word appears elsewhere *(ratio mensurae* for *mensura, est ratio qua mensurantur* for *mensurat)*. The nuances here are elusive, but I cannot see Castrovol's preference for another terminology as accidental or indeed trivial; it is a natural response to Burlaeus's invitation to return to a more primitive conception of *indigentia*.

Albertus de Saxonia declined this invitation, and so did at least one other leading commentator. Chrysostomus Javelli was master of studies and regent of the Dominican convent at Bologna for many years, but gradually withdrew from active teaching to devote himself to his theological and philosophical studies, which gave birth to a large literary output, including a commentary on the *Ethics* published at Venice in 1536, a few years before the author's death. Javelli was a faithful Thomist, and it is more than likely that he had Thomas's *Sententia* at hand when he composed his own *Epitome*, but the direct model for his work is not Thomas but Burlaeus. However, in Javelli's version of Burlaeus there is a change which amounts to a reassertion of the true Thomist interpretation of *indigentia* as *mensura*:

... pretia in rebus statuuntur secundum quod homines eis indigent ad usum; cuius signum est, quod si homines ulla re quam non habent non indigerent, nulla esset rerum commutatio, nullus inter homines contractus; nec ad variationem indigentiae variarentur pretia rerum, et quod indigentia humana sit prima ratio et causa commutationum patet per hoc quod nummisma factum est ...[27]

The functional relation of *indigentia* to price, not to volume of exchange, is reinstated in the very formula where Burlaeus first misrepresented Thomas; it is a return more striking than that of

there is a particularly sense-spoiling *saut du même au même* at 1133a12. Castrovol takes it in his stride with only a feeble attempt at emendation. On this commentator, see Chevalier 3700; DTC II 1837, XII 1895–6; Wadding 278; Sbaralea II 334; Lohr XXVIII 349–350; Gauthier (3) 152–4.

26 *et mensura* omitted in **GB1, 2, 3, 4.**

27 *In X Ethicorum libros epitome*, f.82va. I used a copy in Uppsala UB. On Javelli, see Quétif II 104–5; Jöcher II 1849–1850; EF II 1164; DTC VIII 535–7; LTK 885; Gauthier (3) 161–2.

Albertus de Saxonia, who just dropped this passage. But in the following lines, *indigentia* is not only *ratio* as Castrovol said but *causa commutationum*. It is practically the expression of the ancient Anonymous. So we have come full circle and leave this line of *Ethics* commentaries with the old Greek idea side by side with the more precise and interesting theory of Aquinas.

*

In the course of the sixteenth and seventeenth centuries many authors who treated of commutative justice in moral textbooks drew from the large Thomist and pseudo-Thomist literature and repeated one or both of these ideas. Fabio Albergati, sixteenth century man of letters and castellan of Perugia, whose *Le morali* was published posthumously at Bologna in 1627: *È, dico, il bisogno cagione del permutare, e de' nostri contratti.*[28] Robert Balfour, already quoted on labour: *Duplicem tamen mensuram hoc loco facit, indigentiam et nummum. Vere quidem et natura sua indigentia permutationis et contractus causa est.*[29] Gisbertus ab Isendoorn, professor at Harderwijk, where his *Ethica peripatetica* was published in 1659 (from a table): *Iustitia dividitur in . . . Distributiva . . . ; Commutativa . . . ; Huius obiectum sunt contractus, sive rerum permutationes, de quibus attendenda Causa, quae est humana indigentia . . . ; Medium . . . ; Hic est nummus . . . .*[30] *Mensura* is less self-explanatory than *causa*. Occasionally, authors in the Thomist tradition explain *mensura*. In France, the great humanist Jacobus Faber Stapulensis (Lefèvre d'Étaples) had published a brief summary of the *Ethics* in 1494 and later added a commentary to his edition of the *tres conversiones* in 1497, both confirming the theory of the double measure but otherwise careful not to leave the safe confines of the text.[31] His pupil, the Flemish theologian Jodocus Clichtoveus, reedited the summary in 1502, with a long explanation of his own. This is a much more outspoken

---

28 Ed. 1627, p.176; copy in Copenhagen KB. An edition, Rome 1664, is in London BL, Paris BN; both editions in Italian libraries. On Albergati (1538–1606), see Adelung I 401–2; DBI I 617–9.

29 p. 286; cp. note 2,38.

30 p. 361; copies in Tübingen UB, Göttingen SUB, Basel UB. On the author, see Jöcher II 1995; Gauthier (3) 222.

31 *Ars moralis*, Paris 1494, f.b₁r; *Commentarius*, with *Ethics* translations, Paris 1497, f.g₆v. Both books are in London BL.

commentary and was to exert considerable influence. *Indigentia* is the cause of exchange but also measure in the true Thomist sense: *Crescente siquidem indigentia rerum, augetur earum pretium: et ea decrescente, diminuitur pretium.*[32] More than a century later another leading theologian, Théophraste Bouju de Beaulieu, sums up this position in his *Corps de toute la philosophie*, Paris 1614: *Voila doncques comment l'indigence est cause du commerce, et donne la valeur et prix aux choses qui se permutent.*[33]

Within the German *Kulturgebiet* at least ten works printed between 1575 and 1650 could be quoted in some version of the Thomist theory, mostly confirming the impression of Burlaeus as less influential in the North. But apart from one professor who paraphrases Clichtoveus,[34] they all depend on four or at most five leading authors — direction of influence is in some cases difficult to determine, since some of the works in question may have circulated in these interrelated milieus for many years before publication. An original commentator is at any rate Samuel Heiland, professor at Tübingen, whose *Aristotelis Ethicorum* was first printed in 1578. Exchange and value at *EN*, V, 5 are thus explained:

Cum res permutandae tam dispares, tamque diversae sint: aptior illis mensura adhiberi non potest quam usus et indigentia. Haec enim cuncta continet; nec solum ad contractus impellit: verum etiam pretia rerum aestimat: cum tanto pretiosior quaelibet res habeatur, quanto magis homines illa indigent.[35]

This was paraphrased by Clemens Timpler, professor at Steinfurt, in 1608,[36] and more freely by Henricus Gutberleth, professor at Herborn, in 1612.[37]

32 Ed. 1502, f.29r; rare copies in London BL and in Gonville and Caius College, Cambridge. On Clichtoveus, see Fabricius IV 454–5; Jöcher I 1965; EF I 1461; DTC III 236–243; NBG X 857; Gauthier (3) 156–7.

33 P. II, *De la morale ou éthique*, p. 136; copies in Paris BN, Toulouse BU, Leiden UB, Copenhagen KB. On the author, see NBG VI 933–4; Gauthier (3) 213–4.

34 Hieronymus Praetorius, *Theatrum ethicum*, Jena 1626 (Oxford BodL), p. 85: *Indigentia enim crescente, rerum earum augetur pretium.* Perhaps he has this via Scribonius, cp. note 4,29.

35 p. 110. Edition quoted (Bremen UB) was printed at Leipzig s.a., preface dated Tübingen 1578. Munich SB, Zürich ZB have an edition, Tübingen 1579. There are many later ones. On Heiland, see Jöcher II 1446; ADB XI 310–1; Petersen 169, 172, 179; Gauthier (3) 187, 223.

36 *Philosophiae practicae systema methodicum, Pars prima, Ethica generalis*, Hannover 1608 (Leiden UB), p. 348.

37 *Ethica*, Herborn 1612 (Basel UB), p. 78.

A dominant position in Protestant Aristotelianism in the late sixteenth century was occupied by the academy at Strasbourg, where there were two chairs in Moral Philosophy. For a short period before 1590 they were held simultaneously by Theophilus Golius (1528–1600) and Johannes Ludwig Havenreuter (1548–1618). The former published an *Epitome doctrinae moralis*, Strasbourg 1592, with a pure and simple Thomist interpretation at *EN*, V, 5:

Duo sunt media aestimandi res, earumque pretia: unum est ... a natura, et antiquissimum, nempe ἡ χρεία, usus et indigentia rerum: tanto enim pretiosior quaelibet res esse videtur, quanto magis ea indigemus, et quanto maiorem nobis praestat usum.[38]

Several later authors were to copy this.[39] Havenreuter seems to have taken a particular interest in Book V of the *Ethics*. Most regrettably, his *Analysis* of that book, published at Strasbourg in 1588, cannot be traced, but Heidelberg UB has a collection of disputations *sub praesidio* Havenreuter's, dated in the 1590's, several treating of material from *EN*,V. One of them explains *indigentia*; it is measure and cause: *Indigentia enim tanquam mensura quaedam requiritur, imo, ea ipsa, causa permutationis existit.*[40] But Havenreuter may have had something more interesting to say. A pupil of his was Laurentius Thomas Walliser (1569–1631), a third Strasbourg professor whose own *Analysis* was published in that city in 1597. Influenced by this school was also Johannes Magirus, professor at Marburg, whose comments on *destruerentur* were quoted in Chapter 2. He died in 1596 but his *Corona virtutum moralium* was only published in 1601 at Frankfurt a.M. Magirus seems to combine Golius and Havenreuter:

Quaelibet enim res tanto pretiosior esse videtur, quanto magis ea indigemus, et quanto maiorem nobis praestat usum: imo indigentia, ut Aristoteles ait, est causa permutationis et communicationis rerum, atque adeo vinculum societatis civilis.[41]

38 p. 202. I saw this edition in Marburg UB; other copies: Paris BN, Luzern ZB. There is also an edition, Strasbourg 1597 and later editions. On Golius, see Jöcher II 1060; Petersen 113, 169, 172, 178; Gauthier (3) 199.
39 Cp. Magirus and Walliser below, as well as Anton Deusing, *Synopsis philosophiae moralis*, Harderwijk 1644 (Tübingen UB), f.k₆r.
40 *Disputatio de iustitia et iure, ex libro Ethicorum quinto*, Strasbourg 1594, f.B₃r. On Havenreuter, see Jöcher II 1404; ADB XI 115–7; Petersen 122, 140–3, 149, 198, Gauthier (3) 199–200.
41 Ed. 1601, p. 492; this rare first edition is in London BL, Basel UB, Lübeck SB; there are several later ones. On Magirus, see Jöcher III 37; Gauthier (3) 181, 188. See also above, p. 82.

Walliser's explanation is somewhat similar;[42] perhaps he knew Magirus in manuscript, or perhaps they both drew from the lost *Analysis* of Havenreuter.

But behind Magirus there is also a fourth Strasbourg professor, or rather the first of them all, Obertus Giphanius (van Giffen), who came there from the Netherlands via studies in France and Italy and later taught at other universities before his death at Prague in 1604. His commentary on the *Ethics*, in the form of penetrating and informed analyses of points in the Greek text, was not published until 1608; if he had revised it before his death, he could have used both Magirus and Walliser, but it seems to have been established that it was based on lectures given at Strasbourg in the early 1570's. Giphanius states the theory of the double measure but stresses the role of *indigentia* as *commune vinculum*. This phrase, which is also in our quotation from Magirus above, is due to Philip Melanchthon.[43] On the following page, Giphanius puts the Thomist interpretation of *indigentia* to the test of Greek authorities. Plato and Aristotle, he says, *aliter disputant de indigentia, nempe eam non tam esse medium et mensuram rerum communicandarum, quam principium societatis humanae* . . . .[44] He refers to Plato in Book II of the *Laws*, which may be a mistake for the *Republic*,[45] and to Aristotle in Book VI of the *Politics*, where there is a passage which confirms the Socratic theory of exchange and society already stated in Book I.[46] This material is also in Magirus.

42 *Iccirco Indigentia Commutationis est causa, et quaelibet res tanto habetur praestantior, quanto magis illa indigemus, et quo maiorem etiam usum praestat.* (ed. 1597, f.B$_4$v). This was copied by Andreas Laborator, *Disputationes ethicae*, Tübingen 1604, Disp. II, f.B$_4$v. Both books are in the Bodleian.

43 1133b6–7 in Melanchthon's translation: *Quod autem indigentia coniungat eos velut vinculum, manifestum est* . . . . (ed. 1532, f.Mr).

44 Ed. Frankfurt 1608, p. 382, p. 383. This edition is common; I cannot find an edition 1604 mentioned by Lipenius 996. On Giphanius, see Jöcher II 988–9; Petersen 169, 183; Gauthier (3) 197–9.

45 See above, p. 15, p. 48 and note 1,6.

46 *Politics*, VI, v, 2 (1321b14–18): ". . . it is a necessity for almost all states that people shall sell some things and buy others according to one another's necessary requirements (χρείαν), and this is the readiest means of securing self-sufficiency, which seems to be the reason for men's having united into a single state". (Rackham's translation; Loeb Class. Lib., No. 264, p. 519). The more extensive discussion of exchange and money is in I, iii. (see above, p. 48).

Giphanius would seem to sense a conflict of interpretations. Not so Tarquinius Gallutius (Galluzzi), who had read Burlaeus as well as Giphanius, quoting both frequently. He was an Italian Jesuit who taught for many years in the Collegio Romano and published an enormous *Ethics* commentary in two volumes; the first, up to and including Book V, Paris 1632; the second, Paris 1645. We have already quoted his labour explanation of the bed/house model, which is not from Burlaeus, but another Thomist cost statement is, and there is every reason to believe that his unusual combination of sources determined the *indigentia* analysis of Galluzzi — the last of the Burlaeans:

... permutatio fuerit ante nummum, qui ex hominum consensione substitutus est rebus, ergo tunc aliquod permutationis esse medium debuit, idque non fuit aliud, quam indigentia, quae tamquam communi vinculo continet omnia. Plato quidem in 1.2. de legibus, et ipsemet Arist. in 1.6. Politicorum indigentiam non appellant commutationis mensuram, sed principium societatis humanae, et opificiorum omnium, quibus hominum caetus abundant, cum civitates in eam gratiam institutae sint, ut quod mihi superat, detur alteri; et quod deest, ab altero mihi suppeditetur. Verumtamen huic loco, quem in praesentia tractamus, nihil contrarium dicunt; quia idem potest esse principium convictus et mensura mutuae commutationis; tanti quippe ante nummorum institutionem res permutanda aestimabatur et valebat, quanta erat eius indigentia, qui rem unam cum altera permutabat. Sunt igitur nunc duae commutationis mensurae; indigentia ..., et nummus ....[47]

*

nihil contrarium is at most a dialectical triumph. There is a conciliation of sorts between the two branches of the Thomist tradition, the legitimate and the illegitimate branch. But it does not further economic analysis. The sterility of most of the comments quoted in this chapter is due to their not getting beyond the formal statements of Thomas (or Burlaeus), thereby degenerating into the type of argument over words — if there is any argument at all — for which the inferior strata of late scholastic philosophy are justly notorious. Only if *indigentia* is properly defined does it make sense to discuss its relation to value. If a stronger desire to understand and explain

47 Ed. 1632, p. 937. The book is in B Vat, Brescia BCiv, Paris BN, Copenhagen KB. On the author, see Jöcher II 843; Sommervogel III 1141–4; NBG XIX 346; Gauthier (3) 230–1. See also p. 73 as well as note 2,21.

value had in fact motivated these commentators, they would have tried to find out how *indigentia* must be defined in order to serve as a relevant argument in the Thomist price formula, rather than triumph in the dubious achievement, which was finally Galluzzi's, of effecting a harmony between more or less empty formal propositions. If *indigentia* is taken in the sense indicated by Grosseteste's (and Thomas's) *necessitas*, i.e. as individually experienced, basic need, it will not go far to explain either the actual level of price of a commodity or its normal value. At roughly the time when we are now leaving the Thomist tradition, this issue was brought out in parallel discussions of price formation in two famous Natural Law treatises, one criticizing the other. It is fitting to close this chapter by reviewing this dispute since it not only sums up what has been discussed here but opens a door to each of our remaining chapters.

Mensura eius quod res quaeque valeat maxime naturalis est indigentia, ut Aristoteles recte ostendit, says Grotius in the *De iure belli ac pacis.*[48] This is not a correct interpretation of the *Ethics,* objects Pufendorf in the *De iure naturae et gentium*;[49] according to Aristotle, (*indigentia*) *non est unicum fundamentum pretii, sed permutationis sive commerciorum.* These are both highly conventional observations, as this chapter has proved. More interesting is one of the arguments leading up to Pufendorf's conclusion; for one thing, he argues, we are said to have *indigentia* only for those things *quibus citra grave incommodum carere nequimus,* hence it cannot explain the price of luxuries. This is not quite fair to Grotius, for the latter had made a point of extending the value fundament beyond *indigentia* in the narrow Thomist sense to other factors, desire for luxuries being one of them. Item for item, these are extensions of the *indigentia* concept itself made over the centuries by the Aristotelians. Demand must be extended from pure necessity to other kinds of *hominum voluntas,* says Grotius; Buridan had said this long ago. It must also be understood *communiter* and tied to *copia et inopia*; this is the contribution of Henricus de Frimaria and his branch of the Aristotelian tradition. Finally, account must be taken of *labores et expensae quas mercatores faciunt*; this reflects Albertian thinking which just about this time was bringing

48 Ed. 1646, pp. 232–3.
49 Ed. 1688, p. 458.

off the synthesis of the Odonis branch. What Grotius does not seem to realize any more than Pufendorf, however, is that, as a consequence of these developments, hardly any informed Aristotelian economist of the middle of the seventeenth century would think of *indigentia* as simply *necessitas*.

When Pufendorf criticizes the Thomist theory, he is voicing a more mature view of value determination for which his generation could in fact partly thank the Aristotelians, but a reaction against scholastic philosophy had already started to obscure these debts.[50] It is one of the ironies of intellectual history that the efforts to preserve scholasticism may have hastened this process, in that they preserved mainly orthodox Thomism and let the living branches of it wither. Those who came after Thomas and used him to best advantage, did not often quote him because they did not agree with him as uncritically as many lesser minds did, which is of course part of the reason why they could make constructive contributions of their own. When scholasticism fell upon hard times, these authors and their traditions were forgotten, though not before their seeds had sprouted in the new sciences. But an avenue was kept open at all cost to the glorified Thomas, and it was sometimes forgotten that he had not always had the last word. In economics — and I presume in other sciences as well — Thomist philosophy has come in for some unhistorical criticism on this account. When we now close this chapter of copyists and turn to more inspired authors, let us remember that their inspirations were often taken, in one way or another, from St Thomas Aquinas.

50 De Roover (1) 521–2 stresses the importance of Grotius and Pufendorf as transmitters to Adam Smith of mediaeval doctrines about value and price. Recently, the case for Pufendorf has been restated by Bowley, who concludes (93) that "the *Wealth of Nations* can be regarded as a direct attempt to develop Pufendorf's implications and that Adam Smith can properly be regarded as in the direct line from the schoolmen". Placed in proper perspective, the two seventeenth century jurists can be seen to transmit something of mediaeval value theory and partly in the Aristotelian tradition, but I personally see them as somewhat out of touch with the more vigorous branches of this tradition. If they did indeed inspire Smith, this mainly goes to explain the sterility of early classical value theory as compared to the development, rooted in Italian economics, which drew on Buridan and Odonis and in the early nineteenth century provided a new inspiration for British economists as well.

4. Aggregation and scarcity

The tradition of Henricus de Frimaria

After Thomas, the *Ethics* went underground for a while. It surfaced just after the turn of the century in the monumental commentary by Henricus de Frimaria, a receptacle — in addition to its own contributions — for all that was best in the works of "Eustratius", Albert and Thomas — and of those who had written in the meantime. Systematic search in the present century has brought to light a few scattered manuscripts of a new type of commentary, originating in the Paris arts faculty in the late thirteenth century. They are in question form; the questions at *EN*, V, 5 are in each case more or less the same, and one of them, about *indigentia*, is of great interest for our study. It is to be found fully developed in three manuscripts only, different but evidently deriving from a common origin, the date of which has been disputed — the crucial year being 1277, when the bishop of Paris condemned some of the teachings of the so-called "Averroists".[1] The exact date is not important to us. What can be inferred from evidence at *EN*, V, 5 is that there must have been, at some time between Thomas and Henricus, an unidentified "arch-Averroist economist" at work in the Paris arts faculty, posing for the first time this question about *indigentia*. For it is hard to envisage its being posed without a knowledge of Thomas's commentary. As for Henricus, he may be more or less contemporary with the extant "Averroist" copies, but he is clearly posterior to the original. The point is that in Henricus de Frimaria's long exposition of *EN*, V, 5 based on other authorities,

1 It is difficult to avoid this conventional but not quite appropriate label. On the "Averroist" manuscripts and their origins and dating, see Grabmann (3); Lottin (3); Gauthier (1); Giocarinis (on the Erlangen manuscript).

there is interwoven a series of arguments which is for all practical purposes another version of the "Averroist" questions about *indigentia* and about money. It could not be the original version, and it is not based on any other of the known versions. This adds enormously to the importance of this commentary as a comprehensive early fourteenth century record of the state of Aristotelian value theory.

Suppressed in other versions, the "Averroist" ideas spread with Henricus's commentary and only later with the *Quaestiones* of Buridan. Since we do not know their origin and since they combine with a genuine contribution of his own, it is natural to include them in the basis of the tradition of Henricus de Frimaria. One of the "Averroist" commentaries has survived in the great Amplonian collection at Erfurt, another has come to light at Erlangen, both of these being anonymous. The third is in the Bibliothèque Nationale at Paris and is ascribed to Aegidius Aurelianensis, a master of the Paris arts faculty. *EN*, V, 5 is covered in these manuscripts by two or three questions. The first asks whether simple *contrapassum* is just; it is lacking in the Erlangen version. All three have the question which asks whether *humana indigentia* is a measure of goods in exchange, followed by one which asks whether money is necessary. These questions were destined for fame as Buridan's V,14, V,16 and V,17. In the *indigentia* question, referring to Book X of the *Metaphysics*, the "Averroist" commentators object that measure and thing measured are of one genus and that a measure is the cause of the thing measured,[2] but human need fulfils none of these conditions as related to goods in exchange and so cannot be their measure. The first objection is stated and handled somewhat differently and one suspects a corruption in some versions, but both the Amplonian commentator and Aegidius Aurelianensis say that the condition is fulfilled if the measure has proportionality with the thing measured and *indigentia* has that; as for the second objection, *indigentia* is indeed the final cause of goods in exchange and so fulfils that

2 As in the case of Albertus Magnus, who initiated this line of argument (see above, p. 65), the literal basis of the "Averroist" objections seems to be Averroes's commentary (f.254r–v) rather than Aristotle's own text of the *Metaphysics*.

condition. Measurement by human need is further explained in the body of the question. I quote the Erfurt version, which is the fullest:

Intelligendum est ad hoc quod res commutabiles dupliciter possunt considerari, vel secundum se vel prout veniunt in usum hominis. Si primo modo consideren- tur, tunc dicendum est quod indigentia humana non est mensura ipsarum. Si enim secundum se considerentur, tunc considerantur secundum suas quidditates et species, et secundum hoc illa res tunc dicitur dignior et pretiosior quae maiorem habet dignitatem entis et magis attingit ad finem totius entis. Unde isto modo mensura rerum non est indigentia humana sed species et perfectio ipsarum quae consistit in approximatione ad finem ultimum universi. Unde secundum hoc quodcumque animal dignius est quocumque inanimato, argento vel auro vel margarita. Alio modo possunt considerari res commutabiles secun- dum quod veniunt in usum hominis, et tunc illa sunt digniora et pretiosiora quae magis attingunt ad finem ad quem res sic consideratae ordinantur, qui finis est perfectio imperfecti; unde res sic veniunt in usum hominis ut sint perfectio imperfectionum et indigentiarum quas sentiunt homines. Perficiunt enim sic homines secundum suas imperfectiones, et sic bene indigentia est finis rerum commutabilium ut veniunt in usum hominis et sic mensura. Unde pretiosius et dignius dicitur isto modo illud cuius maior est indigentia. Nisi quod advertendum quod ex indigentia unius hominis respectu rei commutabilis non mensuratur simpliciter pretiositas rei sed ex indigentia totius communitatis. Unde illa pre- tiosiora sunt quorum indigentiam habet tota communitas; unde sunt maioris valoris. Sed uni homini bene est illa res pretiosior cuius habet maiorem indigen- tiam; sed tamen propter hoc non est simpliciter pretiosior, sed illa est simpliciter pretiosior qua magis indiget tota universitas.[3]

Their evident pleasure in syllogistic subtlety cannot detract from the genuine analytical contribution of the "Averroists" to Aristotelian value theory, expressed in the concluding lines above. ... *indigentia humana ut ponitur mensura rerum commutabilium*, says Henricus de Frimaria in the corresponding lines of his commentary, *non debet accipi partialiter respectu huius vel illius personae, sed universaliter respectu totius communitatis, cuius bonum in re publica principaliter est intentum*; the Paris and Erlangen versions of the "Averroist" commentary put it similarly.[4] Historians of economic thought have lauded this insight

3 Erfurt Amplon. F. 13, f.106va.
4 Erlangen UB 213, f.67ra: *Et notandum quod illo modo non mensurantur per indi- gentiam hominis unius, sed etiam totius communitatis et secundum hoc appretiantur.* Paris BN lat. 16089, f.216ra: *Notandum tamen quod valor et pretiositas rerum commutabilium non attenditur solum ex indigentia unius hominis, sed magis ex indigentia totius communitatis politicae.* A fourth commentary, extant in three Vatican manuscripts and one at Paris, has figured prominently in the "Averroist" controversy; it has the question about *indigentia* but passes over the point quoted here. That point does appear in yet another Paris manuscript, lat. 16110, where the anonymous author of a fragment of questions on the *Ethics*

as they have seen it emerge in the writings of later Aristotelians. It is primarily through Buridan that it has come to their attention. He stated the principle elsewhere as well, but is usually quoted in *Eth.* V, 16: . . . *indigentia istius hominis vel illius non mensurat valorem commutabilium, sed indigentia communis eorum qui inter se commutare possunt.*[5] "C'est la notion exacte du marché économique", says Brants. But the many historians who have quoted and praised these lines[6] fail to give credit where it is due, namely to the unknown Paris master who must have conceived the idea half a century before Buridan. It may well seem like a blatant truism to a modern reader, but it was nothing of the sort when it was first written. The way the earlier commentators had left *indigentia*, it expressed a kind of human experience or volition which was still essentially individual. But individual wants or need, while explaining the desire to exchange and thereby also the nature of economic value as opposed to other kinds of value, cannot explain the actual or normal level of price. Only when *indigentia* is conceived as an aggregate phenomenon does its true economic significance emerge, for it becomes possible to view it in another dimension, namely, as Brants points out, in the dimension of market participation; it is the birth of the modern concept of *demand*. As soon as *indigentia* was put on this footing, suggestions began to be made upon which would eventually be built the comprehensive Aristotelian demand theory of value. First out with one important suggestion was Henricus de Frimaria.

*

The man after whom this chapter is named was probably born about 1245 in the village of Friemar in Thüringen (near Gotha). He joined the Hermits of St Augustine while quite young and later studied at Bologna. Henricus had already been German Provincial of his Order when, towards the end of the century, he went to Paris to obtain his doctorate, rising to the Augustinian chair in theology

says that *res non dicitur carior quia unus homo egeat ea (plus?) quam quaedam alia, sed quia communitas magis eget ea.* (f.262rb).
5 On Buridan's version of the "Averroist" question, see below, p. 125. He makes what is essentially the same point in *Eth.* IX, 1 and in *Pol.* I, 11 and I, 15.
6 Brants 71, note 1; cp. Jourdain 46; Negre 119; Kaulla (1) 456; Gelesnoff (1) 206; Rambaud 28; O'Brien 110.

there and remaining at least until 1312. Back again in Germany, he held high administrative and academic positions, with residence at Erfurt, where he died in 1340. It was at Paris that Henricus de Frimaria, like so many others, commented on the *Ethics*; his *Sententia totius libri Ethicorum* can be dated in the first decade of the fourteenth century. It is the only major philosophical work of a man pushing sixty, with the peculiar qualities sometimes (though alas not always) achieved in that kind of undertaking: thoroughly researched, mature in judgments, and unhurried. It is in consequence also too long, the only reason why this central text should have remained unprinted. Fortunately, it is preserved in a handful of excellent fourteenth century manuscripts.[7] Clearly intending to compile a comprehensive source-book of established teaching, Henricus combines all previous authorities, though "Eustratius" seems to have been used partly through Albertus Magnus. The mode of commentary is similar to that of Albert's *First Commentary*, a broad textual exposition with brief questions worked into it, but Albert's teaching as transmitted here is more often that of the *Second Commentary*.

Henricus de Frimaria's exceptional grasp of the Albertian labour theory has been commented on before, as well as his restatement of Thomas Aquinas's labour interpretation of *superabundantias*. Characteristic phrases reveal Henricus's intermediacy in transmission of the labour theory to later authors, of whom Conradus de Susato has been mentioned already. Before 1519, when *superabundantiam damni* came into the printed versions of St Thomas's commentary and caused many authors to quote Henricus through

---

7 I have used **HF1**: Basel UB F.I.14 (economic comments: ff.132rb–135va); **HF2**: Erlangen UB 212 (ff.123va–126va); **HF3**: Brugge Grootseminarie 29/50 (ff.100rb–103ra); **HF4**: Nürnberg SB Cent. IV, 3 (ff.71ra–72vb, incomplete); **HF5**: Toulouse BMun 242 (ff.277ra–278vb). **HF1** and **HF3** are closely related, **HF2** stands a little apart from the rest. A number of known manuscripts are fragments not including Book V, most of the rest are later copies, of which there are three in the Vatican Library. For a manuscript in Vienna, see note 3,20. For a manuscript previously in a Florentine library, see note 4,10. On Henricus de Frimaria, see Stroick; Wulf III 124; Fabricius III 216; Ossinger 952–5; Glorieux II 317; Zumkeller 200–1; Jöcher II 1503; Chevalier 2105; LTK V 188; NDB VIII 408; Grabmann (3) 67–9, (6) 220; Lohr XXIV 221–2; Gauthier (1) 204–6, 209, 264, 305, 320, 333, (3) 134.

him, derivatives of this expression show the direct influence of this author on Nicole Oresme, whom we also met above[8] and to whom we shall return shortly, as well as on the anonymous author of a fourteenth century *Ethics* summary now in Basel UB, who speaks of *ambas superabundantias laborum, expensarum et damni*.[9] In the mid-fifteenth century, Guillelmus Becchius, General of the Augustinians and later bishop of Fiesole, relied in extreme measure on his old confrère for his own commentary, preserved in a Florentine manuscript. At *EN*, V, 5 it is virtually a translation of Henricus from mediaeval to Renaissance scholastic Latin. Curiously, one of the few longer sections which Becchius abbreviates is the "Averroist" borrowing, but the all-important conclusion is there: measurement by *indigentia, . . . non quidem in particulari respectu huius vel illius, sed in communi respectu boni communis et totius communitatis, cuius bonum est principaliter in re publica intentum*.[10] In the original, which I quoted a few pages above, particularly the last line, about the common good, seems to have made a hit. It was copied by Conradus de Susato and by some of the Buridanian commentators at Vienna[11] as well as by Thomas Teufl de Landshut, who taught at Vienna and Ingolstadt in the 1470's and whose commentary *secundum mentem Henrici de Frimaria* combines a late Buridanian influence with the "Averroist" elements in Henricus.[12] Even before turning to his main contribution to Aristotelian value theory, we thus find that Henricus de Frimaria exerted considerable influence throughout that period in which an unprinted commentary could still be influential. This is further underscored by the possibility that his argument against a labour time interpretation of Albertus Magnus may have come to the notice of Odonis.

8 See p. 56, pp. 59–60, p. 72, p. 79, p. 80, p. 84 and note 1,44.
9 Basel UB F. III. 31, f.40rb; work described by Grabmann (4) 90–2.
10 BLaur Aedil. 153, f.57rb. There is no longer any manuscript left of Henricus de Frimaria's commentary in Italy outside the Vatican, but a mid-fifteenth century library list from Florence includes a copy available to Becchius (cp. Gutiérrez 65). On this commentator, see Ossinger 112–4; Zumkeller 176, 237, 249; Jöcher I 887–8; Chevalier 492; LTK X 1134; DBI VII 493–4; Garin 334; Lohr XXIV 195–6; Gauthier (3) 150.
11 Urbanus de Mellico, followed by Thomas Wölfel, see below, pp. 136–7.
12 Munich UB 2° 566, f.127va. On the author, see Lohr XXIX 188. See also below, p. 137.

Henricus is quoted by name in an early sixteenth century printed commentary, the *Moralogium ex Aristotelis Ethicorum libris commentatorumque lecturis*, Leipzig 1509, whose author is Virgil Wellendörfer, of Salzburg, then teaching at Leipzig. His book brings to our source material the distinct flavour of Teutonic humanism, transmitting and reflecting on the ideas of the *Ethics* (in the translation of Argyropulus) in a large number of brief *conclusiones*, each with a rhymed heading, beautified by numerous classical allusions and based on the best authorities: in the conclusions about economics there are references to Eustratius, Albert, Burlaeus, Acciaiolus and Faber Stapulensis as well as to Henricus, but it is the latter's analysis and expressions which are most frequently copied. This may well be his last appearance. But a basic element introduced by him into the analysis of *EN*, V, 5 remained, and an illustration in Wellendörfer may serve to announce it. To demonstrate that *in maiori indigentia atque necessitate res necessariae pro vitae sustentatione plus existimantur cariusque emuntur,*[13] this amazing commentator recounts the fable about the "mouse of Casilinum". It is a story from the Second Punic War, about a man who captured a mouse (or rather a rat), sold it for a large sum of money and died of hunger in the beleaguered city. It is told by Wellendörfer after Valerius Maximus; it is also in Pliny, and in Strabo, from whom Johannes Maior was later to quote it. Economists know it in the version of Davanzati, later criticized by Galiani. Other economists had used it in the meantime, such as Segni and Montanari.[14] The channels through which an illustration like this was actually transmitted are hardly traceable in humanist Italy, but technically they might all have had it from Wellendörfer via Giulio Landi's *Le attioni morali*, an introduction to the *Nicomachean Ethics* in dialogue form, published in

13 *Moralogium*, Conclusio CCXIX, f.75va. I saw this very rare book in Salzburg UB. On Wellendörfer, see Fabricius VI 592; Jöcher IV 1879; Gauthier (3) 158–9.
14 The story is in Valerius Maximus, *Factorum et dictorum memorabilium libri novem*, VII, 6, 3; Pliny the Elder, *Natural History*, VIII, 82; Strabo, *Geography*, V, 4, 10. See below, p. 158 as well as Davanzati, ed. Custodi, Parte antica, II, p. 34; Montanari, Parte antica, III, p. 46; Galiani, Parte moderna, III, p. 68; and Giovanni Battista Segni, *Trattato sopra la carestia e fame*, Bologna 1602, p. 12.

1564. Anyhow, the Aristotelians were bound sooner or later to hit upon this macabre appendix to the Augustinian mouse paradox. It is the perfect classical illustration of *indigentia* as understood in the tradition of Henricus de Frimaria. We can do no better than quote Giulio Landi's introduction to it:

> ... crescendo la carestia delle cose, cresce anco il prezzo loro, e quella scemando, si diminuiscono anco i prezzi; egliè dunque il bisogno overo la necessità, e la carestia delle cose humane la vera e propria misura delle commutationi; che si fanno fra gl'huomini delle cose loro: ilche si pruova manifestamente per uno essempio scritto da Valerio, & anco da Plinio . . . .[15]

carestia is the key word — in the terminology of modern economics, *scarcity*.

*

Aggregation takes *indigentia* close to market demand, and the usual English translation may be appropriate in the case of Henricus de Frimaria even if not in the case of Aristotle himself. But *indigentia* is not yet demand in our technical sense of the word, it is not quantity demanded as a function of price, for it comprises supply as well as demand; *indigentia* is the need or want which results from demand in relation to supply, it is demand in the face of scarcity. Demand may be heavy, but as long as there is sufficient supply, *indigentia* does not raise price, only if there is scarcity. This was implied by all commentators who took the word in an aggregate sense; Henricus de Frimaria was the first to spell it out:

> ... aequalitas non potest semper attendi secundum eandem quantitatem scilicet numeralem et molis, ut quod tantus panis semper detur pro uno denario vel una domus pro uno cultello, sed semper debet attendi secundum eandem quantitatem valoris, qui quidem valor mensuratur secundum proportionem humanae indigentiae et etiam sumptuum illius rei, ut quia magis indigemus domo quam cultello et maior est indigentia panis tempore sterilitatis et famis quam tempore fertilitatis et copiae, ideo plures denarios tempore caristiae oportet dare pro uno pane et plures cultellos pro una domo eo quod pluri constat domus quam cultellus.

It is not that crop failure and famine raise the price of bread, *indigentia* being given; it is rather that they increase *indigentia*, which raises price. Nicolaus Oresmius, known to all economists as the father of modern monetary analysis, not known at all for his

15 Landi, p. 437.

Aristotelian contribution, states this definition of *indigentia* (or, in his own favourite term, *neccessité*) in a note to 1133b10 of his *Ethics* translation. Goods in exchange should be equalized, *En compensant et considerant la neccessité des choses selon le commun cours et la quantité de elles*.[16] Consistent similarity of phrase proves Oresme to be a disciple of Henricus de Frimaria. While no one had read Aristotelian *indigentia* like that before, it is the way it was now to be read by all except those who got stuck on a stagnant branch of the Thomist tradition.[17]

We are in fact as close here as we shall get, to the core of the Aristotelian theory, to what distinguishes it from earlier and contemporary attempts to grapple with the problem of value. The tradition of Buridanus developed further the nature of demand and that of Odonis the nature of supply, but these were developments on a value formula now fixed in its essentials. Value as determined by "common need of something scarce" remained the frame of reference to the Aristotelians for the rest of the scholastic period and is the most certain Aristotelian element in the basis of modern value theory as well. The transition from the Thomist price formula to that of Henricus de Frimaria, definitely stated by Nicole Oresme, is therefore a step of unique importance. Economics textbooks sometimes retrace the historical development of ideas connecting individual need with market value: Human need seeks out certain goods which have the property of being able to satisfy it. If many

16 p. 296; I quote the critical edition of *Le Livre de Ethiques d'Aristote* by A. D. Menut, New York 1940. The unusual spelling, *neccessité*, is confirmed by the manuscripts quoted in note 1,50 (except franç. 206). Preference for this *opus* alternative is one of numerous indications of an influence from Henricus de Frimaria. According to Menut (Introduction, p. 37) the sources utilized by Oresme are Albert and Thomas, Burlaeus and Buridanus. The latter is usually considered to be a main source for Oresme's monetary analysis (Kaulla (1); Roll 51; Stavenhagen 18), but I can detect no such imprint on the value analysis. Henricus is not on Menut's list; not available in print, he may not have been recognized.

17 Historians in general fail to define Aristotelian demand correctly. An honorable exception is Gobbi 348, in a discussion of value theory in late Italian scholastic thought: "Come causa del valore si indicava *l'indigentia*: parola opportuna per esprimere il bisogno combinato colla scarcità dei mezzi per soddisfarlo, ossia l'utilità delle cose combinata colla loro difficoltà di acquisto".

seek the same good, the pressure to obtain it, relative to its available supply at any time, will determine its rate of exchange in the market. A theory of exchange value can start, and has historically started, at any one of the three stages of this deduction. It can start with the conditions of the market, with the abundance or scarcity of goods. This is an explanation based on everyday observation and it is very old; one might compile an anthology of ancient authors who said that "what is scarce is costly".[18] But this explanation runs into difficulties over goods which are scarce and yet have no value and such as are abundant and yet have value of a different kind, and so invariably ends up in the familiar paradoxes without getting any further. Next, a theory may start with the properties in goods which make the market conditions relevant. An example of a value theory of this kind is that of Petrus Olivi, widely known and highly praised as it appears in the writings of St Bernardino of Siena; it seeks to explain value on the basis of properties like *virtuositas* and *complacibilitas* in addition to *raritas*. But any theory that seeks to explain human relations on the basis of the nature of external objects must also break down. In the case of the Franciscan theory — if I may call it that — the very distinction between *virtuositas* and *complacibilitas*, denoting respectively "objective" and "subjective" worth, reveals the chink in its basis. At any rate, nothing much came of this part of Olivi's contribution.[19]

Finally, a theory of exchange value can start with the needs of men which make these properties in things relevant, arguing about market conditions from there. The mediaeval theory which did survive into modern economics had to start that far back; to that extent, at least, it was an Aristotelian theory which survived. The Aristotelians were not alone in discussing economic matters related to human wants, but credit is due to them for taking this concept through aggregation and scarcity into a workable argument in the price formula. Their influence is naturally more easily recognized in those authors who explain value by demand in relation to supply rather than by supply in relation to demand, in other words in those authors who use the Aristotelian term *indigentia* rather than

18 See note 6,23.
19 On his influence on Odonis, see below, pp. 153–7.

the essentially non-Aristotelian *raritas* or related terms. However, the distinction is not clear-cut. Odonis, who was in the Franciscan tradition as well as in the Aristotelian tradition, partly argued in terms of *raritas*, and as a matter of fact the two models, both failing to separate supply and demand, can be taken to express more or less the same idea, as long as it is clearly recognized that *raritas* is also a relative thing, depending on need. This is assured in the case of Odonis by his Aristotelian background. On that assurance, *raritas* served the Odonis tradition well in its analysis of demand and supply in the labour market, on which its approach depended. But in the analysis of product market conditions, *indigentia* is the better term, focusing on the underlying human factor which alone can guide the development towards a modern concept of effective demand. The Aristotelian model was soon to be developed somewhat further along that line in the Buridan tradition, which presupposes the *indigentia* concept of Henricus de Frimaria.

However, its basic failure to separate demand and supply as arguments in the value formula is a defect in the Aristotelian market model which was never quite straightened out in the scholastic tradition. Only when they can be studied as independent variables is it possible to reason conclusively about the processes which bring about harmony between them. The marginal analysis requires a separation of these variables; it can in fact be seen historically as a natural and almost immediate consequence of a strict formal separation, which was thus very slow in coming and hardly an Aristotelian achievement, although some of the most perceptive commentators on *EN*, V, 5 made some preliminary attempts in this area. Langenstein, exponent of one main attitude to the Buridanian analysis, defined *indigentia* in strict accordance with Henricus de Frimaria: price is determined *penes quantitatem indigentiae communis in ordine ad multitudinem vel paucitatem rerum*. This implies two possible dimensions of variation; *indigentia* can be said to increase *extensive* when demand picks up or *intensive* when supply falls off, says Langenstein.[20] It is a surprisingly modern idea; unfortunately, it was not followed up. Later, the Buridan school at Vienna struggled to free *indigentia* from its double role and came up with a mature concept of utility but

20 *Tractatus de contractibus*, I,11, I,10. See below, p. 127.

116

not with hypothetical, aggregate demand as a function of variable price independent of supply, which is the only feasible way out of this methodological hang-up. It was not found until the nineteenth century.

*

While Henricus de Frimaria was in fact the first *Ethics* commentator to relate *indigentia* to scarcity, and thus fathered a tradition, it may be that analysis had reached a stage where this idea was inevitable. As I have pointed out, the relation of price to market conditions, in terms of descriptive pairs like *copia/inopia*, *abundantia/caristia*, *fertilitas/sterilitas*, is the oldest form of value theory; the attraction of the Thomist price formula, with its naked *indigentia*, to this frame of reference would be irresistible. I think this is how we must reconstruct the mental processes of the "arch-Averroist", trying to make sense of St Thomas's double measure. Having thus elevated *indigentia* to an aggregate concept, the "Averroist" model openly invited the connection with scarcity; some would no doubt make this connection independently of Henricus de Frimaria.

It is particularly interesting, considering the modest role assigned to St Thomas in the development of the Aristotelian model, to ask what influence his reference to scarcity in the *Summa theologiae* may have had on post-"Averroist" writers. I refer, then, to the article in II–II, 77 where he admits, answering an objection based on Aristotle at 1135a1, that physical measures of goods may vary *propter diversitatem copiae et inopiae rerum*; in a later article it is allowed that even *pretium rei est mutatum, secundum diversitatem loci vel temporis*,[21] presumably in respect to demand and supply conditions. But Thomas does not seem to have related this to Aristotelian *indigentia*, and it is hardly permissible to argue from the *Summa* to a more mature concept in the *Sententia* than that which can be read from that text as it stands. On the other hand, St Thomas's ideas, as further developed in their respective traditions, were bound to be related by other authors. The *Summa theologiae* created its own voluminous tradition, but external material was seldom allowed to influence its course of development; it is not surprising that we

21 II–II, 77, 2, ad 2; 4, ad 2.

search largely in vain for Aristotelian elements thus at work in the economic articles of the *secunda secundae*; the exceptions are some Odonian and Buridanian offshoots in late works on Justice and Law written in commentary to the *Summa*. But in the tradition of the *Ethics* the economics of the *Summa theologiae* would be a constant source of external influence. An author who made the connection between *copia et inopia* and "Averroist" *indigentia* independently of Henricus de Frimaria would be in the tradition of the latter in the sense of reinforcing it from outside, and more likely than not he would do this on the basis of the *Summa theologiae*. One author who made exactly that connection may in fact have written while Henricus was still at Paris and the "Averroist" element still active there.

He is Guido Terrena (c.1270–1342), of Perpignan, who was to become General of the Carmelites and later bishop of Mallorca and then of Elna in his native region. Three manuscripts preserve his commentary on the *Nicomachean Ethics*, composed about 1313, in question form. Among the questions to Book V are these, *Utrum iustum simpliciter sit per contrapassum, Utrum omnia commutabilia sint una mensura comparabilia, Utrum commutatio pecuniativae sit licita.* The first of these is the "Averroist" question, corresponding to Buridan's V,14. Thomas had asked it in the *Summa theologiae*, with only marginal reference to economics.[22] Terrena, however, both here and in the third question cited, borrows from Thomas's main economic question and particularly the articles quoted above. The middle question is Buridan's V,15, inserted between his "Averroist" borrowings. There may be a common source of this question in Terrena and Buridan, or the latter may have borrowed it from the former. Unlike Buridan, Terrena does not follow it up by another separate question about *indigentia* as a measure, but having concluded that commutables are indeed measurable by a common measure, he asks what this measure is and so appends an analysis of *indigentia* and money in the middle question itself. Thus exposing a non-Aristotelian Thomist model to a post-Thomist Aristotelian model, this commentator brings off an interesting synthesis. Not surprisingly, he concludes in the middle question that *mensura*

22 II–II, 61, 4.

secundum naturam et principalis est indigentia, arguing along the lines of the "Averroists". But he then goes on to further support this by saying that *indigentia*'s being a measure is also proved by the fact that *in terra in qua . . . res multum abundat pro minori pretio commutatur quam in terra ubi parum abundat,* and in the third question he amplifies this in terms which are strictly Thomist:

. . . si res sit mutata de loco ad locum potest vendi plus quam fuerit empta, ut si res sit empta in loco ubi est magnum forum et portetur ad locum ubi propter eius indigentiam est carior, tunc potest vendi plus quam sit empta; cuius ratio est quia res aestimantur secundum indigentiam principaliter ut dictum est. In terra autem ubi est minor indigentia emitur iusto pretio pro minori et in qua est maior indigentia venditur iusto pretio pro maiori; quare res empta iusto pretio delata alibi ubi est carior poterit ibi plus vendi iusto pretio quam sit empta. Item, si mutetur secundum tempus, ut si sit empta tempore quo plus abundabat et minor indigentia eius erat, tunc eam servans tempore quo est maior indigentia potest eam plus vendere, quia tunc plus valet et tunc est iustum pretium plus tali tempore . . . .[23]

Since value is measured by aggregate need in the face of scarcity, it follows that *indigentia,* so defined, can also explain variations in place and time as envisaged in the Thomist just price model. The synthesis is not surprising. The "Averroist" analysis is just one step from Thomas. It is just that he never took that step himself.

The tradition of the *Ethics* and the tradition of the *Summa theologiae* vied for the attention also of those authors who, long after Terrena, sought to build a new economics on the scholastic fundament. Some of them naturally reflect later Aristotelian developments, but others can at least be quoted to demonstrate the survival of the characteristic market model which has served here to define the tradition of Henricus de Frimaria. Thomaso Buoninsegni was the author of a *Trattato de' traffichi giusti et ordinarii,* Venice 1588. He emphasizes that *la giustitia commutativa è ordinata sopra l'equalità della cosa alla cosa,* referring to EN, V. Referring to *tutti i Dottori,* he relates

23 Vat. Borghes. 328, ff.41vb–42ra, f.42rb; Bologna BU 1625, f.34va, f.35ra; Paris BN lat. 3228, f.44va, f.45ra–b. In a question on usury in Terrena's *Quodlibeta* (Vat. Borghes. 39, f.191v) there is a reference to *EN,* V which suggests Albertus Magnus. On Guido Terrena, see the studies by Fournier and Xiberta, as well as Wulf III 106–8; Ueberweg 533, 548–9, 775; Gilson 483–4; Fabricius III 125–6; Jöcher IV 1064–5; Chevalier 4387–8; EF VI 432; LTK IV 1269; Lohr XXIV 190–1; Gauthier (1) 263, (3) 134–5.

price formation to *utilità di tutti communemente* rather than to the utility and *humore* of the individual, and points out that these prices *sogliono crescere, e calare, havuta consideratione intorno al tempo della copia, od inopia della cosa* . . . .[24] Some years earlier, Antonio Maria Venusti had published a *Compendio utilissimo di quelle cose, le quali a nobili e christiani mercanti appartengono*, Milan 1561. He also states the equality principle and goes on to explain how price can be determined:

> . . . per arbitrare il giusto prezzo della cosa solamente si hanno da considerare queste tre cose, L'abondanza ò penuria delle mercantie, de' mercanti, & del danaro ò delle cose che si comutano & cambiano in vece di danaro: si fonda questa dottrina in quella di Aristotele, che dice, Pretium rei humana indigentia mensurat.[25]

In other parts of Europe no comparable literature was as yet developing. Within the tradition of the *Ethics* itself, other branches were pushing that of Henricus de Frimaria aside, his commentary having failed to reach the printing press. As we approach the middle of the sixteenth century, I should be reluctant to ascribe a formal or doctrinal similarity to a knowledge of an unprinted mediaeval commentary.[26] So we cannot know for sure what caused the great Reformer, Philip Melanchthon, to create a virtual sub-branch of this tradition in Protestant Germany. The first commentary on EN, V with Melanchthon's name on the cover appeared in 1531, but it is sketchy and without interest to us. But already in 1532 a new commentary was published at Wittenberg, along with the translation to which I have referred before.[27] This version was frequently reprinted. In 1545, also at Wittenberg, a new version

24 Buoninsegni, f.65v, f.15r–v.
25 Venusti, f.28v, f.30r.
26 In a paraphrase *De moribus* published at Rome in 1600, Laelius Peregrinus says that *rerum copia illius auget valorem, penuria minuit.* (p. 198). This is a statement in the tradition of Henricus de Frimaria in the most general sense, but the author also quotes Buridan (as well as Burlaeus) and often follows Thomas Aquinas. There is no reason to believe that he knew Henricus at first hand, hence conclusion in note 1,44. Copies in Vienna NB and Pembroke College, Oxford. On Peregrinus, see Jöcher III 1380; Adelung V 1881; Gauthier (3) 183–4.
27 p. 45, p. 70, p. 102.

was published again, this time without the text. It was also re-edited repeatedly and underwent some minor changes; it is one of these variants which is included in the *Corpus Reformatorum*. In the 1532 edition Melanchthon says that goods are estimated *ex indigentia quae constituit gradus pretii*; the 1545 edition is more explicit:

... res proportione ad aequalitatem redigandas esse, ut, magis est opus tritico, quam ligno, et minor est copia tritici, ideo tritici est maior aestimatio. Haec analogia invenitur ita, cum consideratur, quae res magis necessaria sit, et cuius sit maior copia.[28]

It is Melanchthon's ideas which are taught when Gulielmus Adolphus Scribonius, of Marburg, asks in his *Philosophia Ethica,* Lemgo 1584: *Quomodo invenitur proportio, qua res ad aequalitatem redigantur? Considerandum, quae res sit magis necessaria, et cuius maior sit copia*.[29] Others also quoted him almost verbatim,[30] the better known authors less so but equally faithfully. Thus Rudolph Goclenius, Scribonius's famous friend and colleague at Marburg, in 1592: *Indigentia igitur vel maior vel minor pro maiore minoreve copia gradus pretii constituit, et res ad aequalitatem redigit*.[31] Wolfgang Heider, professor at Jena, in 1599: *Pluris enim fiunt illa quorum copia minor et usus maior: Sed minoris, quae contra*.[32] Finally, Jacob Martini, pro-

28 Ed. 1532 (Lübeck SB), f.L₈r; ed. 1545 (Oxford BodL), f.O₂v, (cp. *Corpus Reformatorum*, XVI, 383). The 1531 edition of the commentary to *EN*, V is in Munich SB. Melanchthon also composed two freer ethical treatises with an Aristotelian leaning; he treats of commutative justice in them, but when he comes to economics, he prefers to discourse on usury.

29 p. 51. But Scribonius had other models as well, on the following page he paraphrases Clichtoveus as quoted on p. 100 above. The 1584 edition of his book is in Leiden UB, Göttingen SUB, Vienna NB. It was reissued Lemgo 1586, Basel 1588, Frankfurt 1589, etc. On the author, see Jöcher IV 443–4; ADB XXXIII 488; Gauthier (3) 188.

30 Cp. for instance, Andreas Perstenius, in another *Ethica*, Leipzig 1605 (Lübeck SB), p. 120.

31 *Exercitationes ethicae*, Marburg 1592, p. 164; copies in Marburg UB, Kiel UB, Lübeck SB. There are several later editions, the fourth, Marburg 1601, being the most frequent. On Goclenius, see Jöcher II 1031; EF III 301–2; ADB IX 308–312; Petersen 135, 286.

32 *Theses de iustitia, ex V Ethicorum Aristotelis*, Jena 1599, f.Cr. I found these theses in Vienna NB. Heider's better known *Philosophiae moralis systema*, Jena 1629, is less explicit. On Heider, see Jöcher II 1444; ADB XI 306; Gauthier (3) 225.

fessor at Wittenberg, to sum up this branch of the Aristotelian tradition in 1626:

Nascitur autem haec aequalitas ex necessitatis copiae et inopiae consideratione: Res enim maxime necessaria et minus copiosa est carissima: Res vero minus necessaria et valde copiosa est vilissima.[33]

Aggregate need and scarcity are what regulate value. Note also, in conclusion, the preference for *necessitas* in Melanchthon and his imitators. It is Oresme's bleak *neccessité*, prolonging the basic needs of St Thomas, which runs through the tradition of Henricus de Frimaria, setting it off among the flowers of Buridanian analysis.

33 *Synopseos ethicae*, Wittenberg 1626, p. 403; copies in Uppsala UB, Lübeck SB, Basel UB. On Martini, see Jöcher III 229; ADB XX 510; Petersen 126, 136, 200, 218, 266–7, 290.

5. Effective demand

The tradition of Johannes Buridanus

Johannes Buridanus was born in Picardy shortly before A.D. 1300. He was rector of the University of Paris in 1328 and again in 1340, and was still active in 1358. Little is known about his life to supplement the dry academic record, but it was of the material of which legends are made. Violent and colourful, these stories are often capped by reports about his ingenuity and are probably born, like the "Buridan's ass" paradox, of his longlasting fame as a logician. Cheated of a modern critical edition, his genius is only slowly and partially reasserting itself in different fields of science, hampered now by his literary form. Buridan was master of arts and the complete Aristotelian; with few exceptions his important contributions, to social science no less than to natural philosophy, were made in Aristotelian commentaries, of which he composed almost forty, including questions on the *Ethics* and the *Politics*. But from these scholastic writings there emerges an early humanist and empiricist. Quoting the classics to great effect in his *Ethics* commentary, he is also true to these words of the prologue, which some modern economists would do well to heed: *Rationes enim in hac scientia ex actibus humanis sumuntur, quorum notitia non habetur sine experientia multa.*[1]

A larger number of extant manuscripts and more printed editions

1 **JB8**, f.2ra. On Johannes Buridanus, see Faral (1) and (2); Wulf III 129–133, 158; Ueberweg 595–7, 783–4; Gilson 511–6, 794–5; Fabricius I 282–3; Jöcher I 1500; Chevalier 733–4; EF I 1130–1; NBG VII 838–840; LTK V 1013; Grabmann (3) 70–1; Lohr XXVI 161–183; Gauthier (3) 136–7; Walsh; Jourdain 44–7; Graziani 17–8; Brants 69–71, 201; Rambaud 28; Kaulla (1), (2) 57–9; Tarde 35, 41, 50; Schreiber 177–191; Gelesnoff (1) 206; O'Brien 70–8, 109–110; Nègre 118–9; De Roover (1) 497, (2) 163–4; Baldwin 76; Stavenhagen 18, 401–2; Mandel II 413.

(Paris 1489, 1513, 1518 and Oxford 1637)[2] than of any other early commentary, always excepting the *Sententia* of Thomas Aquinas, testify to a continued interest in Buridan's *Quaestiones* to the *Ethics* throughout the scholastic period. In our field it is also one of the few Aristotelian texts whose value is recognized by historians. "Buridanus bedeutet in vieler Hinsicht den Höhepunkt des ökonomischen Denkens des Mittelalters überhaupt", says Schreiber, with reference mainly to the value theory at *EN*, V, 5.[3] To critics like Schreiber, without access to the unprinted material composed in the meantime, it must have looked as though Buridan took the price formula as it came from St Thomas and added the multiple ideas of his own commentary from scratch. Our textual research, bringing to light the works of the "Averroists" and their dependants like Henricus de Frimaria and Guido Terrena, has robbed him of some of this glory. More important, it has revealed the key to his

2 Paris BN has all four editions of Buridan's commentary. For copies of **JBX1**: (1489, Hain 4106, V,16: f.133rb–vb), see GW 5752. The Vatican library has the three later editions; some other locations: **JBX2**: (1513, ff.105vb–106rb): London BL, Paris BMaz, Naples BN, Hannover LB, Munich SB, Copenhagen KB; **JBX3**: (1518, ff.102vb–103rb): Oxford BodL, Milan BN, Naples BN, Munich SB; **JBX4**: (1637, pp. 430–2): BodL, Göttingen SUB, (repr. Frankfurt 1967). The number of extant manuscripts, most of which date from the fifteenth century, is very large but uncertain, for Buridan and his many imitators are sometimes difficult to distinguish and so incorrectly catalogued. Of three *Ethics* commentaries in Vienna ascribed to Geraldus Odonis, only one is in fact by that author, while CVP 5433 is a copy of Buridan and CVP 5149 is Urbanus de Mellico's imitation. Another imitator, Thomas Wölfel, is in CVP 4672, bound alternately with Buridan's original, slightly abbreviated. Similar discoveries are bound to be made elsewhere. Some fourteenth century manuscripts: **JB1**: Auxerre BMun 232 (V,16: f.116ra–b); **JB2**: Cambrai BMun 165 (f.125rb–vb); **JB3**: Paris BMaz 3515 (f.76rb–va); **JB4**: BN lat. 12970 (ff.116rb–117ra); **JB5**: BN lat. 16128 (ff.198vb–199vb); **JB6**: BN lat. 16129 (ff.122vb–123rb); **JB7**: Vat. lat. 2166 (ff. 118va–119ra); **JB8**: Urbin. lat. 198 (f.119rb–vb); **JB9**: Urbin. lat. 1367 (f.109ra–va); **JB10**: Bologna BU 366 (ff.91vb–92ra); **JB11**: Venice BMarc Z. lat. 262 (f.236ra–va); **JB12**: Berlin SB lat. fol. 934 (ff.138rb–139ra). Assuming Buridan to have quoted Seneca correctly (see below), there would be a preference for the group **JB4, 8, 12** which read *sat* as against *satis* in all other manuscripts. **7, 10** elsewhere often follow those three. — There is no reason to think that Buridan commented on the *Ethics* more than once. Lohr lists three items, all in the volume which contains **JB11** on ff.90–357, but the other two are on ff.4–15 the *Summa Alexandrinorum* and on ff.16–83 the *Expositio* by Albertus de Saxonia.

3 Schreiber 178.

contribution. Unlike Henricus and Guido, who drew freely from Albert and Thomas as well, Buridan can only be understood as an economist in the tradition of the Paris "Averroists". They gave him his format and the clues which he developed. But even so, his performance was remarkable.

Buridan's four questions at EN, V,5 are a combination of the three "Averroist" ones with one of Terrena's.[4] All our concern is with V,16, about *indigentia*. It is formally the question as described in our last chapter, with its metaphysical objections and arguments, but it is opened wide in the middle to make room for Buridan's own reflections on the subject of economic value. Objecting to the hypothesis that *indigentia humana* is the natural measure of goods in exchange on the grounds that it implies selling dearer to the poor in greater need than to the rich in less need, Buridan replies in the famous lines already quoted,[5] stating his version of the "Averroist" distinction between individual and *communis indigentia*. But from this objection he goes on to state another one. There are also many things expensive *quibus modicum indigemus, ut ea quibus divites utuntur non in eorum indigentiis sed in superabundantiis voluptatum et apparatuum.* How can *indigentia* be a measure of the value of luxuries? The reply to this objection is the Buridanian essay on the *nature of poverty*, which I must quote in full:

Propter secundum notandum est quod divites et pauperes dupliciter accipiuntur; uno modo secundum habere multum aut modicum de bonis fortunae, et sic accipit eos vulgus; alio modo secundum sufficientiam et non sufficientiam, et sic capiuntur verae divitiae et vera paupertas, de quibus dicit Seneca, Epistula secunda ad Lucilium: Non qui parum habet, sed qui plus cupit, pauper est; quod probat dicens: Quid enim refert, quantum illi in arca, quantum in horreis iaceat, quantum pascat aut feneret, si alieno imminet, si non acquisita sed acquirenda computat? Et addit de divitiis dicens: Quis sit divitiarum modus, quaeris? Et respondet dicens: Primus habere quod necesse est, secundus quod sat est. Manifestum est igitur quod isti divites non indigent sed pauperes oppositi eis indigent semper. De vulgari autem modo divitum et pauperum dicit Aristoteles I Rhetoricae quod utrique concupiscunt. Accidit quidem pauperibus propter indigentiam concupiscere pecunias, divitibus autem propter potentiam concupiscere non necessarias delectationes. Ideo manifestum est quod utrique secundum veritatem sunt indigentes et pauperes, de quo dicit Aristoteles in eodem I Rhetoricae quod dupliciter sunt indigentes, aut enim ut necessarii sicut

4 See above, p. 107, p. 118.
5 p. 109.

egeni aut ut excessus sicut divites. Dicendum ergo est quod non solum indigentia necessarii mensurat apud egenos commutabilia, sed etiam indigentia excessus apud divites.[6]

To explain value in terms of need, since need implies poverty, we must take poverty in its true sense, in which anybody is poor when he desires something which he does not have, be it even a luxury object — *indigentias superfluorum appetituum*, as Buridan says elsewhere.[7] This extension from the type of basic necessities underlying the Thomist analysis and not questioned by the "Averroists" or by Henricus de Frimaria and his branch, at once takes *indigentia* much closer to what we now call *effective demand*. The point is exactly that of the paradox of poverty: "true" poverty in the "vulgarly" rich. The poor may also sorely desire luxuries, but Buridan does not mention that; his value formula is extended only to include *indigentia excessus apud divites*, which is backed by ability to pay — and presumably willingness to pay. Confirming the "Averroist" interpretation of aggregate need, Buridan makes value depend on *indigentia communis eorum qui inter se commutare possunt*; adds one of his imitators: *et volunt*[8], but this condition is clearly implied in the original as well. The analytical strength thus added to value theory by Buridan is formidable. Except that he also fails to separate demand and supply in the argument, as did all the Aristotelians, we now have a general formula. But his contribution involves intangibles of a psychological and ethical nature as well. It is evident that Thomist *necessitas* can be more easily conceived of as just and natural than the luxury wants of Buridan, which are often "wants of the mind" rather than "wants of the body", to anticipate Barbon. By breaking down the partition which had kept one of these classes of economic factors out of consideration, Buridan's analysis permits (if not invites) an attitude to justice in pricing which points far ahead to "subjective" value theory — and to *laissez-faire* economics. Since in this science, explanation must

6 References are to *Rhetorics*, I, x, 9 (1369a11–15) and I, xii, 15 (1372b19–21), and to Seneca, *Epistulae morales*, II, 6. (This locus in Seneca came into English literature in the *Wife of Bath's Tale* by Chaucer, with whom Buridan must have shared many inspirations.) See also notes 5,12 and 6,30.
7 V, 23; cp. **JB8**, f.125rb.
8 The anonymous of CVP 4703; see below, pp. 136–7.

always in some sense keep pace with ethics, these implications cannot be separated from Buridan's analytical contributions, and so there is in V,16 a source of conflict. The best way to introduce a discussion of its impact may be to review the works of two early users of the *Quaestiones*, Henricus de Hassia and Conradus de Susato. Prominent schoolmen both, by taking different stands in relation to Buridan they demonstrate the alternatives left open by him.

*

Henricus de Hassia was born in 1325 at Langenstein (in Hessen, not far from Marburg) and is often named after his native village. He taught philosophy and theology at Paris but had to leave France owing to an untimely initiative in the Great Schism and in 1384 settled in Vienna, where he came to play an important part in reinvigorating the university, of which he was rector in 1393–4. He died in 1397.[9] Langenstein's literary output, still largely unedited, includes a vast commentary on *Genesis* with philosophical excursions, upon which his *Tractatus bipartitus de contractibus emptionis et venditionis*, a late work, is partly based. It was printed once, in the incunabula edition of Johannes Gerson's *Opera*.[10] Langenstein knew the Aristotelian economic model well, as already indicated by

9 On Henricus de Hassia, see Wulf III 183–7, 196; Ueberweg 602, 604, 610–1, 785; Gilson 519–520, 796; Fabricius II 202–6; Jöcher II 1504–6; Chevalier 2087–8; Aschbach 366–402; EF I 850–1; LTK V 190–1; ADB XVII 672–3; NDB VIII 410; Roscher 18–21; Endemann I 25–6; Graziani 11; Brants 20, 38, 42, 58, 71–2, 205–6; Kaulla (1) 461, (2) 58; Tarde 30, 34, 35, 42–3; Schreiber 196–202, 227–8; O'Brien 107, 111–2, 121–4; Ashley (2) 500; Tawney 35, 41; Nègre 119; De Roover (3) 419–420.

10 Vol. IV, Cologne 1484, ff.185r–224r. Still in manuscript is another interesting piece on economics, an *Epistola de contractibus emptionis et venditionis ad consules Wiennenses*, in three parts. The two works overlap to some extent; the material quoted here and drawn from *Tractatus*, I, 11 is also in *Epistola*, II, 10. They are utterly confused in bibliographies. Of the *Tractatus* there are numerous copies in Germany and elsewhere. I have consulted the Vienna manuscripts, viz. CVP 3601, 4; 3825, 1; 3894, 6; 3947, 11; 4173, 19; 4217, 36; 4239, 2; 4409, 33; 4697, 2; 4962, 1. There is a minority (first three) and a majority (last seven) trad⁞tion, to which latter the printed version belongs. There are also at least twelve manuscripts of the *Tractatus* in Munich SB, including five listed by Roth as the *Epistola*, of which I found no copy there. On the other hand, some of Roth's manuscripts of the *Tractatus* in Vienna NB are actually of the *Epistola*; in all, I found seven copies of the latter work, viz. CVP 3947, 12; 4151, 5; 4381, 5; 4659, 29; 4962, 2 (the archetype, according to Heilig 152); 5076, 8 (incomplete); 12671, 2.

quotations from the *Tractatus*,[11] and he knew and recognized the importance of Buridan. In Chapter I,5 he paraphrases V,16 extensively, to lay a foundation for his own arguments about *indigentia* in a later chapter. Our purpose in quoting Langenstein above was to demonstrate an advanced analytical insight. Many examples could be added to confirm this. For instance, copying Buridan on *communis indigentia*, he says that value is measured by the demand of those *qui inter se communicare possunt in uno loco, regione vel civitate*. Defining a limited, operative market is a typical Langensteinian touch, revealing the competent economist. But the moralist in Langenstein is revealed in his choice of words to describe Buridanian non-basic needs, leaving no doubt as to his disgust for the craving of the rich *propter concupiscentiam voluptatum vel propter defectum superabundantiae vel verius propter insatiabilem divitiarum appetitum qui crescit in infinitum*.[12] This attitude is not irrelevant to Langenstein's use of the Buridanian model. Discussing just pricing in Chapter I,10, he classifies *indigentia* in four types:

... consideratio habenda est circa quattuor modos indigentiae, puta naturae, status, voluptatis et cupiditatis, quia in mensuratione iusti pretii ad primos duos indigentiae modos respiciendum est et non sic ad alios duos, licet ut patuit etiam rerum pretium modis illis saepe excrescat. Sed his qui possunt sollerter praecavendum est ne illis modis penuria accidat in regione vel civitate. Confert etiam ad quantificationem valoris rerum utilium quod dupliciter quis non indiget re aliqua, quia vel eo quod de ipsa sufficientiam habet vel quia ad eius statum vel officium non pertinet. Propter quod licet nihil de ipsa haberet, ipsius indigentiam habere non dicitur. Indigentia ergo dicit carentiam rerum cum necessitate vel pertinentia earum ad naturam vel statum aut artem vel officium hominis. Plus enim requirit status aut officium quam natura. Homines ergo diversi status et conditionis diversis indigent etiam distinctis. Sunt etiam quaedam res sustentationi naturae inutiles quae tamen sunt utiles statui, officio vel arti ut papirus et huiusmodi. Et inveniuntur res utiles uni statui aut arti quibus homines alterius artis vel status non indigent ut instrumentis aut materiis.

In a study of the Aristotelian tradition, to which *status* has been applied with a different connotation,[13] it may be appropriate to

---

11 See above, p. 116.
12 The quotation from Seneca follows and is repeated in the same chapter, with an addition: *Non qui parum habet sed qui plus cupit pauper est; et econtra, habitis contentus dives est*. Though Langenstein certainly quotes through Buridan, he seems to have caught this basic theme better; cp. Seneca, loc. cit.: *Illa vero non est paupertas, si laeta est*.
13 See above, pp. 50–1, and below, pp. 150–3.

point out that Langenstein could easily have made his point in terms of *artes* and *officia* alone. His distinction is between *voluptas* and *cupiditas* on the one hand and on the other such needs as to which it is the social planner's task to attend. These are not all basic in a strict physiological sense; there are other needs, the non-fulfilment of which will cause society to suffer. In fact, such social necessaries are the majority in any civilised community, which depends on numerous commodities pertaining to various arts and functions. What Langenstein suggests in the continuation of the text quoted, somewhat optimistically, is that one try to estimate the volume of such needs in a community in a given period and set prices accordingly. In principle he advocates price regulation because, as he says in I,11, *relinquere rerum pretium in arbitrio vendentium est relaxare frenum cupiditati quae fere omnes venditores agitat in excessum lucri.* Thus in Langenstein's analysis two different limitations are made in relation to *cupiditas* and similar Buridanian market phenomena. One is to exclude *indigentia cupiditatis* from consideration, limiting the analysis to markets for necessaries. The other is to keep *cupiditas* on a tight *frenum* in such markets, by strict legal and moral price regulation.

This reaction to Buridan contrasts with that of Conradus de Susato, who first appears in the records of Heidelberg University at his immatriculation in 1387 and frequently in the decades to follow, being rector three times. He left some theological works, as well as an *Ethics* commentary in question form, preserved in three manuscripts. But Susato seems to have been of the breed of professor mainly cut out for administrative and political tasks. He attended the Church councils of the early fifteenth century, first as a member of the Palatine delegation, later as bishop of Regensburg, Albertus Magnus's old diocese. He died in 1437.[14] At Constance, Conradus de Susato took an active part in the legislation concerning usury. An interest in economics is indicated also by his choice of sources in the *Ethics* commentary. The influence of Henricus de Frimaria on

14 Susato's version of V,16 is in **CS1**: Berlin SB lat. fol. 783, ff.296vb–298vb; **CS2**: Munich UB 2° 565, ff.312v–314v; **CS3**: Vienna NB CVP 5340, ff.78va–81vb. On the author, see Ritter 285, 292–8, 330–1, 342–3; LTK VI 474; Lohr XXIII 396; Gauthier (3) 139.

Susato has been mentioned before, as well as his use of Buridan as a basic model.[15] At *EN*, V, 5 almost every line of Buridan's questions is copied, within a rambling commentary to the commentary. But characteristic phrases also reveal a familiarity with Henricus de Hassia, though no adherence to his teaching; in fact, there is an attitude to pricing which would have scandalized Langenstein. Far from ignoring the needs of the rich, Susato takes up the question of aggregation with special reference to then, thus defining a market for luxuries. It is this attitude which enables Conradus de Susato, as the first commentator on record, to see the connection between Buridanian *indigentia* teaching and the old saying that a thing is worth as much as it can be sold for. Breaking with a moral code which must see that *dictum* as being in conflict with Aristotelian justice in exchange, Susato explains one in terms of the other. Paraphrasing Buridan closely and concluding that goods are valued in exchange according as they supply our needs, he makes an addition, as though by an afterthought: *Haec conclusio etiam patet per commune dictum et vulgatum quo dicitur, res tantum valet quantum vendi potest, quod intelligendum est, quantum ad hominum indigentiam, igitur conclusio vera.*

*

When Alfred Marshall says that the "value, that is the exchange value, of one thing in terms of another at any place and time, is the amount of that second thing which can be got there and then in exchange for the first",[16] he is in fact stating one of the oldest "principles of economics" in European thought. Indicated in classical sources,[17] it reached the schoolmen mainly through the *Corpus iuris civilis,* where it is stated in various forms in the *Digest,* one locus introducing the familiar phrase, *aestimandum, quanti valet . . . , hoc est, quanti vendere potest.*[18] It was the influential thirteenth century Romanist, Accursius, who gave the *dictum* its best-known mediaeval form, where there is a significant addition: . . .

---

15 See above, p. 81, p. 111.

16 *Principles of Economics,* II, II, 6; ed. 5, London 1907, p. 61.

17 Cp. for instance, Seneca, *De beneficiis,* VI, xv, 4: *Pretium autem rei cuiusque pro tempore est; cum bene ista laudaveris, tanti sunt, quanto pluris venire non possunt.*

18 Dig. XXXVI, 1, 1, 16; cp. XIII, 1, 14; XIV, 2, 2, 4; XLVII, 2, 52, 29.

communi pretio aestimantur res; quod ergo dicitur, res tantum valet quantum vendi potest, scilicet communiter.[19] There is no direct evidence to show that the "Averroist" *Ethics* commentators based their aggregation of *indigentia* on this *communiter*, but they may have. At any rate, by introducing market valuation these developments had similar moral implications. It may be that some neo-classically trained economists are able to view Marshall's statement as a purely objective definition of value as used in deductive analysis. Others would say that it cannot be entirely cleansed of ethical undertones. What is certain is that a scholastic commentator would be incapable of reading it that way. To say that a thing is worth as much as it can be sold for would imply that somebody selling it for as much as he can get for it is in his right to do so. Hence the immediate need of the schoolmen to modify this inheritance from the Roman Law.

Potest must mean *debet*, says Henricus de Gandavo: *Tantum res valet quantum vendi potest, intelligatur non de potentia facti, sed de potentia iuris, id est quantum de iure pro loco et tempore vendi debet.*[20] After a while, this view was adopted by the leading moralists, such as Gerson, Nider, St Bernardinus Senensis, St Antoninus Florentinus;[21] also Johannes Maior, the Aristotelian: *. . . sequitur iniuste esse dictum res tanti valet quanti vendi potest, nisi subintelligatur quanti iuste vendi potest.*[22] What kind of market price is just? It must be free of fraud; in the words of Aegidius Letinis, *tantum iuste valet quantum sine fraude vendi potest.*[23] But later it also came to be expressly stipulated that it must be free of greed. I quote Hector Forest, another Aristotelian: *Res tantum valet quantum vendi potest, quod intelligendum est sane ad boni viri aestimationem non autem ad ementis indigentiam vel repentinam cupiditatem,*

19 Explaining Dig. XXXV, 2, 63; cp. *Corpus iuris civilis*, comm. *Accursii*, Paris 1559, Vol. 2, col. 1529.
20 *Quodl.* I, 40; ed. Venice 1613, f. 42v.
21 Johannes Gerson, *De contractibus*, II,11. (*Opera Omnia*, Tom. III, Pars 1, Antwerp 1706, col. 179–180); Johannes Nider, *Tractatus de contractibus mercatorum*, Cologne s.a. (Hain 11822), f.9v; St Bernardinus Senensis, Sermo 35, 1, 3. (*Opera*, Vol. IV, Florence 1956, p. 194); St Antoninus Florentinus, *Summa theologica*, Pars II, Tit. I, Cap. 16, §IV. (ed. Verona 1740, Vol. II, col. 258).
22 *Ethica Aristotelis*, Paris 1530, f.82v.
23 *De Usuris*, Cap. IX. This work used to be attributed to St Thomas Aquinas and is printed in the Parma edition of his *Opera*, Tom. 17; quotation is on p. 424.

131

aut vendentis petitionem.[24] Note that *fraus*, while originally to be taken in the same moral sense as the *fraudulentia* of which Thomas Aquinas speaks in II–II, 77, tends to be stripped down to a legal concept. Thomaso Buoninsegni will still state the old *dictum* in terms of the absence of *frode*,[25] but this stipulation was soon to disappear from economic literature, presumably having been taken care of by positive law. The absence of greed is clearly a moral stipulation; greed can be legislated against only by fixing the price. When an Aristotelian commentator is stating the *dictum* in these terms, he is arguing, in the manner of Henricus de Hassia, against an interpretation of Buridan in the manner of Conradus de Susato.

In the decades preceding Buridan the principle of just price as market price free of fraud and greed had been tied to Aristotelian *communis indigentia* in another context as well. Considering the situation of two exchanging parties, a well-established mediaeval maxim of business ethics had stated that a seller whose deprivation at parting with a commodity would be for some reason unusually great could cover this by a higher price, provided that the buyer was in such need of the commodity that he still wanted to buy; but even if the buyer's situation remained the same and he wanted to buy, the seller could not take the higher price if the buyer's need simply meant a larger profit to the seller, his own deprivation being nothing out of the ordinary. Both Thomas Aquinas[26] and Johannes Duns Scotus[27], among many others, made themselves spokesmen of this double rule. Intuitively, it seems quite reasonable even today, at least to the ordinary man, and at least in occasional exchange; it must have seemed so also to those who advocated it at a time when moral teaching was less helped — or hampered — by economic theory. The first part of the rule is based on a principle of cost coverage and does not concern us now. The mediaeval teachers were harder put to make good its second part. Thomas said that profiting *ex conditione ementis* amounts to selling what is not one's own. Duns Scotus said that a thing is not

24 *In quintum Ethicorum Aristotelis*, Lyon 1550 (rare copy in Lyon BMun), p. 50.
25 Op. cit., f.15r; cp. above, pp. 119–120.
26 *Sum. theol.*, II–II, 77, 1, c.
27 *Sent.* IV, 15, 2; ed. 1639, p. 170.

in se pretiosior because of the buyer's *maius commodum*. These explanations are not as fishy as they may sound today, but they were never satisfactory. In retrospect it may seem as though the early advocates of the double rule were reaching for an idea still out of their grasp. The gist of their explanation is that it is wrong to take advantage of a buyer's unusually high need. But what is unusual?

The answer, as it came to be worked out, involves two steps. In the years immediately following the death of Scotus in 1308, the *Sentences* of Petrus Lombardus were read at Paris by Petrus Paludanus, a young Dominican who had been educated in a period full of development in Aristotelian thought. When an occasion offers itself for discussing the second half of the double rule of just pricing, he gives it a new theoretical basis by applying to it an "Averroist" distinction between what he calls *communem hominum indigentiam* and *miserabilem indigentiam unius,* in that *illa quae propter communem infirmorum indigentiam cariora sunt: carius vendi possint: numquam tamen propter istius solius indigentiam.*[28] By thus tying value to aggregate need, Paludanus can rule out overcharging the needy buyer because it is against the natural forces which work to secure a just and normal state of affairs *in the market*. Now ethical teaching can only accept a social basis at some cost to the individual. The buyer, however needy, must now comply with the valuation of the market; there is no room in Aristotelian social ethics for bleeding hearts. On the other hand, the needy buyer cannot be made to pay more than the market price if he is in the market; exploitation presupposes either a singular exchange situation out of reach of a market, where the usual market price can only serve as a benchmark, or else a market situation which is in itself unusual. Hence, again, what is unusual? As the schoolmen were inclined to see it, that which is tampered with for the purpose of gain. *Communis indigentia* is not to be manipulated; the monopolizer, the market operator, *create needy buyers* and are not to be tolerated.

Looking inside the regular commentary tradition of the *Ethics,* we have noted that the tradition of Henricus de Frimaria, prolonging in this respect that of Thomas Aquinas, was disinclined to consider *certain types of need*. We now find that Buridan also inherited a

28 *Sent.* IV, 5, 3; ed. Paris 1514, f.25rb.

133

just price tradition which was disinclined to consider *certain types of motivation*. A consequence of the Buridanian analysis is that by breaking one of these conventions it weakened the other. It makes less sense to condemn sellers' cupidities in markets for "unnecessary" goods sought only for pleasure and entertainment than in markets for necessaries. What about the price of goods *quae vendi solent ad ornatum, splendorem, delicias et voluptates*, asks the Jesuit moralist, *Johannes Azorius*, answering, . . . *in hoc locum habere quod vulgo dicitur : Tanti res valet, quanti vendi potest, et illud; quisque suae rei est moderator et arbiter.*[29] It is a natural idea, still current in countries practising price regulation: certain demands seem to be less deserving of protection — moral and legal — than others. The consequence to the early reader of Buridan was illustrated above. Susato, accepting Buridan on one point, would seem to concede the other. Langenstein, rejecting Buridan, argues against both points. Now Buridan's extension of *indigentia* is an analytical not a moral contribution, but it had moral repercussions. Langenstein's interpretation requires a deliberate stand on socio-ethical principles; taken unawares, the reader may risk being gently pulled in the opposite direction.[30] Such is the dilemma of value theory: formulated as a general explanation of price formation it invites a *laissez-faire* morality.

But the effect of the model on the ethics of the analyst, though sometimes undeniable in economics, can be overestimated. The more frequent connection is for a new morality to find its way to appropriate pieces of extant analysis. That is how Buridan, the empiricist among Aristotelian philosophers, provided a scheme which better than any other survived the fall of scholastic standards. Thomas Hobbes, ethical herald of the classical tradition in England, inherited more of his analytical equipment than he thought; rejecting Aristotle, on economics he inherited Buridan. Fraud is no problem to Hobbes; positive law takes care of that. And greed is

29 *Institutiones morales*, III, viii, 21; ed. Cologne 1612, col. 688.
30 Buridan hints at Susato's interpretation in a truncated phrase in *Pol.* I, 12, where he says that *tantum res valet quantum humana indigentia indiget*. Johannes Langewelt, a contemporary of Susato, who taught at Kraków where there is now a copy of his *Ethics* commentary in the Biblioteka Jagiellońska, supplies the other half of the formula: . . . *de tanto res vendi potest de quanto est eius indigentia*. (cod. 1899, f.90v).

what makes the world go round. Hence the "value of all things contracted for, is measured by the appetite of the contractors: and therefore the just value, is that which they be contented to give".[31] The *just* value. To appreciate the role of Buridanus, one should recognize that it is not only his analysis but also a morality accommodated by it, which find expression in lines like that, or, for instance, in those of Barbon, written just before the scholastic remnants disappeared behind the literary styles of the eighteenth century. Men crave those things that "provide the Ease, Pleasure, and Pomp of Life". "But the Market is the best Judge of Value . . . : Things are just worth so much, as they can be sold for, according to the old Rule, *Valet Quantum Vendi Potest* . . .".[32]

In the long run, Langenstein the moralist has triumphed over Hobbes. But Langenstein the economist had to suffer for it. Precisely because he makes no moral judgment concerning different social and psychological bases of effective demand, Buridan's theory becomes a general one. This is its strength. Now it does not follow that an author such as Langenstein, by rejecting Buridan as an ethical model must also reject his explanation; quite on the contrary, it would seem that his ethical conclusions are based partly on this explanation. But the end result will be a kind of rejection of Buridan's analytical model as well. The point is essentially the one I made in connection with St Thomas. If one is really to understand those aspects of price formation which relate to demand, one would probably do well to look into exactly those types of needs and motivations which a preoccupation with price regulation of necessaries causes one to ignore. Langenstein's attitude puts a break on analytical development, not because his morality renders theory irrelevant, but because it makes him miss the opportunity to explore it.

*

We do not know when Buridan died, he just faded away. According to one legend he went abroad and founded the University of Vienna. This is certainly false. But while he was never there in the flesh, he came and remained there in the spirit. Buridan was read and

---

31 *Leviathan*, I, 15; cp. *The Elements of Law*, I, 16, 5; *De cive*, I, iii, 6.
32 *A Discourse of Trade*, London 1690, p. 15, p. 20.

used all over Europe, but nowhere more constructively than in the eastern universities. In Vienna in the fifteenth century there was a whole group of commentators who asked Buridan's questions on the *Ethics*. Developing the ideas of V,16 in their own manner, they are "the first Austrian school" of economists. Their work is preserved in twelve manuscripts, of which eight are correctly ascribed by Lohr to seven named authors. Three Vienna manuscripts can be added to the documentation of two of these authors, while a fourth Vienna manuscript contains an anonymous commentary clearly belonging in the same group.[33] Thomas Ebendorfer (1388–1464), of Haselbach near the Austrian capital, may be the founder of the school.[34] Theologian and historian, author of the *Chronica Austriae* and a widely travelled man on conciliar and secular missions, he is also one of the great names in the mediaeval history of the University of Vienna, where he was repeatedly rector. His *Ethics* commentary is dated 1424.[35] Urbanus de Mellico, who died in 1436, was twice rector and also influential in conciliar affairs. Reading the *Ethics* in 1429, Mellico sometimes drew on Henricus de Frimaria but was, on the whole, a more conventional Buridanian than Ebendorfer.[36] Taking something from each of these two, Thomas Wölfel melts it down to a most serviceable alloy, by far the fullest and best balanced formulation of the value theory of the school. Wölfel, of Wuldersdorf, also in Lower Austria, three times rector and, like Ebendorfer

33 CVP 5149 is falsely attributed to Odonis. I located CVP 4672, 4914 and 4703 by looking into some likely anonyma in Vienna NB. The enormous Aristotelian source material in this library is by no means exhausted.

34 Comparison of the early representatives of this school cannot fail to nourish the suspicion that they sometimes draw on a common source not included in our group. The Stiftsbibliothek at Melk preserves at Cod. 59 the questions to the *Ethics* by the Vienna master Sebaldus de Wallsee, dated 1417, but the volume is mutilated at the end and V,16 is not preserved. He could well be the real founder of the school; I leave it to others to judge about this from other parts of the commentaries.

35 CVP 4952, ff.188v–189v (location is of *indigentia* question, in this and following notes). On Ebendorfer, see biography by Lhotsky, as well as Fabricius III 181; Jöcher II 259; Chevalier 1260; LTK X 141; ADB V 526–8; NDB IV 223–4; Aschbach 493–525; Grabmann (6) 226; Lohr XXIX 179–180; Gauthier (3) 139–140.

36 CVP 4667, ff.226v–227v; 4914, ff.318r–320r; 5149, ff.262v–264r. On Urbanus de Mellico, see LTK X 548–9; Aschbach 445–6; Grabmann (6) 226; Lohr XXIX 194; Gauthier (3) 139–140. See also above, p. 111.

and Mellico, canon of St Stephan, read the *Ethics* in 1438 and 1442.[37] Jodocus Weiler,[38] Andreas Wall[39] and Stephanus de Brugen[40] drew from Wölfel and sometimes from Mellico. With Andreas de Schärding, who wrote in 1460, the school is about to break up. Some themes are retained, but deliberately rephrased, and there are other influences, for instance Henricus de Langenstein, perhaps quoted through Susato.[41] The anonymous commentary is dated 1466; it is worth studying in V,16 only for a short while until it hitches on to Schärding's commentary.[42]

What occasioned the interesting economic reflections of these authors was Ebendorfer's concern with proper definitions of the market variables. He defines *indigentia* as *carentia alicuius necessarii*, which Schärding has altered to *penuria sive defectus*, a term favoured by authors influenced by this school, for instance Thomas Teufl de Landshut (*defectus boni alicuius*) or Johannes Crell (*defectus rei alicuius utilis*).[43] The latter word may well be original. Wölfel, Wall and the anonymous adopt another definition suggested by Mellico, according to which *indigentia* is *carentia alicuius necessarii vel saltem valde commodosi*, while Weiler says, *necessarii seu utilis*. Mellico's version emphasizes the Buridanian generalization of need; it is against that

---

37 CVP 4672, f.199r–v, f.201r; St Florian St.B XI. 636, ff.276r–278r; Munich SB Clm. 19673, ff.233v–235r. These versions sometimes differ markedly; I usually follow CVP 4672. (The questions in Clm.19848, mentioned in Lohr XXIX 189, are only extreme abbreviations.) On Thomas Wölfel de Wuldersdorf, see also Aschbach 557–8; Grabmann (6) 226; Gauthier (3) 140.

38 Graz UB 883, ff.228v–229v. Jodocus Weiler de Heilbronn, also a rector of the University, taught philosophy from 1419 to 1440. He depends largely on Mellico. See Aschbach 475–7; Lohr XXVI 152.

39 Munich SB Clm. 18883, ff.208v–210r. We know little about this Vienna master, who probably wrote about the middle of the century. See Lohr XXIII 360; Gauthier (3) 140.

40 Melk St.B 801, ff.174r–175r. Stephanus de Brugen is recorded as a *magister artium* at Vienna in 1437; his questions to the *Ethics* are dated 1455. See Aschbach 622; Lohr XXIX 148.

41 Clm. 18458, ff.148v–149v. There are phrases of Susato in the discussion of individual and common need as well as a Langensteinian diatribe about the appetite of the wealthy, *qui in infinitum crescit*, which is also in Susato. On Schärding, see Aschbach 597; Grabmann (6) 226; Lohr XXIII 359; Gauthier (3) 140.

42 CVP 4703, ff.341r–342r.

43 On Thomas Teufl (quoted here on f.127ra), see above, p. 111. On Crell, see below, pp. 159–161.

137

background that we must view the twin sets of definitions which the Austrians now proceed to develop. The duality is posed by Eben-dorfer's observation that, although *indigentia* as a measure of exchange value embraces both need and scarcity, in everyday usage it is often taken *large pro necessitate*, in other words, it is taken for need, regardless of actual scarcity. Hence, to avoid confusion, different definitions are required. In the words of Wölfel, *indigentia capitur duplex, uno modo proprie* (*stricte*, says Weiler at one point) *et sic connotat duo, scilicet carentiam et necessitatem; alio modo capitur large et sic connotat solum necessitatem.* But if it is *indigentia* only in the strict sense which regulates value, does this mean that non-scarce things are valueless? To the philosopher used to the form of the *quaestio*, this *dubium* must suggest itself in objection, since the immediate answer would seem to be negative. Some plentiful things are certainly valuable to us. However, this is in another sense, hence we need different definitions of value also. In Ebendorfer's original version,

> ... duplex est valor rei; quidam valor potest dici essentialis, et est valor quem habet res quae venit in usum humanum etiam ea nullo actualiter indigente, et ille convenit rei praecise secundum se in quantum tamen est indigentiae suppletiva. Sed valor accidentialis est secundum variationem indigentiae communitatis quia eadem res plus valet in caristia quam in abundantia.

Wölfel, the purist, and through him, Wall, repeat this but drop *secundum se*. Words like that came easy to the lips of schoolmen, but there is no question here of an intrinsic value. As developed by the Austrians, essential value turns out to be a kind of potential or latent value in view of changed external conditions; it has no metaphysical properties different from accidental value. What emerges from their discussion is in fact somethings which looks amazingly like a modern concept of *utility*. Two approaches can be distinguished; one is suggested by Weiler: ... *mensuraretur omnis valor penes futuram indigentiam et sic penes indigentiam quae non est sed verisimiliter futura est.* Schärding indicates a similar idea. Essential value, then, to them is a kind of expected value of economic goods occasionally plentiful. Wölfel and Wall, as well as Brugen and the anonymous, adopt another approach, asking about the value of plentiful goods not normally objects of exchange, i.e. what came

138

later to be called free goods. Wölfel: *An aer, aqua, terra, caelum et cetera quae veniunt in humanum usum sint alicuius valoris?* It is clear from their answers that *valor essentialis* should be extended to such goods. But *etiam ea nullo indigente* in all three versions of the twin definition shows that the notion is meant to be general, comprising both classes of goods. Of course air has some kind of value, it is as necessary to human life as food, says Wölfel. How this kind of value is to be understood and measured is explained by him and by Wall and Brugen on the basis of two expressive phrases by Ebendorfer: Plentiful goods may be valuable, since *eis ablatis indigeremus*, hence they are measured by the need *quae esset*. Wölfel:

... quaelibet res quae venit in usum humanum nulla eius indigentia existente actuali proprie loquando, praecise est tanti valoris quanta indigentia esset suppletiva si ea careremus, et per consequens mensuratur valor eius penes indigentiam, non quae est sed quae esset.

Economists from Aristotle in a long line including "the French monk Buridan", says Ernest Mandel, were troubled by a meaningless quantitative concept of utility.[44] Now utility, as defined in economics, is an auxiliary concept, operating within a limited deductive system. The system may be too narrow and so critics may have a point, but this does not mean that utility as used within it is meaningless. The point about utility, however, is that it is not a quantity in a dimension different from exchange value; it is measured, by hypothesis, or by imagination, on the same scale. "... imagine the predicament we should be in, were we deprived", says William Forster Lloyd, the forgotten genius of the classical school.[45] Or in the words of the Austrians, imagine *the demand which might have been*. Imagine a plentiful thing becoming scarce and what one would then be willing to pay to obtain it. The beauty of this idea is that it holds for free and marketable goods alike and that it disposes of the notion of inherent usefulness. The important distinction between goods is not their necessary or luxury character, nor their normally free or normally economic character, but their potential economic character, in case of scarcity. For there are some things which are not missed when lacking: ... *caremus arena et*

44 Mandel II 413.
45 *A Lecture on the Notion of Value*, London 1834, p. 18.

lapidibus qui sunt in fundo maris et tamen propter talium carentiam non dicimur indigentes, says Mellico; *arena maris* became the standard example of goods without essential value, it is in Weiler, Wall, Brugen.

While echoes of the mediaeval Austrians kept cropping up in German commentaries and perhaps elsewhere,[46] they were never printed and the direct influence of their advanced analysis was probably limited. But parallels with other schools and authors serve to place them in a broader pespective. It is impossible not to be reminded of them, for instance, by Galiani's reflections on utility and scarcity. Air and water lack value because they lack *rarità; e per contrario un sacchetto d'arena de' lidi del Giappone rara cosa sarebbe, ma posto che non avesse utilità particolare non avrebbe valore.* In Naples a bag of sand from the beaches of Japan, in Vienna sand from the sea bottom, and, as always, air and water: such is the contrast that will point up the economic character in things. The work to which Galiani did not put his name when first published will hardly prove to have had another author but certainly some interesting inspirations. He would not have read unprinted material in Austrian libraries, but his demand was in the Buridan tradition, carefully extended from the *primi bisogni della vita* to the variety of luxury desires.[47] His kinship with the Austrian school is one of a shared Buridanian ancestry, and it is this ancestry that sheds the best light on the Austrian achievement itself. It is Buridan who carries these authors past the trap into which most early value theorists fell, becoming entangled in the contrast between useful things of no value (such as water) and useless things of high value (such as diamonds). For the "paradox of value" is only a product of analytical schemes which cannot assign utility to diamonds. But luxuries pose no more of a problem to the Austrians than they do to Galiani; since they are desired, they have utility in an operative sense. So the Buridanians of all ages will be more interested — coincidence of examples apart — in comparisons that permit

46 The early seventeenth century French economist Montchrétien distinguishes *la valeur essentielle* and *le prix accidentel*; cp. *Traicté de l'oeconomie politique,* Rouen 1615, p. 184. But expressions like that would be sufficiently common for coincidences to occur.

47 *Della moneta,* I, ii; ed. Custodi, p. 59, p.61ff.

utility to reveal itself, for instance in water as against ocean sand. Perhaps the main significance of the Buridanians at Vienna was just to demonstrate the potential of a demand model which did not get involved in irrelevant paradoxes but invited a line of analysis of which further insight could come, given time and better techniques: variation in scarcity, given utility; variation in utility, given scarcity.

Like the Aristotelians, Galiani lacked marginal utility. As far as demand theory is concerned, that is what separates him from Menger, says Schumpeter.[48] But even in Menger, professor at Vienna from 1873 and member of another Austrian school, the same examples mark the analytical takeoff: "die atmosphärische Luft, der Sand in einer Wüste", "Quantitätenverhältnis" revealing their "ökonomischen Character". How long can a model be inherited in a university, from one professor to the next? Hardly for four centuries. But it is fascinating to reflect that Menger, instead of lambasting Aristotle for his allegedly primitive ideas about value,[49] could have walked down to the Hofburg and there found in the Aristotelian commentaries of his mediaeval colleagues, fragments of a theory far advanced along the lines he himself worked so successfully to complete and perhaps — who knows? — even heard the voice which echoes faintly in his own examples.

*

From the invention of the art of printing down to the end of the scholastic era, the economic ideas of Johannes Buridanus were kept alive in a number of summaries and paraphrases, the total circulation of which must have been considerably larger than that of the original *Quaestiones*.[50] In the 1490's, Claudius Felix, of Langres, prepared an edition of the *Ethics* in the mediaeval translation, with brief textual explanations and some questions. There

48 Schumpeter 301.
49 Aristotle's equality principle is criticized on p. 173 of the first edition (see note 17 to Introduction) and on p. 183 of the second edition, 1923. The examples quoted here appear on p. 66, in a revised section, of the second edition.
50 Other unprinted commentaries also reflect Buridan, for instance that of Nicolaus de Amsterdam (two copies in Nürnberg SB) and two commentaries mentioned in note 6,6.

were later editions in 1500 and 1509. The questions at *EN*, V, 5 are
borrowed from Buridan, V,16 appearing as a brief *dubium*. This is
the best summary of his economics: nothing corrupted and nothing
essential left out.[51] Petrus Tartaretus, of Lausanne, rector at Paris
in 1490, composed questions on the *Ethics* of which there are three
editions in or shortly after 1496; the fourth appeared in 1504 and
was followed by at least ten more in the sixteenth century and some
in the seventeenth. This book, then, rather than the original, has
the version in which a late student of Aristotle is most likely to have
encountered Buridan's value theory. There are questions corresponding to V,15 and V,17; the former incorporates the *indigentia*
analysis of V,16, somewhat less compressed than in Felix, quite
intelligent, but unfortunately marred by errors in some editions.[52]
A third summary is in the commentary by Johannes de Celaya, of
Valencia, who studied at Paris and left shortly after publishing his
book in 1523. It is a textual exposition based on Argyropulus, rather
than a set of questions, but the author relies wholly on Buridan at
EN, V, 5.[53] So does also, much later, another Spaniard, Joseph
Saenz de Aguirre, who paraphrases V,16 in a long section of his
De virtutibus et vitiis disputationes ethicae, Salamanca 1677.[54] Johannes
Casus, who taught at Oxford, wrote central parts of Buridan up in
what Petersen once called the "grässlichen Tabellenform",[55] so
characteristic of Protestant Aristotelianism. The *Speculum moralium
quaestionum in universam Ethicen Aristotelis*, where this remarkable
material is to be found, first appeared at Oxford in 1585 but was
reprinted half a dozen times in Germany where it became a highly
popular textbook.[56] On the whole, however, the German Protestant

51 First and second editions (GW 2377–8) both in Copenhagen KB.
52 First three editions, slightly different: Hain 15343 (H. E. Huntington Library); Reichling 1877 (Freiburg UB); Madsen 3826 (Copenhagen KB,
   Freiburg UB). Editions, Paris 1504, 1509, 1513, are in Paris BN. Numerous
   later editions at Venice, as well as Basel 1514 (Munich SB) and Vienna 1517
   (Vienna UB).
53 Copies in Oxford BodL and Paris BMaz.
54 pp. 496–9. On this author, see Jöcher I 161–2; Gauthier (3) 232. He is
   quoted in another work on p. 73 above.
55 Petersen 325.
56 The table is on p. 216 of the Oxford edition, of which there are copies in
   Oxford BodL, London BL, Vienna NB. The book was reissued at Frankfurt
   in 1589, 1591, 1594, 1604, 1609, 1625. On Johannes Casus, see Jöcher I 1767;

tradition, dominated by Thomas Aquinas and Melanchthon,. remained outside Buridan's sphere of interest which shifted to the south of Europe as a new interest in economics was stirring there. The juridical literature written in comment on the *secunda secundae* of St Thomas, on which Schumpeter places such reliance in his analysis of late mediaeval economics, sometimes drew on the Aristotelian tradition and mainly in the Buridan branch. Schumpeter's choice of writers to represent this genre, based on a book by Dempsey, is arbitrary; at least two others, Soto and Salon, are as relevant as Molina, Lessius and Lugo.[57] Dominicus Sotus, professor at Salamanca and earliest of these authors, quotes Aristotle in his *De iustitia et iure*, Salamanca 1556, to the effect that *indigentia* is *causam mensuramque*; however, *ubi . . . indigentiam nominamus, ornatum etiam reipublicae intelligimus: ut cuncta complectamur quae hominibus praeter vitae necessitatem etiam ad suam voluptatem et splendorem usui esse possunt.*[58] Towards the end of the century, Michael Bartholomaeus Salon commented on St Thomas; in different sections, both referring to *EN*, V, he uses Odonis and Buridanus, the latter in phrases similar to Soto's. Molina, one of Schumpeter's authors, says much the same.[59] But I think the importance to economics of these late Thomists has been overestimated. Davanzati wrote before Molina,. initiating another genre (initiating, some would say, modern economics); the value analysis of the Italian monetary theorists, founded on Davanzati's *appetito* and *bisogno*,[60] could still for a long time draw directly on the mediaeval Aristotelian sources.

In Geminiano Montanari, writing almost a century later, these ideas find a definite expression. Like any knowledgeable seventeenth century author, Montanari is careful to establish his interpretation of *l'indigenza ed il bisogno* on the authority of Aristotle; what he

EF I 1243; DNB III 1171–2; NBG VIII 958; Gauthier (3) 190. There is an arrangement resembling part of his table in *La science morale d'Aristote* by Jean Crassot, Paris 1617, p. 146.

57 Schumpeter, *History*, 95–9, using Dempsey (1). I cannot accept Schumpeter's description of these authors as "representative Schoolmen" (Introduction to Dempsey, p. viii); they are representative only of a particular Thomist genre.

58 Soto, p. 547.

59 Salon, *Commentariorum*, Tom. II, Valencia 1598, col. 22–3; Molina, *De iustitia et iure*, Tom. II, Disp. 348; ed. Cuenca 1597, col. 563. See also note 6, 6.

60 *Lezione delle monete*, ed. Custodi, p. 33.

expounds at length is Buridan's Aristotle. Having quoted *EN*, V, 5 at 1133a25–28 (in an adaption of Perionius), Montanari goes on to point out the relativity of human wants (once using a phrase strongly reminiscent of the mediaeval Austrians) and concludes with a broad operational definition:

> ... siamo costumati a dire di aver bisogno di tutti ciò che non l'avendo desideriamo, e le cose stesse ad uno possono dirsi voluttuose e superflue che ad un altro saranno necessarie ed oneste ....
>
> Volle dunque intendere in questo luogo Aristotile non dell' indigenza delle cose necessarie solamente, ma di ogni desiderio che ci muove a dare stima alle cose e misurar il loro valore col soldo.[61]

The success of the value theory which was to be developed in the line extending from Montanari through Galiani to the Italian and French economists of the eighteenth and early nineteenth centuries is in no small part explained by its emphasis on utility as a psychological experience, playing down considerations of the properties in goods which cause men to desire them, a preoccupation which is sure to take theorists away from the main point. It is the lasting merit of the Aristotelian model, as the main mediaeval source of seventeenth century value theory in Italy, that it permitted the restatement by Buridan in terms which made one concept, *indigentia*, comprise indiscriminately "every desire which moves us to set store by things".

61 *Della moneta*, ed Custodi, p. 44, p. 45.

6. Synthesis

The tradition of Geraldus Odonis

Geraldus Odonis was born about 1290 at Camboulit, a small hilltop village near Figeac (Lot), where he joined the Franciscan Order. He was a *magister theologiae* at Paris by 1326 and lectured there as well as in the Franciscan convent at Toulouse, but he left teaching early and embarked on a rapid and successful though sometimes controversial ecclesiastical career. In 1329 Odonis was elected Minister General of his Order to ward off growing trouble from the Spirituals, and remained in this position for thirteen years. For his services to the Holy See the Pope rewarded him with the patriarchate of Antioch and later also made him bishop of Catania. That is where he died in 1349, of the Plague, and was buried in the cathedral.[1] An assortment of written material has been ascribed to Odonis: letters and official documents, sermons, a versified catechism for a young boy, as well as a commentary on the *Sentences* with an Aristotelian principle of just pricing at IV, 15: ... *in commutationibus attenditur aequalitas secundum valorem rerum in comparatione ad usum et indigentiam hominum.*[2] There has also recently come to light a treatise on economics from the hand of Geraldus Odonis; not itself in the Aristotelian tradition, it is essential for a full understanding of his contribution there and we shall deal at length with this treatise and its background later on. In the field of philosophy

---

1 On Geraldus Odonis, see Langlois; Bartolomé; Jöcher III 1028; Chevalier 3401–2; Fabricius III 41–2; Wadding 145; Sbaralea I 324–5; EF III 79; DTC XI 1658–1663; LTK IV 708; Moorman 321–331, 394, 402; Grabmann (3) 70; Heidingsfelder 53, 75–8, 129–130; Stroick 57; Lohr XXIV 163–5; Gauthier (3) 134–5; Walsh.
2 Paris BN lat. 3068, f.42va.

proper only some fragments on logics exist besides a commentary on the *Nicomachean Ethics*, which is without doubt Odonis's main work and earned him the honorific title of *doctor moralis*. It can be read in two early editions, Brescia 1482 and Venice 1500, and in a handful of manuscript copies in Italy and a few scattered elsewhere.[3]

The Venice edition describes the commentary as a *Sententia et expositio cum quaestionibus*. Lecture 9 to Book V, which includes the value analysis, has no question but is a detailed explanation of the text, informed and critical of previous contributions. Terminology proves without doubt that Odonis knew Thomas Aquinas and Albertus Magnus. The literal use of one of Grosseteste's notes, *ad opus hoc est ad necessitatem et indigentiam*,[4] in comment to 1133b18–20, as well as *opus id est necessitas* at 1133a25–27, suggest that he had a copy of the pure *Lincolniensis* and so also knew "Eustratius" (as quoted below) directly. Thanks, then, perhaps to Grosseteste, Odonis had no problem with the different meanings of the key word and even suggests an elegant and most proper example of *opus* as need by citing the Palm Sunday story of the ass and her colt: "The Lord hath need of them".[5] Though he quarrels with St Thomas elsewhere, he follows the earlier *Sententia* closely at this point, adopting the Augustinian valuation paradox (with a worm in contrast to all the gold in the world) and taking Thomas's essential point about need as measure: . . . *opus secundum veritatem et naturam omnia continet, id est omnia in valore tenet.* That is certainly an ingenious

---

3 Vienna NB CVP 2383 (XIV, economic comments: f.71va–b); Florence BLaur Plut. 13 sin. 3 (XIV, ff.151vb–152va); Vat. Palat. lat. 1027 (XIV, ff.171rb–172va); Paris BMaz 3496 (XIV, f.139rb–vb); BN lat. 16127 (XIV, f.91rb–vb); Assisi BCom 285 (XIV, f.98rb–vb); Padova BAnton XVIII 389 (XIV, f.97ra–va); Boulogne-sur-Mer BMun 111 (XV, ff.184rb–185rb); Vat. lat. 2168 (1439, ff.145rb–146ra). The text is less certain and the choice between early traditions more difficult than in commentaries of equal importance. I find that I often agree with the late Vatican manuscript; "nitidus exaratus" (Maier) at Nürnberg, it is far better than the sub-contemporary printed editions (Hain 11968–9). Some locations: Brescia 1482 (economic comments: ff.X$_4$vb–X$_5$vb): London BL, Freiburg UB, Vienna NB, B Vat (Palat. lat. 1020); Venice 1500 (ff.105va–106ra): Paris BMaz, Vienna NB, Giessen UB, Uppsala UB.

4 See above, p. 44.

5 *Math.* 21, 3, which reads in the Vulgate: *Dominus his opus habet.*

twist to Aristotle. On the question of the value of labour, where Odonis, as we shall see, represents an analytical break-through, there are indications, but no unassailable evidence, of an inspiration from Henricus de Frimaria. At any rate, Odonis has received a market model developed beyond St Thomas and squarely in the tradition of Henricus. In continuation of the last lines quoted, significantly changing his terminology, Odonis illustrates by several examples how value is regulated by aggregate need in the face of scarcity: *Videmus enim quod quando est magna indigentia rerum tunc plus valent, sicut tempore messium sunt cariores famuli conducticii et tempore infirmitatum medici et tempore belli arma et sic de similibus.* Considering the nature of his own main contribution, it is interesting to note that two of these examples relate to labour or professional services and only one to commodities.

This latter example reappears in various later economic texts, indicating an Odonian influence, which is worth noting because his tradition, in terms of later *Ethics* commentators using him, is modest.[6] Circumstances were against Odonis; in his own Order all the interest was in the non-Aristotelian works of Scotus; elsewhere an old-fashioned exposition like his would have trouble competing with the handy formats of Burlaeus and his imitators. Fortunately, some of those who did use Odonis were first-rate minds able to appreciate what he said and develop it further. The following is the crucial part of his commentary, where he argues against Thomas on *superabundantias*. What he says about *superabundantiam doni* may be only linguistic bickering, but to *superabundantiam laboris* he brings

---

6 There are traces of Odonis in Orbellis (see above, p. 97) and, according to Gauthier (3) 137, n. 159, in Sélestat BMun 113, an anonymous commentary where Buridan is more in evidence in the economic sections. Paulus de Worczyn, an early fifteenth century professor at Kraków (Lohr XXVIII 322–5) copies all three of Odonis's examples in an otherwise unremarkable Buridanian question. (cp. BJag 720, f.136va; 741, f.143vb; 2000, f.222v). The third example reappears in Salon, the Jurist, also an author elsewhere influenced by Buridan (see above, p. 143); explaining *communis indigentia* he says that *tempore belli arma cariora sunt, et equi, et alia quae ad usum bellicum necessaria sunt, vel utilia.* (col. 64). Again, there are related phrases in Molina. (col. 564). Even Vincentius Filliuccius, the seventeenth century moralist and economist, has found his way to these lines; cp. *Quaestiones morales*, Tom. II, Lyon 1626, p. 565.

a real objection; it amounts, in one way or another, to a rejection of the Alberto-Thomist labour theory:[7]

Si autem non fiat talis transportatio, alterum extremum habebit utrasque superabundantias; puta si coriarius est pretiosior et carior artifex quam agricola et opus eius erit pretiosius et carius quam agricolae opus. Et secundum hoc exponit quidam quod alterum extremum haberet utrasque superabundantias, quia et plus laborasset et plus donasset et sic haberet superabundantiam laboris et superabundantiam doni. Sed quantum sit talis expositio irrationalis etiam sine rationis discussione, apparet primo quia non dator sed acceptor doni dicitur habere donum, secundo quia neque labor artificis venit ad aestimationem commutationis. Plus enim laborat agricola pro una parva quantitate tritici quam advocatus pro formatione unius libelli, et tamen dabit advocato agricola multum de tritico in quo laboraverit in centuplo pro illo parvo libello, et sic de quibuscumque artificibus secundum quod sunt rariores et in magnis negotiis necessariores, et hoc bene consonat sententiae Philosophi plus quam illa expositio. Eustratius vero exponit ubi nos habemus alterum utrumque, et est in summa intentio sua ... quod inconveniens est utrumque extremum habere superabundantiam, quia pone duos artifices, unum rariorem et cariorem et alium viliorem — primus habet superabundantiam et alter defectum — et eodem modo intellige de ipsorum operibus. Modo, si fiat commutatio operis ad opus simpliciter, ille carior habet superabundantiam artificii et ministerii sui, alter autem habebit et recipiet superabundantiam operis pretiosioris. Hoc autem est inconveniens et iniustum ....

*

Using once more the technique of approaching a text through the eyes of its readers, we may start with two Renaissance commentators who happened to pick up Odonis. Nicolaus Tignosius (1402–1474), of Foligno, practised medicine and taught at North Italian universities. His commentary on the *Ethics*, preserved in two manuscripts in the Laurentian Library, is based on the translation of Aretinus and on the mediaeval *Sententiae* of Aquinas and Odonis; paraphrasing both, he re-opens the old controversy.[8] Antonius Silvester,

7 On the *superabundantias*, see above, p. 53ff. *Quidam* in the fourth line is most certainly Thomas Aquinas. The likelihood of Odonis's knowing the pure *Lincolniensis* might for a moment lend support to the hypothesis that *quidam* is Grosseteste in his note, *in labore et dono*, but this is ruled out by the literal use of Thomas's expression, *superabundantiam laboris et superabundantiam doni*. The reference to "Eustratius" may be original or derive from Albertus Magnus; the two are clearly mixed up in the reference to *inconveniens*, which is Albert's expression. Henricus de Frimaria similarly confuses the two.

8 Quotations are from Plut. 76, cod. 48, f.100r, f.99r, and cod. 49, f.87vb, rb. On Tignosius, see Jöcher IV 1196; Chevalier 4527–8; EF VI 471; Garin 325; Lohr XXVIII 306; Gauthier (3) 150.

a Paris master who in 1517 published an *Ethics* commentary with the text of Argyropulus, also paraphrases Odonis but omits the *superabundantias* arguments.[9] It is Tignosius's reaction to these arguments which gives us our best clue. In the central lines of his much shorter version, he says that

> ... cum labor non veniat ad aestimationem valoris, nam plus agricola laborat ad modium messis quod daturus est medico quam medicus in medendo, fortassis melius est sic exponere, ut dicamus: utrumque extremum habebit alterum excessum; nam pone duos artifices quorum alterius ars existat nobilis, alterius ignobilis; primus habebit excessum, secundus defectum ....

Having both texts before him, Tignosius may have realized that Odonis is attacking Aquinas, but he could not have known who or what is behind the reference to "Eustratius". Following Aretinus who reads, at 1133b2, *utrumque excessum habebit alterum extremum*, he seems to believe that Odonis suggests a reversal. Anyhow, he proceeds to state the case against Thomas, but in his words this comes to read like a simple rejection of the labour theory, missing the explanation which imports analytical significance to that inference in the original. This reading is confirmed elsewhere in Tignosius. Following Thomas Aquinas into *EN*, V, 5 before switching over to Odonis, he comes to the point where the former, in some oft-quoted lines, makes a house exchange for shoes according to *quot plures expensas facit aedificator*.[10] In a section otherwise identical except for terminology, Tignosius makes this read, *quot plura meretur aedificator*, dropping the reference to cost. He does not say what he means by *meretur*, but he stresses the operation of the market in his commentary, and one way to read Odonis would be thus to play up the other half of the value analysis at *EN*, V, 5, at the cost of the Albertian explanations. It looks as though we can also read Silvester that way. Presumably rejecting the labour theory on what he believes to be Odonis's direction just as Tignosius did, Silvester brings the *indigentia* explanation into the cross-conjunction formula where the labour explanation usually reigned supreme:

... *tunc dicetur contrapassum esse quando erunt quae commutantur aequata,*

9 Silvester is quoted on f.133v. The book (IA 107.843) is in London BL, Paris BMaz, Munich SB. On the author, see Jöcher IV 587; Villoslada 107, 364, 429; Élie 230; Gauthier (3) 163.

10 See above, pp. 71–2.

149

ut pote opus agricolae ad opus sutoris . . . , *sed in tali aequatione indigentia est consideranda* . . . .

Posing the labour and demand explanations in mutual conflict is always a blind alley in value theory; it is not what Odonis meant to do. Neither does he reject all reference to labour, but only what he takes to be a labour quantity theory;[11] nor does he bring in demand in a manner that can justify a simple change of reference. To gainsay Thomas, what he points out is not demand for the goods exchanged, but rather some properties in the producers. Behind this, of course, is demand for these properties; *indigentia* in the factor market, as it were, is what will in the final analysis reconcile the seemingly conflicting explanations. But this is not an easy point to take. It is the most difficult link to forge in the entire Aristotelian chain of reasoning. On the face of it, Odonis only points out the empirical fact of different factor reward associated with different professions and so with social position. To most authors reading Odonis on *superabundantias*, this rather than a rejection of labour for product demand is what suggests itself as an alternative to St Thomas's interpretation. From this viewpoint, Tignosius's *mereor* assumes a new significance. What is the nature of the builder's merit as compared to the shoemaker? In the author's own words, as quoted, it has something to do with his practising a *nobilis ars*, but he stops short of telling us in what this nobility consists. So do most others who explained Aristotle in such terms. As always with the Aristotelians, an outright "status" interpretation is arrested before the brink of acceptance, but some commentators allowed it to come very close.

Best known of those who chose this line of interpretation, and one of the most influential of all commentators on the *Nicomachean Ethics*, is Donatus Acciaiolus, the Florentine humanist and statesman whom we have already quoted in a tantalising remark about labour. First printed in the year of the author's death, his commentary was reissued, after a long delay, in the important printing centres (Venice 1535, Paris 1541, Lyon 1544), and was subsequently to be printed more than fifteen times, having become a standard companion to the translation of Argyropulus. Not primarily interested in economic *realia*, Acciaiolus lectured his

11 See discussion on pp. 75–9.

numerous readers on the technicalities of commutative justice in exchange, sometimes in a way reminiscent of the pre-Albertian commentators.[12] But he also used mediaeval sources and one of them must have been Geraldus Odonis. Thus, as I would read historical influences, a curious quasi-Odonian tradition has developed since the Renaissance, partly and perhaps mainly from Acciaiolus. Extending into modern Aristotelian exegesis, this tradition would seem to be responsible for the "status" interpretation occasionally voiced by economists attempting to judge the contributions of their ancient and mediaeval colleagues.

Read in his own words, Acciaiolus does not permit of an interpretation like that. He explains cross-conjunction by saying that the builder is a *praestantior artifex* than the shoemaker, but points out that this has nothing to do with personal worth: . . . *non attenditur hic personarum dignitas, quia non videntur altera alteram excedere, nisi ratione operis* . . . . In economic exchange, regulated according to commutative justice,[13] there is never a question of personal differences per se; any difference relevant to the terms of exchange must rest in the products or rather in men's evaluation of them. This principle was accepted by all scholastic commentators; only inexcusable ignorance of the old tradition in some modern critics has allowed it to be questioned. Acciaiolus stressed it again and again. However, coming to grips with *superabundantias* and taking the line of Odonis, he fails, like Tignosius, to state the economic conditions which alone can make sense of what he calls *excellentiam artis* or, in concluding, *dignitas*:

. . . agricola haberet unum calceum, id est minus, et habebit plus in eo quod excedit sutorem dignitate artis, posito quod sit dignior. Item sutor, minus in eo quod exceditur dignitate artis, habebit plus quia habebit alimentum quod est pluris pretii.

12 Some manuscripts of Acciaiolus's commentary are listed in note 2, 33. He is quoted here from the first edition (Florence 1478; GW 140, Hain 33), ff.q₁r–q₂v. Later editions in Cranz. The cross-conjunction formula alternately in the direct and the reverse form (see above, pp. 51–2), is one of several features common with the Greek commentators of the *Translatio Lincolniensis*. Most often in evidence of scholastic commentators is Thomas Aquinas (at *EN*, V, 5 not through Albertus de Saxonia, as suggested by Dyroff 345, nor through Burlaeus, as suggested by Heidingsfelder 147). On Acciaiolus, see Jöcher I 56; EF I 39–40; DBI I 80–2; Lohr XXIII 400–1; Gauthier (3) 150–1.

13 See above, p. 14. I now pick up a line from Chapter 1, p. 50.

While this commentary accompanied the translation of Argyropulus, another much used Renaissance translation, by Dionysius Lambinus, came equipped with that translator's own notes, where an explanation of *superabundantias* in terms of *excellentiam artis* and *excellentiam operis*, clearly based on the Florentine commentator, further extended the influence of the latter.[14] Guilielmus Wilkinson, who published a Greek and Latin combined text of the *Ethics* at Oxford in 1716, reproduced much of Lambinus in a note but added a labour explanation, perhaps deliberately seeking to avoid a misunderstanding.[15] Strictly speaking, and given the full context, what these quasi-Odonian commentators say does not contradict the Aristotelian principle of personal equality in commutative justice, but *dignitas* is a word which should be handled with the greatest care since it is bound to call up in some readers a misleading association with social criteria, while Acciaiolus obviously means to refer to worth in some vague economic sense. Authors who join this tradition at the next remove without taking the explanatory model along and perhaps write in the vernacular, can hardly expect to avoid the wrong association. In Italian, for instance, *degno* would seem to be a dangerous word to use. Felice Figliucci, scholar, philosopher and native of Siena, in 1551 published a paraphrase of the *Ethics* with traces of Odonis. Explaining cross-conjunction, he introduces *due artefici, uno più degno, e l'altro men degno*.[16] To the less watchful reader, this is a "status" interpretation.

And so we arrive at those modern economists who believe that Aristotle and his scholastic interpreters intended to compute prices on the basis of "social rank" (Sewall) or "dignity or rank" (Bonar) or "status" (Polanyi). Presumably relying on information about social structure they forget that men of other ages could also reason realistically about empirical phenomena. An economic interpreter can less than the layman be excused for reversing the causal relation between earning power and social status of a much sought after artisan. There is a redeeming appendix to Bonar's comment: "We

14 Ed. Venice 1558, p. 351.
15 See note 1,44. The Latin version is based on Lambinus, sometimes in the original, sometimes in the adaptation by Bergius (cp. note 1, 24), as at 1133a27.
16 *De la filosofia morale*, Rome 1551, p. 211.

might make Aristotle's adjustments easier to understand if we supposed that the regard he insists on paying to the respective status of the producers was a regard paid to the respective skill and difficulty of their trade."[17] "Dignity or rank", which becomes "status" overleaf, is obviously Acciaiolus's *dignitas*. Had Bonar had access to the original material of which the Renaissance *Ethics* commentaries are but a pale reflection, he would have been able to confirm that this ranking of producers has indeed something to do with skill. But to the economist it is also clear that there is no ranking of productive skills except by demand for what they produce.

*

Turning now from these developments to a truer interpretation of Odonis's analysis, we must first look into its full background. Besides being an Aristotelian, Odonis belonged to the Franciscan tradition in value theory and drew upon it to explain Aristotle. Some of those who did not know this background had trouble following him, but he had some highly capable followers who were familiar with it. By applying the ideas of a Franciscan genius in the analytically fruitful context of the *Ethics*, he showed them the road to a synthesis in value theory. Two volumes in the municipal library in Siena, U.V.6 and U.V.8, contain the treatises *de contractibus* by Petrus Johannis Olivi and Geraldus Odonis, both annotated in the hand of a third Franciscan who worked in that city, the great fifteenth century preacher, St Bernardino of Siena. The former treatise is extant in two other copies as well, the latter only in this one copy. Neither was printed. But Olivi's analysis of exchange and value is copied almost verbatim into the economic sermons of St Bernardino, which have seen numerous editions. Only quite recent research has unearthed this source of the value theory expounded by St Bernardino and after him by St Antonino of Florence who also borrowed some of it from the former. They base much of their considerable reputations as economists on this loan. Petrus Olivi (c.1248–1298), of Sérignan in Languedoc, was one of the really brilliant economic minds of the Middle Ages. His ideas reappear in

17 Bonar 39, 40; Sewall 8; Polanyi 107.

some of the leading treatises on value all through the scholastic age and later.[18] But particularly after his death, when he came to be associated ever more strongly with the Spiritual Franciscans, it was not opportune for perceptive confrères who recognized his brilliance to acknowledge him as a source, even in economics. St Bernardino, a reform leader himself, who used both of the Siena manuscripts in his sermons, quotes only Odonis.[19] The latter, on his part, was an advocate of a more liberal interpretation of the Franciscan Rule, and any association with Olivi would have been unthinkable, but he uses him freely in his own *Tractatus*, though less verbatim than St Bernardino.[20]

The famous triplet of value determinants previously ascribed to the Tuscan Saint, *virtuositas, raritas, complacibilitas*, appears among his marginalia in Siena U.V.6 and the text to which they refer contains the prototype of his own analysis in Sermon 35. I do not think highly of the idea of separating subjective and objective utility and have had occasion to criticize this part of the Franciscan theory.[21] Significant here is the definition of *raritas* in Aristotelian terms. In economic exchange, says Olivi, valuation is made

... secundum quod res ex suae inventionis raritate et difficultate sunt nobis magis necessariae, pro quanto ex earum penuria maiorem ipsarum indigentiam et minorem facultatem habendi et utendi habemus.

18 The three known manuscripts of Olivi's economic treatise are, Siena BCom U.V.6, ff.295r–316r; Bologna BU 129, ff.170r–196r; Naples BN VII.D.39, ff.218r–249v. See Pacetti (1) and (2). A treatise published at Rome in 1556 in the name of Gerardus Senensis, includes some of the Olivi material but not the value analysis, which is on the very first folios of the manuscripts. (Pacetti knew two copies of that book, at Genova and Palermo; I found a third copy in the Biblioteca Classense at Ravenna.)

19 St Bernardino's economic sermons (32–45) are in Vol. IV of the *Opera* edition (8 vols., Florence 1950–1963); Sermo 35, which has the material quoted here, is on pp. 189–202. The economic sermons were printed as a separate treatise, *De contractibus et usuris*, as early as 1474 at Strasbourg (GW 3881, Hain 2835).

20 His treatise on contracts (Siena BCom U.V.8, ff.77r–124r) is not included in Langlois's bibliography of Odonis; it is in Sbaralea but not in Wadding and has come to light mainly through the work of Pacetti and the editors of St Bernardino who note the Saint's use of this source.

21 See a discussion of this, and of the Franciscan concept of *raritas*, on pp. 115–6 above.

Olivi had also been educated at Paris; his terminology proves that he knew the Aristotelian economic tradition,[22] and he may have read "Averroist" material. At any rate, his *raritas* is scarcity in the face of need and reflects, in reverse, the *indigentia* concept which Henricus de Frimaria was soon to establish on the basis of the "Averroists". Expressing a development also shared by this branch of the Aristotelian tradition, Olivi emphasizes community need and valuation and goes on to explain further the influence of scarcity on *communis taxatio et aestimatio*. Among factors to be observed in just pricing are

... communem cursum copiae et inopiae seu paucitatis et abundantiae. Unde et commune verbum est quod omne rarum est pretiosum et quod nimia familiaritas et abundantia parit contemptum. Quanto enim rarius et difficilius adire possumus et habere, tanto supra nostram facultatem altius et admirabilius aestimamus; ardua enim nobis et insolita admiramur. Et ideo ubi aurum vel triticum communiter multum abundat non tanti pretii aestimatur sicut quando communiter grandis inopia est ipsorum. Et idem est ubi est communis copia vel inopia medicorum vel advocatorum aut pugilum vel fossorum.

There is an abbreviated version of this in Odonis's treatise while St Bernardino copies extensively, coining from the second line the more striking phrase, *omne rarum est carum*; St Antonino contributes to our references by ascribing the saying to St Jerome.[23]

The concluding lines (from which Odonis obviously borrows the example of the *advocatus* in his *Ethics* commentary) introduces a salient feature of the Franciscan analysis of value, namely its focus on the relative *raritas* and *pretiositas* of human productive skills. Olivi repeatedly returns to this subject in other examples, and we easily recognize the source of Odonis's analysis of *superabundantias*. He who quarries or cuts the stones, *quamquam plus corpore laborans,*

22 Commutative justice, he says, consists *in aequivalentia ad nostrum usum et utilitatem.*
23 Op. cit., col. 256. Bowley 66 provides a short list of ancient authors, including Plato and Sextus Empiricus, who said that rare things are valuable. Since this is as close to a truism as any economic statement and the shallowest basis on which to construct a value theory (see above, p. 115), it makes no great difference where Petrus Olivi hit upon the phrase. What counts is the use made of it. However, I think St Antonino must be correct in assuming that it was taken from St Jerome, who may of course have had it from one of Bowley's sources but is himself a more likely scholastic source. At any rate, the statement is made (at least) twice by St Jerome in his commentary on Isaiah, namely in V, xiii, 12: *Pretiosum autem dicitur omne quod rarum est,* and in VI, xiii, 12: *Pretiosior autem intelligitur pro eo quod est rarior. Omne enim, quod rarum est, pretiosum est . . . .* (PL, Tom. 24, 161, 219).

gets less than the architect who guides and instructs the labourers *cum altiori peritia et industria*. This is at once a rejection of the labour quantity explanation of value and a clue to the true role of productive labour in the value model. That is estimated higher, *ceteris paribus* (an expression adopted by St Bernardino and subsequently much beloved by the economic profession), which needs more skill. It is not only that higher functions require *amplior sollicitudo mentalis et etiam multo et diuturno studio atque experientia et labore*; skills are difficult and costly to come by: ... *multisque periculis et expensis communiter acquiritur peritia et industria talis*. Such skills, then, *pauci sunt et rari sunt* and, says Olivi, *ideo in maiori pretio reputantur*. It is Odonis in his *Tractatus* who most firmly links up that final deduction, explaining *why* it is that rare skills are better paid. In his version, the first example quoted from Olivi above has an appendix: ... *est penuria advocatorum, medicorum, pugilum sive fossorum, sequitur quod tales possunt carius locare sua opera*. This is a first indication of the clue to a synthesis of the labour and demand explanations; it lies in the power of scarce labour to command a higher product price (through product scarcity). Olivi does not say it clearly; it is Odonis's inference, which St Bernardino copied, and a crucial element of the Franciscan analysis. It can also be taken to finish Odonis's analysis of *superabundantias* in the *Ethics* commentary. Two artisans are compared, one cheap, the other *rariorem et cariorem*. An artisan is expensive when he is rare, and he is so because he will be in demand; in a phrase reminiscent both of Olivi and of Grosseteste, some artisans are *rariores et in magnis negotiis necessariores*. We know from his treatise on contracts what he means: being needed, they have bargaining power in the product market and can ask more.

It may well be that the analysis of relative productive skills offered the most feasible approach to the central problems of microeconomic adjustment in pre-capitalistic societies. It was to be taken by many early economists and is as typical of Galiani, for instance, as it is of Olivi, on whom Galiani very obviously depended. The Franciscan analysis can lead to a theory of wages and, in so far as it involves a balancing of simple labour against the capital costs of acquiring skills, to a primitive theory of distribution. But it did not reach a full synthesis in value theory in any author I can name outside the Aristotelian tradition. The reason for this would seem to be the very emphasis on wage differentials, on which the whole approach depended. The essential point as regards labour in the explanation of product value is not differentiated reward for particular scarce labour skills, but the value, because of inherent scarcity, of *all labour* which brings forth a needed product. In the Aristotelian tradition, the Albertian generalized concept of labour kept rubbing against the demand theory, and I have no doubt that this is what conditioned the synthesis which was in the end achieved by exposing the Franciscan arguments to Aristotle. But when Odonis received the *Ethics* for commentary, the *indigentia* explanation was just struggling to accommodate the improvements of the "Averroists" and Buridan had not yet written. Moreover, the precise task which caused Odonis to use Olivi's approach was that of arguing against the Albertian labour theory as he read it in St Thomas. This may have obscured his view of the general synthesis to which he came so close. A century afterwards, St Bernardino made Odonis's source available to a larger audience. In the course of the following centuries two other prominent *Ethics* commentators found their ways to it, Johannes Maior in the sixteenth and Johannes Crell in the seventeenth.

*

Johannes Maior (Mair) was born in 1469 at Gleghornie in the parish of North Berwick in Scotland. He wrote a famous history of England and Scotland and taught in periods at St Andrews, but more than thirty years of his academic life he gave to the University of Paris, where he taught at Montaigu and later at the Sorbonne and became widely renowned for his erudition. It was at Paris that he published, in 1530, his *Ethica Aristotelis*, a textual commentary with the translation of Argyropulus.[24] As an economist, Mair has been

24 The economic comments in the *Ethica Aristotelis* are on ff.80v–82v. The book (IA 107.922) is rare, but some of the copies are well placed: London BL, Paris BMaz, Munich SB, Vienna NB, B Vat. On Mair, see the Life by Mackay, prefixed to the 1892 English edition of Mair's *History*, as well as Fabricius IV 383–5; Jöcher III 56; Chevalier 2965; EF IV 219; DTC IX 1661–2; LTK VI 1308; Wadding 213–4; Sbaralea II 99; DNB XII 830–2; NBG XXXII 934–6; Villoslada 127–164, 459; Élie 205–212 and *passim*; Ashley (1) II 341, 443–6, 452, 485–6; Gauthier (3) 164.

praised for his realistic views on usury in his commentary on the *Sentences*.[25] Opening his *Ethics* commentary to the chapter on exchange, one finds that he has studied both Odonis and Buridanus. The chapter is headed by a long exposition structured on the mediaeval Franciscan commentary; appended are six *dubia*, one of which paraphrases some of Buridan's V,16. But many other sources intervene; not for nothing was Mair described as a "storehouse of all the learning of the Middle Ages". To illustrate Buridan he relates the tale of the "mouse of Casilinum" and elegantly couples it with the story of Cleopatra and the liquefied pearl, thus giving Thomas's old champions on the scales of natural and economic valuation their definite classical representations.[26] From another of the *dubia* I have previously quoted Mair on *res tantum valet*.[27] Burlaeus is paraphrased in the early part of the main exposition, while in the central part the analysis is unmistakably that of Olivi, who has in all likelihood reached Mair through the sermons of St Bernardino, now available in print.

Odonis is used to explain value measurement in the face of scarcity: . . . *tempore belli arma cara, pacis tempore minoris veneunt*; and to disprove the labour quantity theory: *Advocatus aut scriba pro literis signandis plus lucri in die consequitur quam sutor fortasse in mense.* In the *superabundantias* analysis, this source is combined with the source by which it was itself at one time inspired:

. . . alioqui continget alterum extremorum utrumque excessum habere in nobilitate et caritate. Aliquis est artifex rarus propterea carus, nam omnia rara (ut inquiunt) cara; ut politor lapidum pretiosorum, quia de suo artificio degit et rarenter ei operis locatio occurrit, ut operam suam carius vendat necesse est. Similiter opus rei arduae est carum, ut opus advocati qui pro dominiis et amplis possessionibus litem arcere solet. Requiritur enim illic ingenium cum literis, quare carus est. Vult Philosophus ergo dicere quod nisi sit comparatio rationum, alterutrum extremum habebit excessum in raritate et pretiositate . . . .

While Odonis had had the *advocatus* work for a farmer, Mair has him supply the needs of the rich. It is an obvious Buridanian

25 See particularly Ashley (1). An Aristotelian argument of Mair's was quoted from his commentary on the *Sentences* on p. 30 above.
26 On Thomas Aquinas's adoption of St Augustine's paradox, see pp. 87–8. The story of the mouse which saved the life of the buyer is mentioned on p. 112 with references in note 4,14. The story about Cleopatra who drank a pearl dissolved in vinegar is in Pliny the Elder, *Natural History*, IX, 58.
27 See above, p. 131.

influence, evident also in the other prototype of the rare artisan, a gem polisher (*rarus propterea carus*), who recurs in the Buridanian *dubium* where *lapides pretiosi* exemplify objects which *sunt cara quibus parum indigemus*, as Mair says, paraphrasing the original. Products of exceptional skills are often luxuries and the power of skilful artisans to affect price would normally be greater in luxury markets; the Buridanian element therefore takes Mair closer to the essential point in the Odonian analysis. When he fails to spell it out the way Odonis did (and the way he must have read it in St Bernardino, copying Odonis), it may be because it is self-evident in the Buridanian context. Anyhow, what Mair prefers to emphasize is not the artisan's power to raise the price but his need to do so in order to live by his chosen art; this clearly recalls the Aristotelian *destruerentur* and so provides another important link with the Albertian labour theory which is lacking in Odonis. However, in the final reckoning Mair, like Odonis, stops short of the complete synthesis because labour as a value-determinant per se, owing to the fundamental *scarcity of all labour*, is never suggested; it is all along a question of comparing different kinds of labour. For that suggestion there is still a century to wait, until another *Ethics* commentator combined these sources.

Johannes Crell was born in 1590 at Helmetzheim in Franken. While studying at Altdorf he was won over to the teaching of the Socinians, and in 1612 Crell went to Raków to become rector of their school recently founded there. In this remote Polish town he worked and wrote for a few years, but died in his early forties. This obscure sectarian theologist is the author of the most perceptive chapter on economic exchange in the entire Aristotelian tradition. It was printed posthumously at Amsterdam in 1650 in Crell's *Ethica Aristotelica*, of which a second edition appeared in 1681. As early as 1635 a brief *Prima ethices elementa* had been published at Raków. It contains a very much abbreviated version of the *indigentia* analysis now to be quoted from the larger work:[28]

---

28 *Ethica Aristotelica*, II, 16; ed. 1650, pp. 130–1. I have been able to locate only three copies of this book, viz. in London BL, Hannover LB, and Zürich ZB. The 1681 edition is in Oslo UB, London BL, Paris BN, Amsterdam UB, Leiden UB, Göttingen SUB, Wolfenbüttel Herzog-Aug. B, Geneva BU, Bern

... ad hoc, ut exaequentur res inter se, requiritur ut sint comparabiles; ut autem comparari possint inter se, opus est communi aliqua mensura, quae res permutandas metiatur et aestimet. Quare quae sit haec *mensura communis* quaeritur. Haec vero *duplex* est: *naturalis* una; altera *hominum ingenio excogitata*, illius prioris veluti vicaria. *Naturalis mensura* est *Indigentia*, quae est defectus rei alicuius utilis. Ea quo maior minorve est, eo quoque res pluris minorisve habetur. Et haec etiam nos ad permutationem instituendam impellit; ut si frumento egeat locus quispiam aut regio, vino abundet, maioris erit frumentum quam vinum. Ad indigentiam autem duo requiruntur; primum ut res ipsa usum aliquem ac fructum quem appetamus nobis praebere possit. Nam re inutili non dicimur indigere. Deinde ut illa careamus. Utraque res pretium rerum mutat. In usu spectatur potissimum necessitas, commoditas (quo nomine voluptatem quoque complectimur), dignitas; addi potest etiam communitas; quorum enim usus latius se extendit, ea pretiosiora sunt. Singula ex his pretium augent, quo sunt maiora; si minora minuunt, caeteris paribus. Dico, *caeteris paribus*; quia interdum id quod est magis necessarium, vilioris est pretii, quia ad dignitatem non pertinet, aut minus pertinet. Ea enim quae ad commoditatem aut dignitatem pertinent, fere solent esse pretiosiora, quamquam id ob copiam aut paucitatem seu penuriam rei videtur accidere. Nam quae prorsus sunt ad vitam necessaria, quae sane genere pauca sunt, (paucis enim natura contenta est) eorum copiam fere maiorem produxit natura; aut eorum conficiendorum ratio est facilior, quam eorum quae ad commoditatem ac dignitatem; qualia sunt supellectilia pretiosiora, aedes amplae, magnificae, et similia. Ad carentiam, ut ita loquar, pertinet raritas, quae pretia semper vehementer auget; *quae rara cara*; et hanc ob causam ea quae maiori labore, periculo, artificio parantur, cariora sunt, quia rariora.

Crell is the definite scholastic commentator, in whom all branches come together. Of background and training he is a Thomist of the German Protestant branch;[29] there is a double measure of goods in exchange, human need is the natural measure, but also cause of exchange. But unlike his numerous German colleagues, Crell has received Buridan, extending need to *voluptatem*, stressing "Averroist" *communitas*. Most ingeniously, he draws on Boethius[30] rather than Seneca to voice the sentiment about contentedness from which Buridan had launched his essay on poverty, taking the opportunity for some edifying remarks about the wisdom of nature. Several Buridanian elements bear the unmistakable imprint of the "Austrian school"; through some untraceable channel, material originating

SUB. Cp. also *Prima ethices elementa*, pp. 79–80. This book is in Copenhagen KB, Paris BN. There is a *Vita Joannis Crellii* prefixed to his *Opera omnia exegetica*, Tom. 1, Amsterdam (*Biblioteca Fratrum Polonorum*) 1656. See also Jöcher I 2184–5; LTK IX 929; ADB IV 586; Gauthier (3) 204.

29 See above, pp. 100–2.

30 Cp. *De cons. phil.*, II, pr. V: *Paucis enim minimisque natura contenta est ....* (PL, Tom. 63, 692).

with the fifteenth century Buridanians in Vienna must have reached Crell at Kraków; cp. the definition of *indigentia* already mentioned in Chapter 5,[31] the separation of utility (*appetamus*) from scarcity (*careamus*), the characteristic *commoditas*. (*Dignitas*, repeatedly paired with *commoditas* to describe luxuries, is not an Aristotelian term.) As in the case of Mair, insight comes of joining Buridan and Odonis, the latter perhaps not in his *Ethics* commentary but at least as an element in St Bernardino's sermons, which have clearly been at the disposal of the impressively resourceful Crell. Rare objects are expensive, hence that which is made with more *periculum* and *artificium* will be more expensive, he says, using Olivi's term. But then he adds something which takes him one definite step beyond the others who joined the Franciscan symposium on wage differentials, and I suggest that what enabled him to find it was his broader Aristotelian support. Like all who commented on the *Ethics* through St Thomas, Crell was an Albertian, raised on the principle that value in exchange must comply with labour and expenses in the most abstract and general sense. At any rate, we have finally met the commentator who saw the essential point that labour spent in production not only influences value in so far as some artisans are rarer and so able to charge more than others, as Odonis had said, but regulates value of any useful product in production of which labour is spent because all labour is necessarily to some extent scarce and so brings forth a scarce product: . . . *ea quae maiori labore . . . parantur, cariora sunt, quia rariora.*

*

I have quoted a few who commented on Aristotle after Crell, but this scholastic tradition was by now in rapid decline. His result was reached in its last hour and was not repeated. But less than two centuries afterwards, the young professional science of economics, growing vigorously from scholastic roots, regained Crell's position. The circumstances under which this happened recall in some respects those of the Aristotelian synthesis. A labour theory of value states that the relative exchange value of any two commodities varies with the labour spent in producing these commodities.

31 p. 137.

A demand theory of value states that this relative value varies with the demand for each of these commodities. Historically, an economist can be said to have solved the problem of value when he understands that these theories are really partial statements of a unique theory, the unifying principle being a double one, namely, (1) that labour is a relevant value regulator only in so far as it is spent on producing something useful, and (2) that labour is always to some extent scarce. For then the useful object on which scarce labour is spent will also be scarce and so have value, which means that the labour spent on it will be in demand and have value as well. This rudimentary solution still leaves to be explained the problem of distribution between factors of which labour is only one and the problem of general equilibrium, but it provides an elementary insight conditioning these further advances. To read chronologically the analytical attempts of early economists is to wait for somebody finally to say something which proves that he has this insight. This takes a long time indeed.

The line of able Italian and French economists of the seventeenth and eighteenth centuries, including Galiani, is searched in vain; they have the two theories marching separately, scarcity and utility usually taking the burden of explanation. The classical tradition in Britain, shifting the emphasis, at first failed to effect a union, but then suddenly in the next generation there is a flash. Priority should perhaps be given to Malthus, but this sometimes surprisingly scholastic author still emphasizes the "rarity" of work "of a nature to require an uncommon degree of dexterity and ingenuity" rather than the fact of labour as such, whose reward is explained in a manner which recalls the Aristotelian *destruerentur*.[32] However, the idea that labour regulates product value through scarcity, is clearly emerging. In Senior's brief statement it is fully established:

... wherever there is utility, the addition of labour as necessary to production constitutes value, because, the supply of labour being limited, it follows that the object, to the supply of which it is necessary, is by that very necessity limited in supply.[33]

32 Op. cit., pp. 74–5; cp. above, pp. 82–3.
33 *An Outline of the Science of Political Economy*, London (1836) 1938, p. 24.

Senior's position, once reached, was soon crowded and left behind. His kind of insight belongs to a definite stage in the development of value theory. It is interesting to note here that this insight was all but forced upon Senior's generation by two conceptual matrices working against one another in the analytical material which this generation had inherited, namely the Continental demand theory developed in a long tradition and the classical labour theory suddenly clamped against it by Smith cum Ricardo. Malthus and Senior were in fact experiencing something like the situation of the Aristotelians, called upon to comment on a brief text where partial labour and *indigentia* explanations had been rubbing against each other since the first expositions in the thirteenth century.

To the historian of the Aristotelian tradition it is also curious, to say the least, that Senior, as one of really quite few modern economists, should bring the exchange model of the *Nicomachean Ethics* into his economic teaching, paraphrasing it extensively in his *Lectures* in an interpretation supporting his own theory of value published elsewhere and comparing Aristotle favourably to Smith.[34] This happened rather less than a century before the first "status" interpretation by an economist quoted above, but in the course of that century there took place the final, formal burial of the scholastic Aristotle and the birth, with Bekker, of modern exegesis — for better and for worse, as far as philosophy is concerned. Reading Senior on Aristotle one finds that he, like the best of the schoolmen, looked for the economist. Principally, and not surprisingly, he picks up the demand theory: "The real standard of value, the real connecting link of society is demand, or the desire for what we do not possess". This he compares with a more recent value theory:

... Aristotle's description of value as depending on demand, χρηα (sic), approaches much more nearly to perfect accuracy than Smith's who, by adopting labour as a measure of value, and talking of labour as never varying in its own value, has involved himself and his followers in inextricable confusion.

34 The Aristotelian material in Senior consists of the paraphrase with some comments added. It is published in *Industrial Efficiency and Social Economy* (ed. Levy), Part VII, Chapter I, Section 1, New York 1928, Vol. II, pp. 43–5, and is from Lectures, Old Series, First Course (1826–7).

But labour is a factor to Senior's Aristotle as well, not indeed labour quantity as autonomously causing product value but labour value as being equalized by the product market:

When the value of men's labour has been equalized, they exchange with equal advantage; and the husbandman receives from the shoemaker shoes bearing the same proportion in value to a given quantity of food which the labour of the husbandman bears to that of the shoemaker.

The Aristotelian principle of equality — or of "equal advantage" in Senior's excellent term — can be interpreted so as to indicate the nature of his synthesis reached elsewhere, namely the operation of demand, in the face of scarcity, bringing about equilibrium allocation of labour resources. Let us not be misunderstood on this important point: the notion of equilibrium is of course strictly anachronistic even as referred to Senior when taken in the sense of positive analytical history, but it is legitimate in terms of a vague final idea which analytical development grappled for and which proved not too difficult to formulate once Senior's kind of insight had been reached. In the modern history of economics, Nassau W. Senior is a primitive. I have sometimes in these pages tied a late Aristotelian form to an early modern one; this indication of continuity on various points of theory has been a main theme. So also in the central synthesis of the labour and demand theories of value itself: by tying Crell to Senior, this study demonstrates the mediaeval preconditioning of an early modern insight on which could soon be erected the elaborate neo-classical edifice which we still inhabit.

That which is made with more labour is costly because it will be scarce. Such is the simple verbal form of Johannes Crell's synthesis as stated in the *Ethica Aristotelica*, and it is precisely what Senior says: ". . . the addition of labour . . . constitutes value, because . . . it follows that the object . . . is . . . limited in supply". When Crell's *Ethica* was reissued in 1681, the Aristotelian commentary was already an outmoded literary form, and Aristotelian economic reasoning hardly any longer seriously pursued; Hobbes had fired his volleys at commutative justice as a relevant concept in price analysis, and economists were arguing in terms of other models. But the Aristotelian tradition did not immediately die. The new economists also had classical educations. If they turned to a Latin

Ethics commentary, there were few published after 1650 of greater general authority than Crell's. Published and republished at Amsterdam, it could have reached the hands of almost any of the savants who set in motion the new economics of the eighteenth century. None of them seems to have discovered his solution to the problem of value. But at the very least, and in a general sense, the Aristotelian influence must have facilitated its nineteenth century rediscovery.

Appendix

Aristotle's exchange model in the *Translatio Lincolniensis*; the pure text (**L**¹) with variants of revision.

1132b 31 Sed in communicationibus quidem commutativis
concomitationibus **Rp**
continet tale iustum, contrapassum, secundum

proportionalitatem, et non secundum aequalitatem. In contrafacere enim proportionale
Per **Rp, T**
commanet civitas. Vel enim hoc male quaerunt. Si autem
hoc *om* **Rt**
133a I non, servitus videtur esse, si non contrafaciat. Vel quod bene. Si autem
quod *om* **Rt**
non, retributio non fit. Retributione autem commanent. Propter quod
commanet **Rp**
et gratiarum sacrum prompte faciunt, ut retributio sit.

Hoc enim proprium gratiae. Refamulari enim oportet ei qui gratiam

5 fecit, et rursus ipsum incipere gratiam facientem. Facit enim
incipere ipsum **R, T**
retributionem eam quae secundum proportionalitatem secundum diametrum

coniugatio. Puta aedificator in quo A, coriarius in quo B, domus

in quo G, calciamentum in quo D. Oportet igitur accipere aedificatorem
autem **Rp**
a coriario illius opus, et ipsum illi

10 retribuere quod ipsius. Si igitur primum sit secundum proportionalitatem

aequale, deinde contrapassum fiat, erit quod dicitur.

Si autem non, non aequale, neque commanet. Nihil enim prohibet

melius esse alterius opus, quam alterius. Oportet igitur utique haec
haec utique **R, T**
aequari. Est autem hoc, et in aliis artibus. Destruerentur

15 enim si non fecit faciens et quantum et quale, et
fecerit **Rp, T**; *om* **Rt**
patiens passus est hoc et tantum et tale. Non enim ex
pateretur **Rt, T**; *om* **Rp**
duobus medicis fit communicatio, sed ex medico et agricola,

et omnino alteris et non aequalibus. Sed hos oportet aequari.

Propter quod omnia comparata oportet aliqualiter esse, quorum est commutatio. Ad
 Rt   comparabilia **Rt, T**

167

20 quod nummisma venit, et fit aliqualiter medium. Omnia enim

mensurat. Quare et superabundantiam et defectum. Quanta

quaedam utique calciamenta, aequale domui vel cibo. Oportet igitur quod

aedificator ad coriarium, tanta calciamenta ad domum

vel cibum. Si enim non hoc, non erit commutatio neque communicatio.

25 Hoc autem, si non aequalia sint aliqualiter, non erit. Oportet ergo uno aliquo omnia
   Haec **R**   sunt **Rp**   enim **T**
mensurari, quemadmodum dictum est prius. Hoc autem est secundum

veritatem quidem, opus quod omnia continet. Si enim nihil indigerent,
                    indigentia quae omnia **Rt**, **T**; *om* **Rp**
vel non similiter, vel non erit commutatio, vel non eadem; puta propter
                        communicatio **R**   indigentia quae *post* eadem **Rp**
commutationem necessitatis nummisma factum est, secundum compositionem:

30 et propter hoc nomen habet nomisma, quoniam non natura sed nomo,
                        nummisma **R**, **T**
est; et in nobis transmutare et facere inutile. Erit

utique contrapassum, quando aequata sunt. Quare quod agricola ad coriarium,

hoc opus coriarii ad quod agricolae. In

1133b 1 figuram autem proportionalitatis, oportet ducere quando commutabuntur. Si autem
   formam **Rt**   non oportet **Rt**; opera non, secundum duos libros graecos, oportet **Rp**
non, utrasque habebit superabundantias alterum extremum. Sed

cum habeant quae ipsorum, sic aequales et communicantes, quoniam haec

aequalitas potest in ipsis fieri. Agricola A, cibus G,
                    autem **Rp**
5 coriarius B, opus ipsius aequatum D. Si autem sic
              ipsi **R**
non erat contrapati, non utique erat communicatio. Quoniam autem opus
   circa pati **Rp**   indigentia **R**, **T**
continet quemadmodum unum quid ens, ostendit quoniam cum non in necessitate sint
                  unum quidem **Rt**; quidem **Rp**   sunt **R**, **T**
ad invicem vel utrique vel alter, non commutant, quemadmodum
              uterque **Rp**, **T**   communicant **Rp**
cum quo habet ipse, indiget quis, puta vino dantes frumenti eductionem.
             non indiget **Rp**   uno **R**
10 Oportet ergo hoc aequari. Pro futura autem commutatione

si nunc nihil indiget, quoniam erit si indigeat, nummisma

puta fideiussor est nobis. Oportet enim hoc ferenti esse
   quasi **T**; quale **Rt**; *om* **Rp**
accipere. Patitur quidem igitur et hoc idem; non enim semper aequale

potest; verum tamen vult manere magis. Propter quod oportet omnia

15 appretiari. Sic enim erit semper commutatio. Si autem hoc, communicatio.

Nummisma utique quemadmodum mensura commensurata faciens, aequat.

168

Neque enim utique non existente commutatione communicatio erat; neque commutatio,
erit **T**
aequalitate non existente; neque aequalitas, non existente commensuratione. Secundum

veritatem quidem igitur impossibile tantum differentia, commensurata fieri.
veritatem *om* **Rp**

20 Ad opus autem, contingit sufficienter. Unum utique aliquid oportet
Ad indigentiam autem **Rt, T**; *om* Rp convenit **R**
esse. Hoc autem, ex suppositione; propter quod nomisma vocatur. Hoc
quod et nummisma **R, T**
enim omnia facit commensurata. Mensurantur enim omnia nummismate.

Domus in qua A, mnarum quinque, lectus in quo B,
quo **R, T**
mna dignus. Lectus autem quinta pars domus utique
minus **Rp**
25 erit. Manifestum igitur quanti lecti aequale,

domui, quoniam quinque. Quoniam autem sic commutatio erat ante quam nummisma

erat, manifestum. Differt enim nihil vel lecti quinque pro domo,
nil **Rp**
vel quanti quinque lecti.

169

Select bibliography

Arias, Gino "Ferdinando Galiani et les physiocrates", *Revue des sciences politiques* 45 (1922) pp. 346–366.

Aschbach, Joseph: *Geschichte der Wiener Universität im ersten Jahrhunderte ihres Bestehens.* Vienna 1865.

Ashley, W. J. (1): *An Introduction to English Economic History and Theory.* Parts I–II. New York (1888–1893) 1966.

— (2): "Justum pretium", *Palgrave's Dictionary of Political Economy.* Vol. II. London 1926. pp. 500–1.

Baldwin, John W.: "The Medieval Theories of the Just Price", *Transactions of the American Philosophical Society* 49, 4 (1959).

Bartolomé, León: *Fray Gerardo de Odón,* Murcia 1928.

Bonar, James: *Philosophy and Political Economy, in Some of their Historical Relations.* New York 1893.

Bowley, Marian: *Studies in the History of Economic Theory before 1870.* London 1973.

Brants, Victor: *L'Économie politique au Moyen-Âge.* Louvain 1895.

Burke, Peter: *Tradition and Innovation in Renaissance Italy.* London 1974.

Callus, D. A. (1): "The Date of Grosseteste's Translations and Commentaries on Pseudo-Dionysius and the Nicomachean Ethics", RTAM 14 (1947) pp. 186–210.

— (2): "Robert Grosseteste as Scholar", *Robert Grosseteste, Scholar and Bishop. Essays in Commemoration of the Seventh Centenary of his Death.* Oxford 1955. pp. 1–69.

Dempsey, Bernard W. (1): *Interest and Usury.* London 1948.

— (2): "Just Price in a Functional Economy", *The American Economic Review* 25 (1935) pp. 471–486.

De Roover, Raymond (1): "Monopoly Theory Prior to Adam Smith: A Revision", QJE 65 (1951) pp. 492–524.

— (2): "Scholastic Economics", QJE 69 (1955) pp. 161–190.

— (3): "The Concept of the Just Price", *The Journal of Economic History* 18 (1958) pp. 418–434.

— (4): *San Bernardino of Siena and Sant'Antonino of Florence. The Two Great Economic Thinkers of the Middle Ages.* Boston 1967.

Dognin, Paul-Dominique: "Aristote, Saint Thomas et Karl Marx", *Revue des sciences philosophiques et théologiques* 42 (1958) pp. 726–735.

Dunbabin, Jean (1): "The Two Commentaries of Albertus Magnus on the Nicomachean Ethics", RTAM 30 (1963) pp. 232–250.

Dunbabin, Jean (2): "Robert Grosseteste as Translator, Transmitter and Commentator: The 'Nicomachean Ethics' ", *Traditio* 28 (1972) pp.460–472.

Dyroff, A.: "Über Albertus von Sachsen", BGPM (1913, Suppl.) pp. 319–346.

Elías de Tejada, Francisco: "Derivaciones éticas y políticas del Aristotelismo salmantino del siglo XV", *Miscellanea mediaevalia* 2 (1963) pp. 707–715.

Élie, H.: "Quelques maîtres de l'université de Paris vers l'an 1500", AHDLMA 18 (1950–51) pp. 192–243.

Endemann, Wilhelm: *Studien in der romanisch-kanonistischen Wirtschafts- und Rechtslehre*. B. I–II. Berlin 1874–1883.

Faral, Edmond (1): "Jean Buridan. Notes sur les manuscrits, les éditions et le contenu des ses ouvrages", AHDLMA 15 (1946) pp. 1–53.

— (2): "Jean Buridan", HLF 38 (1949) pp. 462–605.

Fournier, Paul: "Gui Terré", HLF 36 (1927) pp. 432–473.

Francheschini, Ezio (1): "Roberto Grossateste, vescovo di Lincoln, e le sue traduzioni latine", *Atti del Reale Istituto Veneto di scienze, lettere ed arti* 93, II (1933–4) pp. 1–138.

— (2): La revisione moerbekana della 'translatio lincolniensis' dell'Etica Nicomachea", *Rivista di Filosofia Neo-Scolastica* 30 (1938) pp. 150–162.

Garin, Eugenio: "La fortuna dell'Etica aristotelica nel 400", *Rinascimento* 2 (1951) pp. 321–334.

Gauthier, René Antoine (1): "Trois commentaires 'averroïstes' sur l'Éthique à Nicomaque", AHDLMA 16 (1947–8) pp. 187–336.

— (2): "La date du Commentaire de Saint Thomas sur l'Éthique à Nicomaque", RTAM 18 (1950) pp. 66–105.

— (3): "Introduction" (Tom. I, 1), *L'Éthique à Nicomaque, introduction, traduction et commentaire*, par R. A. Gauthier et Jean Yves Jolif. 2. éd. Louvain/Paris 1970.

— (4): "Praefatio", *Sancti Thomae de Aquino Opera Omnia*. Tom. 47. (*Sententia libri Ethicorum*). Rome 1969.

— (5): "Saint Thomas et l'Éthique à Nicomaque" (Appendix), *St Thomae Opera*. Tom. 48. Rome 1971.

Gelesnoff, W. (1), *Grundzüge der Volkswirtschaftslehre*. Leipzig 1918.

— (2): "Die ökonomische Gedankenwelt des Aristoteles", *Archiv für Sozialwissenschaft und Sozialpolitik* 50 (1923) pp. 1–33.

Gilby, Thomas: *The Political Thought of Thomas Aquinas*. Chicago 1958.

Gilson, Etienne: *History of Christian Philosophy in the Middle Ages*. London 1955.

Giocarinis, Kimon: "An Unpublished Late Thirteenth-Century Commentary on the Nicomachean Ethics of Aristotle", *Traditio* 15 (1959) pp. 299–326.

Gobbi. Ulisse: *L'economia politica negli scrittori italiani del secolo XVI–XVII*. Milan 1899.

Gonnard, René: *Histoire des doctrines monétaires*. Tom. I–II. Paris 1935–6.

Grabmann, Martin (1): "Forschungen über die lateinischen Aristotelesübersetzungen des XIII. Jahrhunderts", BGPM 17, 5–6 (1916).

— (2): "Die wissenschaftliche Mission Alberts des Grossen und die Entstehung des christlichen Aristotelismus", *Angelicum* 6 (1929), pp. 325–351.

— (3): "Der lateinische Averroismus des 13. Jahrhunderts und seine Stellung zur christlichen Weltanschauung", SBAW 1931, 2.

— (4): "Methoden und Hilfsmittel des Aristotelesstudiums im Mittelalter", SBAW 1939, 5.

Grabmann, Martin (5): "Die Werke des hl. Thomas von Aquin" (3. Aufl), BGPTM 22, 1–2 (1949).

— (6): "Der Anteil Deutschlands am Aristotelismus des Mittelalters", *Mittelalterliches Geistesleben*. Band III. Munich 1956. pp. 219–231, pp. 449–450.

Graziani, Augusto: *Storia critica della teoria del valore in Italia*. Milan 1889.

Gutiérrez, David: "La biblioteca di Santo Spirito in Firenze nella metà del secolo XV", AA 25 (1962) pp. 5–88.

Hagenauer, Selma: *Das 'justum pretium' bei Thomas von Aquino*. Stuttgart 1931.

Hardie, W. F. R.: *Aristotle's Ethical Theory*. Oxford 1968.

Heidingsfelder, Georg: "Albert von Sachsen. Sein Lebensgang und sein Kommentar zur Nicomachischen Ethik des Aristoteles", BGPM 22, 3–4 (1921).

Heilig, K. J.: "Kritische Studien zum Schrifttum der beiden Heinriche von Hessen", RQ 40 (1932) pp. 105–176.

Hohoff, W.: "Die Wertlehre des heiligen Thomas von Aquin", *Monatsschrift für Christliche Social-Reform* 15 (1893) pp. 431–8, pp. 471–489.

Jourdain, Charles: "Mémoire sur les commencements de l'économie politique dans les écoles du Moyen Âge", *Mémoires de l'Institut National de France* 28 (1874).

Joachim, H. H.: *Aristotle. The Nicomachean Ethics. A Commentary*. Edited by D. A. Rees. Oxford 1951.

Kaulla, Rudolph (1): "Der Lehrer des Oresmius", *Zeitschrift für die gesamte Staatswissenschaft* 60 (1904) pp. 453–461.

— (2): *Die geschichtliche Entwicklung der modernen Werttheorien*. Tübingen 1906.

— (3): *Staat, Stände und der gerechte Preis*. Basel (1936) 1951.

Kristeller, Paul Oscar: "The Aristotelian tradition", *Renaissance Thought*. New York (1955) 1961. pp. 24–47.

Langlois, C.: "Guiral Ot, frère mineur", HLF 36 (1927) pp. 203–225.

Lhotsky, Alphons: "Thomas Ebendorfer", *Schriften der Monumenta Germaniae historica* 15 (1957).

Lottin, O. (1): "Saint Albert le Grand et l'Éthique à Nicomaque", *Aus der Geisteswelt des Mittelalters*, BGPTM (1935, Suppl. III, 1) pp. 611–626.

— (2): *Psychologie et morale aux XIIᵉ et XIIIᵉ siècles*. Tom. I–VI. Louvain/Gembloux 1942–1960.

— (3): "A propos de la date de certains commentaires sur l'Éthique", RTAM 17 (1950) pp. 127–133.

Mandel, Ernest: *Traité d'Économie Marxiste*. Tom. I–II. Paris 1962.

Martin, C.: "Walter Burley", *Oxford Studies Presented to Daniel Callus*. Oxford 1964. pp. 194–230.

Mauthner, Fritz: *Aristoteles. Ein unhistorischer Essay*. Berlin 1904.

Moorman, John: *A History of the Franciscan Order from its Origins to the Year 1517*. Oxford 1968.

Nègre, Pierre: *Essais sur les conceptions économiques de Saint Thomas d'Aquin*. Aix-en-Provence 1927.

O'Brien, George: *An Essay on Mediaeval Economic Teaching*. New York 1920.

Pacetti, D. (1): "I codici autografi di S. Bernardino da Siena della Vaticana e della Comunale di Siena", AFH 29 (1936) pp. 501–538.

— (2): "Un trattato sulle usure e le restituzioni di Pietro di Giovanni Olivi, falsamente attribuito a Fr. Gerardo da Siena", AFH 46 (1953) pp. 448–457.

Pelzer, Auguste (1): "Les versions latines des ouvrages de morale conservés sous le nom d'Aristote en usage au XIIIe siècle", RN 23 (1921) pp. 316–341, pp. 378–412.

Pelzer, Auguste (2): "Le cours inédit d'Albert le Grand sur la Morale à Nicomaque recueilli et rédigé par S. Thomas d'Aquin", RN 24 (1922) pp. 333–361, pp. 479–520.

Petersen, Peter: *Geschichte der aristotelischen Philosophie im protestantischen Deutschland.* Leipzig 1921.

Polanyi, Karl: "Aristotle Discovers the Economy", *Primitive, Archaic, and Modern Economics.* Boston 1968. pp. 78–115.

Powicke, F. M.: "Robert Grosseteste and the Nicomachean Ethics", PBA 16 (1930) pp. 85–104.

Rambaud, Joseph: *Histoire des Doctrines Économiques.* Paris 1899.

Ritter, Gerhard: *Die Heidelberger Universität. Das Mittelalter.* Heidelberg 1936.

Roll, Eric: *A History of Economic Thought.* London 1953.

Roscher, Wilhelm: *Geschichte der Nationalökonomik in Deutschland.* Munich 1874.

Rose, Valentin: "Über die griechischen Commentare zur Ethik des Aristoteles", *Hermes* 5 (1871) pp. 61–113.

Roth, F. E. W.: "Zur Bibliographie des Henricus Hembuche de Hassia dictus de Langenstein", *Centralblatt für Bibliotekswesen* (1888, Beiheft.) pp. 97–118.

Sandoz, A.: "La notion de juste prix", RT 45 (1939) pp. 285–305.

Scheeben, H. C.: "Albert der Grosse", *Quellen und Forschungen zur Geschichte des Dominikanordens in Deutschland* 27 (1931).

Schreiber, Edmund: *Die volkswirtschaftlichen Anschauungen der Scholastik seit Thomas v. Aquin.* Jena 1913.

Schumpeter, Joseph A.: *History of Economic Analysis.* London 1954.

Sewall, H. R.: *The Theory of Value before Adam Smith*, New York 1901.

Soudek, Josef: "Aristotle's Theory of Exchange", *Proceedings of the American Philosophical Society* 96 (1952) pp. 45–75.

Stavenhagen, Gerhard: *Geschichte der Wirtschaftstheorie.* Göttingen 1964.

Stegmüller, Friedrich: "Pedro de Osma", RQ 43 (1935) pp. 205–266.

Stroick, Clemens: "Heinrich von Friemar", *Freiburger Theologische Studien* 68 (1954).

Tarde, Alfred de: *L'Idée du Juste Prix.* Paris 1907.

Tawney, R. H.: *Religion and the Rise of Capitalism.* London (1926) 1964.

Thomson, S. Harrison: "The 'Notule' of Grosseteste on the Nicomachean Ethics", PBA 19 (1933) pp. 195–218.

Ueberweg, Friedrich: *Grundriss der Geschichte der Philosophie.* B. II, (B. Geyer) *Die patristische und scholastische Philosophie.* 11. Aufl. Basel/Stuttgart 1928.

Van Steenberghen, Fernand: *Aristotle in the West. The Origins of Latin Aristotelianism.* Louvain 1954.

Villey, Pierre: *Les sources et l'évolution des Essais de Montaigne.* Tom. I–II. Paris 1908.

Villoslada, R. G.: "La Universidad de Paris durante los estudios de Francisco de Vitoria O. P. (1507–1522)", *Analecta Gregoriana* 14, B (N.2) (1938).

Walsh, James J.: "Some Relationships between Gerald Odo's and John Buridan's Commentaries on Aristotle's Ethics", *Franciscan Studies* 35 (1975) pp. 237–275.

Weisheipl, James A: *Friar Thomas d'Aquino. His Life, Thought, and Works.* Oxford 1974.

Whitaker, Albert C.: *History and Criticism of the Labor Theory of Value in English Political Economy*. New York 1904.

Whittaker, Edmund: *A History of Economic Ideas*. New York 1940.

Wulf, Maurice de: *Histoire de la Philosophie Médiévale*. 6. éd. Tom. I–III. Paris 1934–1947.

Xiberta, B.: "Guiu Terrena, carmelita de Perpinyà", *Estudis Universitaris Catalanis*. Sèrie Monogràfica II. Barcelona 1932.

Yanaihara, Tadao: *Catalogue of Adam Smith's Library*. New York (1951) 1966.

Žmavc, Johann: "Die Werththeorie bei Aristoteles und Thomas von Aquino", *Archiv für Geschichte der Philosophie* 12 (1899) pp. 407–433.

Zumkeller, A.: "Die Augustinerschule des Mittelalters", AA 27 (1964) pp. 167–262.

Abbreviations

AA	Analecta Augustiniana
ADB	Allgemeine Deutsche Biographie, 1875–1900
Adelung	Supplements to Jöcher, 1784–1819
AFH	Archivum Franciscanum Historicum
AHDLMA	Archives d'hist. doctr. et litt. du Moyen Âge
AL	Aristoteles Latinus
BGP(T)M	Beitr. z. Gesch. d. Phil. (und Theol.) d. Mittelalt.
Bolduanus	Bibliotheca Philosophica, 1616
CAG	Commentaria in Aristotelem Graeca
Chevalier	Répertoire; Bio-bibliographie, 1905–7
Cranz	Aristotle Editions 1501–1600, 1971
DBI	Dizionario biografico degli italiani, 1960–
DNB	The Dictionary of National Biography, 1921–2
DTC	Dictionnaire de Théologie Catholique, 1902–1950
EF	Enciclopedia Filosofica, 1967
Emden	Biographical Register, Oxford, 1957–9
Fabricius	Bibliotheca Latina, 1858–9
Glorieux	Répertoire, Paris, 1933–4
GW	Gesamtkatalog der Wiegendrucke
HLF	Histoire littéraire de la France
IA	Index Aureliensis
Jöcher	Allgemeines Gelehrten-Lexicon, 1750–1
Lipenius	Bibliotheca Realis Philosophica, 1682
Lohr	Aristotle Commentators. Traditio XXIII–XXIX
LTK	Lexikon für Theologie und Kirche, 1957–1965
NBG	Nouvelle Biographie Générale, 1857–1866
NDB	Neue Deutsche Biographie, 1953–
Ossinger	Bibliotheca Augustiniana, 1768
PBA	Proceedings of the British Academy
PL	Patrologia Latina
QJE	The Quarterly Journal of Economics
Quétif	Scriptores Ordinis Praedicatorum, 1719–1721
RN	Revue néoscolastique de philosophie
RQ	Römische Quartalschrift
RT	Revue Thomiste
RTAM	Recherches de théologie ancienne et médiévale
Sbaralea	Supplements to Wadding, 1908–1936
SBAW	Sitzungsberichte d. Bayer. Akad. d. Wissensch.
Sommervogel	Bibliothèque de la Compagnie de Jésus, 1890–1932
Tanner	Bibliotheca Britannico-Hibernia, 1748
Wadding	Scriptores Ordinis Minorum, 1650